"The Successful Spirit *will inspi*[...] strive for more in your own life. 1[...] [...]ity of authors keeps you engaged and provides proof of the power of one's mindset in overcoming challenges. I found myself taking notes and highlighting countless sentences in this powerful book. A must-read for those who are on the journey of personal development!"

—KYLE COLETTI, Winner of SPIKE TV's Sweat Inc., Founder of Focusmaster Fitness

"The Successful Spirit *will help you uncover untapped potential and performance. Within the three planes of human beings, mind-body-spirit, mind and body receive most of the focus in regards to performance. However, the human spirit is an almost untapped potential full of possibilities, resources, and creative energy that can help even elite performers get to their next level. The most inspiring leaders in history weren't known for their mind or body but for their unimpaired spirit. If you are already successful and wonder if there is more in you,* The Successful Spirit *is your answer.*"

—GILAD KARNI, Former Professional Basketball Player, Coach for Inspiring Leaders and Entrepreneurs

"The Successful Spirit *is inspirational on many levels. As I was reading the chapters, I was impressed with how authentic the authors were with their personal journeys to success and how the lessons they learned while enduring hardship and overcoming obstacles will teach all of us how to overcome adversity, strengthen our identity, and continue to feed our peaceful and powerful spirit.*"

—TONI DELOS SANTOS, Sport Psychology Coach, Founder of 90% Mental

"Each one of us has a special light within; a beacon that shines even in the darkest of nights. Learning how to tap into your spirit and let it guide you as no one else can—that is one of the greatest secrets to happiness on this journey called life. That is exactly what The Successful Spirit *helps you do. From the lessons of others' journeys, this book is a toolbox of gifts to help you to find your way."*

—KIRSTEN JONES, Peak Performance Coach, Co-Host of #RaisingAthletes podcast

*"*The Successful Spirit *explores the human condition and not only outlines trials and tribulations but successes across the globe. We all must choose a path in life and decide, as we follow that path, if we view our cup half full or half empty. Mindset and determination make anything possible, and this book helps us see the cup as full.* The Successful Spirit *breaks down the fundamentals of finding the positivity and strength we all covet, and it may be utilized as a playbook as we weave others' ideas about performance strategy into our own journey."*

—PAUL SCIANNA, Professional Boxer, Owner of Empowering Punch Fitness

*"*The Successful Spirit *has something for everyone! Giggling whilst yelling PLOT TWIST all the way to grabbing my heart whilst taking a deep breath! I laughed! I nodded! I reflected how each person was (and is) a true embodiment of resilience. Most of the chapters offer a tangible idea or strategy to apply to your personal journey. Other chapters tug on just the right heartstrings reminding you of what is truly possible. My favourite moment... when each author made a promise to themselves. Honouring a promise to self is the highest form of self-care. I recommend this book to anyone and everyone! Time well spent! Inspired!"*

—JESSICA M. CORVO, Resilience Coach, Fitness Instructor, Mental Health Advocate

THE
SUCCESSFUL
SPIRIT

THE SUCCESSFUL SPIRIT

Top Performers Share Secrets to a Winning Mindset

Authored by:
Erik Seversen, Jessie Adams, Richard Bowling, Veronica Carlson, Danny P. Creed, Dartanyon Crockett, Barbara Daoust, Brett Elena, Nathaniel Errez, Dr. Elena Estanol, Dr. Jen Faber, Jory Hingson Fisher, Fabian Florant, Mandi Freger, Susanne Grainger, Drs. Annemieke Griffin, Jeroen Keymolen, Dr. Tarryn MacCarthy, Tim Wayne Medvetz, Stephen Miller, Emmanuel K. Nartey, PhD, Tom Perrin, PhD, Emily Perrin, Theo Pickles, April Qureshi, Ahad Raza, Flemming Rontved, Stefan Due Schmidt, Scott Span, Jenny R. Susser, PhD, Kamille Rose Taylor, Gabrielle Thomas, Joey Wagman, Kendrick Williams

THIN LEAF PRESS | LOS ANGELES

Disclaimer—The advice, guidelines, and all suggested material in this book is given in the spirit of information with no claims to any particular guaranteed outcomes. This book does not replace professional physical or mental support or counselling. Anyone deciding to add physical or mental exercises to their life should reach out to a licensed medical doctor or therapist before following any of the advice in this book. The authors, publisher, editor, and organizer do not assume and hereby disclaim any liability to any party for any loss, damage, or disruption caused by anything written in this book.

Library of Congress Cataloging-in-Publication Data
Names: Seversen, Erik, Author, et al.
Title: *The Successful Spirit: Top Performers Share Secrets to a Winning Mindset*
LCCN 2021910374

ISBN 978-1-953183-02-6 | ISBN 978-1-953183-03-3 (ebook)
Nonfiction, Mind, Body & Spirit, Self-Help, Performance
Cover Design: 100 Covers
Interior Design: Formatted Books
Editor: Nancy Pile
Copy Editor: Rebecca Lau
Thin Leaf Press
Los Angeles

THIN
LEAF

Thank you for reading this book. There are tools found within the following pages that can greatly benefit your life, but don't stop there. Make sure you get the most you can from this book and reach out directly to the 33 expert authors who want to help you enjoy life with a healthy mind, body, and spirit. Contact information for each author is found at the end of their respective chapter.

To the free spirits in the world and to those dedicated to pursuing positive changes within themselves and others.

CONTENTS

INTRODUCTION

By Erik Seversen
Author of *Ordinary to Extraordinary* and *Explore*
Los Angeles, California

After the publication of *The Successful Mind*, I've received countless thanks and feedback from readers, ranging from struggling students to high-powered executives, about how something in the book sparked a positive change in their lives. I decided I didn't want the influence of those positive changes to stop there, so the second book, *The Successful Body*, was created. Again, seeing the fantastic responses by readers, I knew another book was needed, and it was obvious that to complete the project, this book should be *The Successful Spirit*.

As the third book in *The Successful, Mind, Body, and Spirit* trilogy, I was apprehensive about starting *The Successful Spirit*. With an all-star cast of writers for both *The Successful Mind* and *The Successful Body*, and with each book reaching best-seller status in multiple countries, I wondered if I'd be able to complete the series with an equally impressive and impactful book. As soon as I began meeting with potential authors for *The Successful Spirit*, I knew this book would also be filled with the magic embedded in the first books.

As with *The Successful Mind* and *The Successful Body*, I reached out to a variety of experts who could contribute something unique to the book, and I intentionally looked for individuals who are extremely successful in their fields, who come from a variety of different backgrounds, and who work in diverse areas of expertise. The goal was not to have a group of authors with the same opinion about focus, drive, determination, and peak performance, but rather to have multiple perspectives. As a result, *The Successful Spirit* was created by a group of 33 top experts in sports, coaching, entrepreneurship, business, and wellness, who each help answer the question: *what is the most important thing a person can do to create more success in their sport, business, and life by harnessing the power of the inner spirit that drives us to peak performance?*

As mentioned, this book's 33 contributing experts hail from a variety of backgrounds. They come from all over the USA, all over Canada, the United Kingdom, the Netherlands, Belgium, Denmark, and the United Arab Emirates. These authors' areas of expertise include peak performance, the military, athletics, team sports, individual sports, coaching, business, entrepreneurship, mindset, psychology, counseling, energy, neuroscience, wellness, meditation, yoga, Pilates, holistic health, neuro-linguistic programming, organizational change, stress management, and more.

The authors composing this book are Olympic athletes, Paralympic athletes, professional athletes, world record holders, PhDs, multiple best-selling authors, international keynote and TEDx speakers, Forbes Council coaches, workshop facilitators, gym and fitness center owners, military officers, pastors, podcast hosts, filmmakers, CEOs and founders of coaching and consulting companies, martial arts experts, competitors on reality TV shows including *American Ninja Warrior, American Gladiators,* and *Broken Skull Challenge,* Mount Everest summiters, Ironman triathletes, ultra-marathoners, NCAA coaches, strength and conditioning coaches, scientists, and transformational experts.

The authors composing this book have been featured on ABC, NBC, CBS, CMT, ESPN, CNN, Fox, Discovery, and National Italian, Spanish, Australian, and Chinese television and radio programs, in *Forbes, New York Post, Chicago Tribune, Los Angeles Times,* and in many more internationally recognized media outlets. In summary, the individuals who contributed to this book are people who have gone beyond the normal levels of sport, business, and life. They are leaders who all want to help you become the best you can be. With this said, we should note that a foundational idea of this book is that peak performance is something that some people seem to be born with, but it is also a skill that can be developed by anyone.

A note about the name of the book. While I think there is a bit of an intangible quality to the "successful spirit," this book is not about finding success through Buddha or Jesus. Rather, the spirit as shown in this book is a powerful inner spirit that drives people to success, to win. The foundations of this fighting spirit include focus, drive, and determination. In turn, this book is divided into the three areas of focus, drive, and determination. Also, there are chapters about the importance of slowing down, of balancing life, and of allowing quiet and mindfulness to be present as we strive for peak performance.

While this book is organized around the united themes of accomplishment, success, and personal growth, each chapter is totally standalone. You can read the chapters in any order. I encourage you to look through the table of contents and begin wherever you want. Even still, I urge you to read all the chapters because, as a whole, they provide a tremendous array of perspectives with each one proving valuable in providing you tools for the development of a successful spirit.

While I'm extremely proud of the information contained within the chapters in this book, nothing can replace the real communication and accountability offered through face-to-face or online consultation. If you connect with something in this book, I encourage you to reach out to the author directly (you'll find their contact information provided in each chapter). Each author wants to help you live the best, most successful, satisfying life you can. I pray that this book is instrumental in helping you unlock your full potential, so you can perform at the highest levels to reach your goals.

Email: Erik@ErikSeversen.com
Website: www.ErikSeversen.com

CHAPTER 1

TRAIN YOUR MIND. FUEL YOUR BODY. RENEW YOUR SPIRIT.

By Jessie Adams
Founder of BelieveinU Fitness, American Ninja Warrior
Bettendorf, Iowa

The mind is everything. What you think, you become.
—Buddha

There are three things you have the power to control in your life: your mind, body, and spirit. You are never in control of what happens around you, but you are always in control of what happens within you. I would like to explain the importance of all three and how you can create a powerful mind, build a strong body, and renew your spirit in order to lead and live the incredible, joyous life you truly desire and ultimately deserve.

My life has never been without setbacks and challenges just as yours has not. But I view my past not as composed of obstacles but rather as opportunities for growth and expansion. Perspective is a beautiful thing, and I know we all have the power to change the way we see our world through our thoughts and beliefs.

Many people who don't know my past and see me now might think my life has always been filled with ease and adventure. That is how I live my life now, but it wasn't always that way.

Grow Through What You Go Through

In 2006, I was a young stay-at-home mom living what looked like the American dream, but I was living a lie. My husband and I had a nice house with a white picket fence in a middle-class neighborhood, several cars, two children, and one on the way. However, my husband was secretly abusing pain medications and other prescription drugs after a short-lived season as an NFL football player. He was visibly a strong man who looked put together with a solid build and large stature, but he was spiritually weak and mentally insolvent. When I first discovered his addiction, I tried interventions, treatment facilities, meeting with church members, pastors, and counseling. The more I tried to help him overcome his addictions, the worse it all seemed to get.

I didn't realize it at the time, but my husband's addiction was also affecting my own health and well-being. I was overwhelmed, overweight, afraid of other people's opinions and judgment, and deeply fearful of our future. My world changed forever the day he packed a single suitcase and left a letter on the kitchen table that said I didn't understand his struggles and that it was too much for him to be a husband and a father. I was five months pregnant when he walked out of our lives and left us penniless, and shortly after, bankrupt.

That day was a defining moment in my life that not only shook me to the core but awoke something inside of me. I vowed to never let any challenge be bigger than my ability to overcome. I never wanted my kids to see me give up when life gets hard. It drove me into taking massive action. I picked up the pieces, failed forward, and wrote a new story. I was determined to become mentally, physically, and spiritually strong enough to handle any challenge life threw at me. I never wanted to fear failing again.

I not only stopped fearing challenges, I embraced them. And once I did, everything in my life changed. I went from an out-of-shape, broke single mother to a professional fitness coach, UFC gym owner, career firefighter, reality TV show competitor on shows—including NBC's *American Gladiators*, *American Ninja Warrior*, and CMT's *Broken Skull Challenge*—and founder of BelieveinU Fitness.

By working through the challenges in my life, I am now a peak performance coach helping people believe in themselves and break through mental barriers, so they can create bucket-list life adventures with a successful mind, body, and spirit.

Developing a Powerful Mind

Mindset is everything. Everything begins inside our mind. What we believe and how we view the world determines our life experience. If we live with a fixed mindset or limiting beliefs that are not challenged, our very existence will be a reflection of those beliefs. If, however, we have a growth mindset or belief that we are in control of our own abilities and have limitless potential, our life experience will be one of abundance and endless possibilities.

> *Whether you believe you can do a thing or not, you are right.*
> *—Henry Ford*

No one has a powerful mindset by accident. You have to train your mind as much as you do your physical body. Just like you can't outtrain a bad diet, you can't outtrain a weak mindset. Let me share my seven principles for a powerful mindset. These seven principles are a way of life that, once adopted, will strengthen your mental toughness, build your confidence, and create a powerful mind.

Principle 1—Believe It's Possible

In order to develop a powerful mind, the first thing is to BELIEVE that it's possible. Whatever your religious or spiritual background, a key element in every religion is believing in something greater through faith. What is the definition of faith? Faith is complete trust, confidence, and certainty in someone or something. It is a strong belief in God or the doctrines of a religion, based on spiritual apprehension rather than proof. It is the assurance that things will come to pass even though they are unseen.

If you have a desire, but you don't BELIEVE a positive outcome is possible, how much effort are you going to give that goal? Your expectations and beliefs about your desire have to line up in order for you to achieve your goal. Let your faith be bigger than your fears. Anything is possible, you just have to believe it.

Principle 2—Take Your Power Back

Often, people give their power away by not accepting responsibility for their own life. We blame other people or circumstances for why we can't do something and give our power away. No one is in control of your emotions or decisions but you. Decide today that you are going to take responsibility for where you're at in your life.

When we can take ownership of our life, we have the power to control our destiny.

Principle 3—Challenge Your Fears

Most people don't take risks in their life because of one ugly little word we all know too well: FEAR. What is fear anyway? Fear is just a limiting belief. And what is a belief? A belief is just a thought you keep thinking.

If you want to change your belief about something, you have to challenge it. And in order to challenge it you must take action. Inaction only creates doubt and more fear. Action breeds confidence and courage. Challenge your fears by taking them head-on. When you face your fears, you are able to expose them for what they actually are: **F**alse **E**vidence **A**ppearing **R**eal.

The only thing you have to fear is fear itself.
—Franklin Roosevelt

Principle 4—Make Failure Your Friend

Everyone who's made something truly great of their life has failed their way to success. Failure is our friend. We learn from all of our failures, and when we stop fearing them and, instead, embrace them, our life transforms.

So many people have a negative relationship with failure. But we can't achieve success in life without failure. Failure plays a massive role in reaching success. We must be willing to fail in order to succeed.

When I'm training clients in the gym and they're lifting weights, I want them to hit failure because that's where adaptation and growth happens. In order for the muscle to grow, we want to take it to the point of failure. Failure also helps us recognize the areas that we need to work on in order to evolve.

Get comfortable with failing and remember failure is your friend. You will never know your limits or what you're truly capable of unless you push yourself to them. Embrace your fears. Fail early. Fail often. Fail forward. Your fearless future self is waiting for you!

Principle 5—Forgiveness

If you are thinking about the past and holding on to grudges or anger, you are cluttering your mind with negative thoughts and harvesting negative energy within the body.

You also cannot move forward in life without letting go of the past. It's like trying to drive your car down a highway but only looking in the rearview mirror. You can't go forward by looking backwards. Forgiveness is a gift you give yourself. It's not for someone else, it's for you. Forgiving someone may not change the past, but it will certainly enlarge your future.

Most importantly, learn to forgive yourself. You will NEVER be perfect! You learn from every life experience. It may be hard when you're going through it, but life lessons only prepare you for bigger and better things. You grow through what you go through.

I could have chosen to dwell in my past circumstances and allow them to define me, to be the reason I never tried or felt worthy; or I could learn from the lessons, forgive myself, move on, and create the life I deserved. I chose the latter, and you can too.

Principle 6—PPO: Positive People Only

Keep your circle small. Surround yourself with people who inspire and uplift you. Find the people who are mastering what you want to achieve.

Sometimes we have very well-meaning people in our lives. Some may be our family, who are dream killers, but understand that people who can't see a dream for themselves can't see one for you. It's not their dreams to dream, they are yours.

Principle 7—Attitude of Gratitude

Gratitude is not only a practice, but a way of life. Every morning when I wake up and start my day, I begin it with an attitude of gratitude. Whether I write it down or say it out loud, I go through all the things I can think of that I'm grateful for.

Sometimes life feels uninteresting because we take for granted all that we have. When we focus on the things we are grateful for in our life, we are asking for more things like that to come into our experience through the power of our thoughts. The more thankful we are, the more things we will have to be grateful for. Living a life of gratitude creates a beautiful mind of strength and love.

Write a list of ten things you're grateful for each morning.

Building a Strong Body

Our physical health is just as important as our mental strength. Essentially, we all want to be healthy and to look and feel our best. Too often, when new clients come to me, they have a belief that taking care of their physical body is too much work or too time consuming. They look at it as a chore they have to do, rather than being grateful that they have the ability to care for their body.

Fall in love with taking care of your body. It's the only place you have to live. Building a strong body builds confidence, creates vitality, gives you more energy, and allows you to achieve other goals you've set. If you are not taking care of your body, you are not able to fully enjoy what life has to offer.

There are five areas of health that we have the power to control in our life when building a stronger body: exercise, nutrition, sleep, water, supplements. When all five of these systems work together, we can optimize the way our body functions and create homeostasis (balance) in our body.

Exercise

Exercise is what burns energy and speeds up our metabolism while muscle is what controls our metabolism. Our fat is burned in the muscle, and each pound of muscle burns approximately 30 to 50 calories per day. The more muscle we have on our body, the more accelerated are our fat-burning capabilities. This is why it is important to incorporate both strength training and cardiovascular exercise into our normal exercise routine.

Nutrition

Food is energy. We need to fuel our physical bodies with the proper nutrients. We need sufficient macronutrients—proteins, fats, and carbohydrates—and micronutrients—vitamins and minerals—as well as water in order to function at an optimal level, both physically and mentally.

A healthy diet should consist of a variety of nutrient-dense foods, mostly plants, fruits, vegetables, lean proteins, raw nuts and seeds, and whole grains.

Some of the benefits of a healthy diet consist of delayed aging, weight loss or maintenance, increased energy and focus, a reduced risk of chronic disease, and an overall better quality of life.

Water

Water is vital to every function of our body and probably the most underestimated essential nutrient in regards to nutrition. The human body can survive for up to five weeks without protein, carbohydrates, and/or fats, but only five days without water. Our body is made up of about 60 percent water. Hydration is a key component in the five parts of health, and when we don't get a sufficient amount of water, it puts strain on every system in our body.

I encourage you to drink a gallon of water a day, and if you need some motivation, know that water can provide you with more energy, clearer skin, weight loss, less bloating, and fewer headaches. Water also helps digestion, improves brain function, and increases performance.

Sleep

Sleep is an essential function in your physical health that allows your body to repair and your mind to recharge. Not getting an adequate amount of sleep prevents the brain from functioning optimally and the body from proper metabolization of nutrients, and it slows fat loss. Research suggests that seven to nine hours of sleep is an appropriate amount.

Supplements

Although getting your micronutrients from whole foods should be the foundation of a balanced nutrition program, it is very challenging to get all the essential nutrients you need through diet alone. Having deficiencies in any essential nutrient can lead to a variety of physiological or biological issues. I recommend checking with your health care professional before taking any supplements to make sure it's individually right for you.

Six supplements that most people will benefit from include a multivitamin, vitamin D3, fish oil, magnesium, probiotics, and turmeric.

Renewing Your Spirit

You are soul-spirit. You are made up of vibrational energy and have an inner spirit, an inner being or God within.

When we don't feel our best or feel out of alignment, we are disconnected from our inner being, ourselves. Our inner being is pure positive radiant energy and sees only the perfection of who we truly are—love. Here are some ways to connect to your higher power and renew your spiritual well-being. Choose one or more of the following suggestions to bring the light back into your eyes, return you to the knowing of who you are, and set your spirit on fire.

Prayer/Meditation

Prayer and meditation not only can influence our spiritual state but can enhance our mental and physical health as well. It can lower blood pressure, relieve stress, influence our thoughts and emotions, and reconnect us to God and ourselves. It takes the pressures of the world off of us and gives it to a higher power. Meditation teaches us how to respond rather than react. It helps us to control our emotions and release resistance so that we can become more purposeful and live in the moment. Meditation requires discipline to remain still, focus on our breathing, and quiet the mind, but if practiced daily, it will become an intricate part of our life.

Read a Book

If you're reading this right now, you're already mastering this step. When you spend time reading or listening to positive, inspiring messages, you flood your mind, lift your spirit, and raise your vibrational energy. You're creating expansion in your life.

Get in Touch with Nature

We have a spiritual connection to nature. When we go out into nature, mountains, valleys, rivers, forests, the sun, and the moon, and we reconnect, we find a greater sense of peace and connection with ourselves and others around us.

Slow down, spend some time outside in silence, and reconnect to nature and your spirit.

Music and Dance

Music and dance are two forms of emotional language that touch your soul and uplift your spirit. Listen to something that is going to raise your emotions and vibrational energy, that makes you want to jump off of your feet and dance. Turn up the music and sing at the top of your lungs, dance like no one's watching, and let yourself be free!

Laughter

You've heard the old wise saying, laughter is the best kind of medicine. There is definitely truth behind that. Laughter is scientifically proven to decrease stress hormones, increase immune-boosting cells, trigger the release of endorphins, and create an overall sense of well-being. You can't be sad or in pain and laugh at the same time. Watch a funny movie, tell jokes, share stories, or hang out with positive friends who make you laugh and bring the best out in one another. Life is too short not to laugh.

*

We cannot always understand why bad things happen, but it's what we do with our challenges that can either break us or make us stronger. I am now happily married to the absolute love of my life, with three healthy incredible teens who are all powerful creators and living life to the fullest. You know I've had adversities in my life, but I want to use these to fuel my purpose in life. To inspire others to never give up, to have courage, and to believe in themselves.

You have limitless potential in what you create in your reality, and my desire for you is that it is a reality with a powerful mind, a strong body, and a successful spirit. I hope that these words have resonated with you and that you never stop growing, learning, evolving, and expanding. Nothing is impossible, and it's never too late to believe in yourself.

I BELIEVEINU. Enjoy the journey, my friend!

With much love and gratitude,

Jessie

About the Author

Jessie Adams is a nationally recognized health and fitness coach, specializing in helping people who've struggled with weight loss in the past to transform their bodies through mindset and peak performance coaching in order to achieve the body they've always desired and live the life they ultimately deserve. She is known as the "Transformation Fitness Expert."

After going from an out-of-shape, broke single mother to a top fitness and professional athlete performance coach, a UFC gym owner, reality TV show competitor, career firefighter, and founder of BelieveinU Fitness, Jessie uses her experience and knowledge to help others overcome their struggles around transformation to show them what they are truly capable of. Jessie has been featured on NBC, CMT, Fox, KLJB, and in the *Chicago Tribune*, and competed in shows such as NBC's *American Gladiators*, NBC *American Ninja Warrior*, and CMT's *Broken Skull Challenge*—just to name a few. Jessie will be speaking at TEDx June, 2022.

Email: jessie@believeinufitness.com
Website: www.believeinufitness.com
Facebook: facebook.com/believeinufitness
Instagram: @believeinufitness

CHAPTER 2

DELIBERATELY CONSTRUCT A FUTURE SUCCESS PERSONA

By Richard Bowling
High Performance Entrepreneur's Coach
Gaithersburg, Maryland

There is always a future version of ourselves calling us forward, whether we feel it or not. Every several years, each and every cell in our body will be replaced, and so will our identity be replaced. A totally different you. For better or worse.

The only question then is—do we actively want to participate in creating who we will become, to deliberately construct our future success persona? Others have done it, and so can you.

Matthew McConaughey says he'll never actually catch his "hero," his future successful self. But in constantly chasing this hero, McConaughey maximizes his potential in the here and now. This is certainly in line with Tony Robbins' definition of success, which claims that success is essentially progress. What both McConaughey and Robbins realize is that the spirit of success lies not in the end-result, but in the path we take toward our future self. It is up to each of us to harness our inner-spirit to continually steer our current selves in the direction of our future success—that continually changing image that we strive to become as we grow in each present moment.

Successful people in multiple arenas have always had systems for bringing out their best selves. And while the world simply saw the hard work and the results of their efforts, it was actually the mental rituals of the successful that drove them to become their best.

Identity is at the very core of our behavior and actions. Identity is the very reason why a person can adopt a new diet and lose weight, and then regain that weight. Without an identity shift, this person often returns to the previous weight.

If you can consciously upgrade your identity, your future self can do amazing things.

I want to challenge you, here, to consider taking the plunge in not leaving your future self to chance, but to deliberately create a future success persona that has the capacity to achieve your next big goals in life.

Let's start by breaking down the process of achievement:

Step 1: There is what you need to KNOW.
Step 2: There is what you need to DO.
Step 3: There is how you need to THINK.
Step 4: There is who you need to BECOME.

Those who achieved moderate success did so by following the first three steps. But those who hacked the fourth step—the *BECOMING*—launched themselves into the realm of extraordinary success.

This is why personal development and transformation is at the heart of every major teaching success on the planet. Trying to avoid this simple truth is like trying to escape from gravity. You don't get in life just what you know, do, and think. You essentially get what you *become*.

But why would anyone in their right mind resist transforming into a better version of themselves? Well, that's simple. The resistance is from your ego. Your ego will most often attempt to convince you that who you presently are is all you are supposed to be. And while that's true on some level, what the ego leaves out is that you *can* become a better version of yourself regardless of who you are today.

In the world of basketball, Kobe Bryant had a phrase to represent his future success persona. He called it Mamba Mentality. The symbol of this was the mamba snake. And Kobe had an insatiable work ethic that drove him to become his best—in line with this symbol.

Michael Jordan didn't have a catchy phrase or symbol to represent his future success persona, but he was constantly chasing it. Regardless of how good or how famous Jordan was, he was never satisfied if he wasn't giving 100 percent in his training and competition. And he often found *triggers*—i.e., trash talking competitors or inspiring a young fan—that drove him to incredible performance levels, far above his natural talent.

But exactly how did these superstars flip the switch to step towards that future success persona? The short answer is that each person did it differently. Ultimately, you will need to find a recipe that works for you. Soon we will address various ingredients you can use to form your own unique system.

First, let's start at the very beginning of the process. Everything begins with intention. You must first make a commitment that you will attempt the process to actively transform into your future self—even with the resistance of your ego, something that you will surely experience along the way. Are you willing to commit to this process?

Next read a few stories of people, who against extraordinary odds, became mega successes in their respective fields. People like the actor Sydney Portier, who made a conscious decision to completely change his accent, so that when he spoke, he would be well received in the theater world. What a transformation!

Part of creating a success persona for yourself also begins with a no-matter-what commitment to the journey. The actor Michael Cane was told, when he started his career, that he simply wasn't talented enough to be an actor. But Michael's passion for acting was so intense that he simply refused to do anything else.

In addition to reading great success stories of others, there are at least two ways you can begin to construct your success persona. The first is by having strategic profound life experiences, and the second is practicing neuroscience-based mindset exercises.

Strategic Profound Life Experiences—imagine for a moment that you could take a year off from normal life and travel around the world, going on adventures through jungles; climbing the highest mountain peaks; and interacting with the locals from numerous countries, fully immersing yourself in their cultures, eating the food, learning their languages, and embracing their customs. At the end of the year, the new perspective that you will have gained will literally transform you into another person—and hopefully for the better.

Can you think of similar profound life experiences that you might create that would bring out the best in your future self? Check out the film *The Game* for even more ideas in this direction, and then make them happen.

Neuroscience-Based Mindset Exercises—now consider the absence of such profound life experiences to construct your future success persona. How might you make a powerful transformation in the midst of your ordinary life? Well, just as going to the gym each day can transform your body, practicing neuroscience-based mindset tools can transform your thinking and identity.

As a professional coach, I work with my clients weekly on this very thing. Here's a tiny sample of these exercises that you can try to explore your consciousness and create a future success persona.

Let's start with a little basic neuroscience. Because of the neuroplasticity of the brain, we can literally rewire our brains to become the person we want to be. Just as you lift weights to shape muscles, there are simple question-based exercises that can rewire your brain to reshape your identity. And this reshaping of your identity will trigger the actions you take towards greater levels of success.

Does this sound scary? Are you worried that you could do this wrong and create a Frankenstein out of yourself? Well, not to fear. In fact, with your conscious or unconscious self-talk, you are *already* shaping your future identity. What we are attempting to do is simply get behind the wheel—to be in control of the process.

Here's a quick sample. Let's say you want to become the best salesperson in your department. Every morning you look in the mirror and recite the affirmation, "I am the best salesperson my company has ever seen." Will this work? Sure, if you repeat this enough over a long period of time.

But the problem here is that you are going in through the front door of your mind, where the ego is standing to resist your "I'm the best salesperson" affirmation with the simple response of, "Oh, no, you're not." With repetition, you *can* eventually wear down the ego's defenses. But it's a battle, and it usually takes a while.

A faster process is what I call using a "back door to the mind" where the ego is more defenseless. The above scenario would then look like this. In front of the same affirmation you simply add a "why." So, the question you would ask yourself becomes, "Why am I the best salesperson in my company?" As your brain searches for answers, you trick your brain into believing this affirmation is true. And—*bam!*—you rewire your brain with the new identity belief in a much shorter time.

Here's the thing: theorizing about how weights can transform your muscles doesn't actually transform your muscles. You must *use* the weights and exercise on a regular basis. It's the same with brain rewiring exercises. To reshape your identity, you must *use* these exercises. Information alone is *not* transformative.

A summary of the two basic ways to create your future success persona include: 1) a profound life experience and 2) a brain rewiring question, "Why am I such an amazing salesperson?" (Or whatever it is you are trying to become.)

While deliberately changing ourselves into who we want to be is possible, it isn't common. However, there are real and fictional characters who have each made their journey to their future success personas.

Clark Kent became Superman.

Neo from the Matrix film became "the ONE."

Muhammad Ali stepped into the description of himself as "the greatest."

Steve Jobs said that he would "become the world's next greatest storyteller." And, he did!

The examples are endless.

Creating your future success persona is everything because you don't get what you want in life; you get what you *become*.

A few more simple ways you can begin crafting your future success persona: get creative! Think of a name for yourself as your future self.

What is it that you're wearing? How do you speak? How do you think? How do you make decisions? Where do you live? What resources do you have access to?

What influence do you have on others? What are your specific superpowers and weaknesses? Add as much detail as possible and practice visualizing and feeling these daily. Experiencing the feeling of what you want to become is actually where the transformation takes place.

Do these things feel abstract or elusive to you? If so, you are intellectualizing the process. And unfortunately intellectualizing won't actually help you in this arena. Find a way to *practice* it.

Think of creative ways that you can daily remind yourself of your new identity, your successful spirit. Find triggers to step into this identity. Will you need a cape?! Try one on! There is always a future version of ourselves calling us forward, whether we feel it or not.

The only question then is: do we actively want to participate in creating who we will become to deliberately construct our future success persona?

Others have done it, and so can you. *BECOME the superhero that you were meant to be!* The world is waiting.

About the Author

Richard Bowling is professional coach, serial entrepreneur, filmmaker, and emerging thought leader on personal development and entrepreneurship.

Richard bounced into this unique path literally because of a ping pong ball. Twenty years ago, he walked away from a lucrative electrical engineering career with multinational corporations to follow his passion for table tennis, becoming a table tennis entrepreneur, Olympic-aspiring athlete, and inventor of the *iPong*—a table tennis ball machine that is sold worldwide.

Richard later enhanced his entrepreneurial skills bringing dozens of products to market as global product manager for one the world's largest table tennis brands: *JOOLA*.

In 2019, Richard founded *Amar Neo Consulting*, which today predominantly coaches engineers to leap from their careers into their own tech startups.

In 2021, Richard launched two additional startups: *Atomic Maids,* a disruptive/online residential cleaning startup; and *Coach Vision Media,* a cinematic marketing film startup for coaches and consultants.

Email: Richard@AmarNeo.com
Website: www.AmarNeo.com

CHAPTER 3
WARRIOR'S SPIRIT

By Veronica Carlson
Chair of USA Wrestling's AAC, Coach
Arvada, Colorado

*The spirit of a warrior is not geared to indulging and complaining,
nor is it geared to winning or losing. The spirit of a warrior is geared
only to struggle, and every struggle is a warrior's last battle on earth.
Thus the outcome matters very little to him. In his last battle on earth
a warrior lets his spirit flow free and clear. And as he wages his battle,
knowing that his intent is impeccable, a warrior laughs and laughs.*
—Carlos Castaneda

It usually piques a stranger's interest when they learn that I was a wrestler. When I started wrestling in seventh grade, I was the only female on my team. It was a recurring theme for a few years. At the turn of the century, not everyone thought a girl belonged on the wrestling mat, but I didn't care. I wore my black eyes and cauliflowered ears with pride. I never complained. And I gave a heroic effort in whatever was asked of me.

When I think back to my days as a young warrior, I smile. I hope to never lose that revolutionary spirit. I'd wager it's still there.

My name is Veronica. I would like to share with you what grit looks like, feels like, acts like.

I do not believe in limitations. The second someone tells me no is the second I stop listening and start crafting an alternative. In wrestling, no matter the odds, the score, or the time left on the clock, there is still a chance to turn things around before the final whistle blows. You find a way to win. In life, you do the same.

As an athlete, I was known for my heart. My toughness. My drive to conquer and give everything I had at any and all cost. Head down, eyes forward, I was a warrior. I lived for the battle. I relished the fight.

As an emerging professional finding my way in the world, I'm now known for the same things. Just in a more socially acceptable, every-day mien. What do I do with my time now? I follow my passions. Fervently. I serve as an athlete leader, soak up everything I can that will help me pivot into a business professional, and I obsess over making the perfect cup of coffee. I employ what has worked for me in the past: hard work, vision, and endless passion for every budding challenge. My fighting spirit has not changed, but the road I'm traveling certainly has, and I have had to adapt accordingly.

In taking this notion of redirection into account, I'd like to point out that there's a relative attitude and approach that absolutely carries over from success as an athlete to success in life. I've climbed a few mountains, and I'll climb many more. These expeditions are all very different in nature, but it is the mindset I have secured that allows me to adapt confidently and energetically into new roles on my journey.

I am done wrestling competitively, but my spirit still yearns for the grind. It is when I am pushing boundaries that I feel most in my element, most alive, most free. I refuse to be stagnant.

Outside of the Comfort Zone

To be uncomfortable, that is, to step outside of your comfort zone, is a space that few explore without some form of resistance. But this lonely space, I have discovered, is my precious sanctuary and greatest teacher. As I became accustomed to venturing outside of my comfort zone at a young age, I grew fascinated with how far I could push myself. What were my limitations? I wanted to know what it would take to break me.

I knew that if I could bring myself to levels of discomfort that nobody else would go, then no person and no situation could ever defeat me. I worked through pain to fortify my body, mind, and spirit. I mastered sovereignty over my own will. In my quest to be unbreakable, I learned how to be mentally tough.

When first exploring your own personal limits, this space breeds pain, discomfort, uncertainty, and fear. This space exists with constant begging of the question, "Should I quit or keep fighting?" The longer I exist in the space, the more moments I have chosen the latter. The more moments I have chosen the latter, the lesser my mind begs me to quit. The more moments I have chosen the latter, the more my spirit strengthened. In time, I could sit with pain and discomfort like an old friend. Discomfort let me know that I was growing. Pain let me know it was time to push even harder. Moment to moment, I chose to fight through.

To outlast this test of will in any given situation was to emerge in humble satisfaction. No money, fame, gold, nor glory. Simply knowing I did not give up was enough. The true reward was the opportunity to let my spirit rise in the face of adversity. I learned to enjoy the struggle.

To further define what stepping outside of your comfort zone looks like, it is a temporarily unbearable situation where each passing moment presents a choice to continue or not. I'm sure you've been in many of these situations in your life, perhaps without even realizing that you had a choice to continue.

This moment of choice, as I will refer to it, rears its head when things have become too heavy, too hard, too painful. "What is the point of enduring this? Is it worth it?" And then, the mind weakened by intrusive questions, convinces you that you cannot continue. "Just quit. Who cares? Save yourself for another day. It's not worth it."

In this split-second decision, space and time pauses. Your mind and your heart are at odds. Your mind asks for you to walk away in defeat. Your spirit wants to press on. You must choose.

Do you choose to stop? The feelings multiply and consume you. You quit. Instant relief from pressure, discomfort, and pain, but a mist of disappointment lingers. Is your spirit's palette for victory refined enough to notice? Is this choice of stoppage so ingrained in you that it's unrecognizable from any other thoughtless day-to-day action?

Or, back to our moment of choice, in a valiant attempt to thwart the mind and follow your heart—do you opt to continue?

This split-second decision begs immediate action. We meet this crossroads continuously in life in both large and small expressions. I would like to share a personal anecdote that most adequately illustrated this moment of choice as it unfolded for me.

At the 2015 USA Wrestling National Championships, I was battling back for third place, having lost earlier in the tournament. Wrestling through the repechage for bronze is a tough path. You still must give your full effort for a sliver of the glory. Your opportunity to win the tournament is soured, and yet, quitting is not ever an option. Point being, I already had a chip on my shoulder heading into this bronze medal match, and I was not about to lose again.

The match started off great for me. Four minutes in, I had an 8-0 lead.

Excerpt from USA Wrestling article:

With two minutes left in the match at 69 kg/152 lbs., the wrestlers were side-by-side in the neutral position. [The opponent] was fighting to gain control and Carlson's right arm got trapped in an awkward position.

The match was quickly stopped as Carlson was in severe pain.

"I heard it snap in three places," Carlson said of her right arm. "It was just crazy. I was screaming in pain and pounding my fist on the mat."

Medical staff quickly came onto the mat.

"When it first happened, I thought there was no way I could continue. I knew my arm was broken," Carlson said. "I knew it was really bad. I told the trainers that I thought it was broken, and they asked if I could move it and I could actually move it. My arm was hanging at a weird angle, but I could move my fingers."

So there you have it. A literal breaking point.

- Physical—*my arm is broken and useless.*
- Mental—*even if I gut through this pain, how can I perform without an arm? It's impossible.*
- Emotional—*why did this have to happen now? I was so close to winning.*

There was my moment of choice. The influx of doubt and the annoying voice of reason pleading with me to walk away and lick my wounds. Nobody would blame me for stopping. Hell, nobody expected me to continue.

Nobody except for me.

"When I got on my feet, I looked at the score and looked at the clock. I just had something in me that said I can't let her win and I can't walk away from this."

Carlson asked the trainers to tape up her badly damaged arm. And she elected to continue wrestling.

"I felt like the injury couldn't get any worse," she said. "It was my call. I decided to keep wrestling."

The match resumed, and [the opponent] mounted a comeback, but Carlson gutted it out to earn a gritty 10-8 victory.

"I was in a lot of pain," she said. "It was excruciating. I was bawling through the entire last two minutes of the match. It was terrible."

Carlson's suspicions were confirmed that night when she went to a Las Vegas hospital to have the injury examined further.

"I tore the tendons right off the bone and I tore the radial collateral ligament at the elbow," she said. "When all of the tendons tore, all of the muscles snapped and balled up in my arm. My arm looked deformed.

… "Going through the end of that last match was really hard," she said. "Obviously, I wish the injury didn't happen, but I'm glad I got the opportunity to show what I was made of. I think I made the right decision to keep wrestling. I was aware of my body and what I could handle. The biggest obstacle was the pain."

A breaking point is an opportunistic stage for the warrior's spirit to shine through. By looking into your own soul, trusting what you are made of, and deciding to keep fighting, you begin to develop a new habit in the name of mental fortitude. There's no time for pity or inaction. You find a way to win. And in doing so, you fortify your spirit.

This is how you build mental toughness. With every test or impossible challenge, you create a new pattern of action by capitalizing on, as well as appreciating, the opportunity to overcome the hand life throws at you. You choose to persevere no matter what because your spirit is unbreakable.

Mentality Is a Secret Weapon

This mentality that carried me through the broken elbow situation is my secret weapon, and I use it every day although I'm no longer an athlete. I've assumed many new skins as I navigate the world with fresh eyes. Leader, advocate, entrepreneur, coffee person. My new ventures and passions transcend my previous persona as an elite athlete. And I believe it to be a reintroduction of my most authentic expression of self. I'm no longer tied to a single identity or path.

Many people commit themselves to a goal or dream in a way that supersedes their own true self. This fascination with the outcome is all-encompassing. I feel this is important to include because I fell into this trap of thinking for many years. The biggest mistake I made in my athletic career was intertwining my own identity with an outcome that felt so important: an Olympic gold medal. When I stepped away from the dream, I stepped away from the self-image I had spent over a decade cultivating. My identity was gone, and I felt hollow inside and out of place with the world I had just previously felt so in control of. I had never envisioned what life could look like a moment past my anticipated victory.

My breach in identity taught me a great lesson: measurable goals are useful tools that help to establish direction and motivate our spirits, but to risk life and limb for a specific goal is a selfish conquest of the ego. We must reexamine our attachment to specific goals.

The goal is never the end goal. An accomplished goal is a ripple of the greater quest of seeking lifelong excellence. The successful spirit is unclouded by superficial conquests of glory, riches, or fame, and aligns with a higher path and purpose. The successful spirit realizes that all of these things happen as a result of committing to excellence in all areas of life.

To quote Aristotle: "Excellence is an art won by training and habituation. We do not act rightly because we have virtue or excellence, but we rather have those because we have acted rightly. We are what we repeatedly do. Excellence, then, is not an act but a habit."

The Successful Spirit

This successful spirit, this *warrior's spirit* exists within each of us. How you harness it looks different for each individual, but there are key similarities in the internal framework of those who have mastered this strategy of the soul. Here are some takeaways that I have forged into habits. I believe these components of my approach have been paramount in my success and maintenance of mental toughness.

Courage—the courage to acknowledge a dream and the conscious decision to dedicate your efforts to it.

Identity—you must identify with the warrior's spirit, see yourself in the warrior's spirit, and then adopt this empowering identity as your own. You must then act in accordance with this adopted identity. *There is a quiet knowing that you are the victor before you ever enter the arena.*

Discipline—unwavering commitment to align every action with excellence.

Enthusiasm—choose to display unrelenting enthusiasm in the mundane because every moment is a gift. Fully embrace every struggle, big and small. Invite every challenge with open arms because it is a chance to show what you're made of.

Trust—belief and trust in your preparation to allow the warrior inside to rise to the occasion. Action does not require thought when preparation has been sufficient.

Detachment—separation from any outcome, good or bad. Success comes as a side dish to a well-lived journey. The emphasis here is on relishing the process. Acceptance, gratitude, and the will to either keep going or flawlessly pivot to the next dream defines the unbreakable spirit. Not the outcome.

In closing, life is filled with highs, lows, and infinite opportunity to reinvent ourselves in-between. To align ourselves with our own spirit of will and grit, if only for the sake of giving our best in every moment of struggle and triumph, is an expression of our truest nature.

The warrior's spirit is a successful spirt. The warrior's spirit never retires and never rests. The warrior's spirit simply is.

About the Author

Veronica Carlson, who also goes by Vonnie, is well known for an accomplished career in the sport of freestyle wrestling. Having recently retired from sport, her sights are set on entrepreneurial ventures, leadership, and pouring the perfect cup of coffee.

Veronica serves on USA Wrestling's Executive Committee and chairs USA Wrestling's Athletes' Advisory Committee. Veronica is vocal about athlete advocacy and creating opportunity for active and retired athletes. She also coaches wrestling locally and nationally.

Veronica currently manages café operations at an organic coffee roastery in Colorado. On Veronica's days off, she visits other cafes because she appreciates coffee so much.

Veronica is vegan, lives a sober lifestyle, and practices meditation. She is currently working towards a degree in Business. Her interests include listening to 90's music, watching documentaries, and tending to her plants.

Veronica resides with her other half, Kodey. The two met as training partners, became life partners, and aspire to be business partners someday.

Email: vcarlson@live.com
Website: www.veronicacarlson.com

CHAPTER 4

LIGHT YOUR FIRE

by Danny P. Creed
Master Business and Executive Coach, International Speaker
Phoenix, Arizona

The human spirit can endure a sick body, but who can bear a crushed spirit?
—Proverbs 18:14

The successful spirit of a person says everything about them without a single word spoken.

My mother died a few years ago. By all accounts, everyone who ever met her said she lived with a spirit of kindness and love. In turn, I've met people throughout my life who exuded a spirit of meanness and hatred.

The successful spirit is a feeling. It's a vibe you get when you're around someone who has it. You can see it in the confidence of their walk. You can hear it in the passion of their voice. You can see it in the happiness of their smile and the twinkle in their eyes.

The successful spirit is our heart and our soul. It's that magnetic "something" that attracts us to some people and repels us from others. You can sense the successful spirit. It's that invisible something, but something that is real.

The power of a person's spirit is the foundation of heroism's tales and overcoming odds for hundreds if not thousands of years. We cheered the spirit of Rocky Balboa, overcoming all odds to become the champ. Movies like *Chariots of Fire*, *Norma Rae*, or *Gandhi* tell stories of people with an incredible spirit to change the world against all odds.

We screamed and shouted at our living room television as we were inspired by the team spirit of the outmanned and outgunned US men's hockey team as they beat the Russians in the *Miracle on Ice* in the 1980 Winter Olympics. We salute our veterans of war and conflicts around the globe, whose patriotic spirit drives them to serve our country.

Spirit and soul is in my grandmother's apple pie. The spirit of life, survival, and patriotism is my father getting both feet frozen in World War II at the Battle of the Bulge. And, the true human spirit of life and possibilities was with my mother who suffered a stroke that left her paralyzed from the neck down. She could barely talk. She could no longer walk or feed and clean herself. Yet, the last time I visited her in the hospital and asked her how she was doing, she looked at me with her now beautiful yet crooked smile and whispered in my ear, "I'll be dancing by Christmas."

That's spirit.

The human spirit is said to include our intellect, emotions, fears, passions, and creativity. Scientifically, Daniel Helminiak, noted theologian and author, and Bernard Lonergan, a Canadian Jesuit priest and philosopher, consider spirit a mental function of awareness, insight, understanding, judgment, and other reasoning powers. Others view the human spirit as representing the qualities of purpose and meaning. Scientists and philosophers alike can puff on their pipes and debate the issue for decades. But, for me, spirit is much simpler. It is a fire in the belly, the twinkle of an eye, or a sly smile.

My advice to other disabled people would be, concentrate on things your disability doesn't prevent you from doing well and don't regret the things it interferes with. Don't be disabled in spirit as well as physically.
—Stephen Hawking

The successful spirit translates into many different forms. Spirit is the prime ingredient of perseverance. Simply translated, perseverance is the ability to achieve something despite difficulties, failure, or opposition. It is a discipline. It is sticking to a plan. Elbert Hubbard described it as "Doing what you need to do; when you need to do it; whether you want to or not." Spirit is the fuel that drives perseverance and discipline. It can cause us to succeed, and it can be the fire that forces us to bounce back after failure. It is what drives us to take one more step and try one more time, to continue pushing forward. Just remind yourself of Steve Job's story.

The founder of Apple built the empire from his parents' garage. It soared into a multi-billion-dollar company. Yet, Steve Jobs found himself without a job after being ousted by Apple's Board of Directors. Jobs later said that getting fired was the best thing that ever happened to him. Instead of lying in a corner and becoming bitter and feeling sorry for himself, he did the opposite. He acquired new creativity levels, started new companies, and soon regained his position at Apple and drove it to new heights.

One of the most famous personalities of perseverance is Thomas Edison. To many people, he was a nutcase. Seven days a week, many without sleep, Edison was driven by his indomitable spirit to create things that others could not even envision. Can you imagine being presented an investment idea in 1880 and being shown the prototype for a light bulb? But Edison always found a way. While no one else on earth believed in him, his spirit of success and innovation never waned. He had immense belief in himself.

Edison was queried once about how he could ever persist after failing a rumored 10,000 times. How could anybody have the grit and perseverance to continue? He became famous for saying, "I have not failed 10,000 times. I have not failed once. I have succeeded in proving that those 10,000 ways will not work. When I have eliminated the ways that will not work, I will find the way that will work."

His spirit changed the world.

There are, of course, other incredible examples of a never-give-up spirit.

- If you love coffee, you can thank Howard Shultz, Starbucks' founder, for his spirit and perseverance. Schultz went to 242 different banks looking for his original loan to start the business.
- WhatsApp founder, Jan Koum, grew up without running water. He found his way to Silicon Valley. He tried to get a job at Facebook but couldn't. He never gave up on his vision and, driven by his inexhaustible successful spirit, later sold his WhatsApp company to Facebook for a reported $21.8 billion.
- Jack Ma, the founder of Alibaba, is worth about $50.6 billion and change. But success wasn't instantaneous or easy. His biography says that he applied and was turned down for over 30 different jobs. He applied and was rejected by many colleges, including Harvard, who famously declined him ten times. Throughout all of the rejection, he knew that he had a certain spark that lived deep in his soul. Others

couldn't see it, but he knew it was there, and he persevered. He pushed and found a niche in mining the potential of the internet and e-commerce. And, if there is such a thing as karma, Mr. Ma proved it. He later in life was asked, and he accepted an invitation to deliver the commencement address at Harvard.

How Do I Maintain a Successful Spirit?

The maintenance of a successful spirit can sometimes be a challenge. The world we live in can be a very hostile place, and staying strong is harder for some than others. Your ability to have and maintain a positive spirit is essential to short-term and long-term success. No matter your profession, your successful spirit will be challenged. Your spirit is like a flame. It can be robust, powerful, and create light for yourself and all around you. Or, your flame can be delicate and extinguished with the slightest breeze, never to be relit. You have full control over the brilliance of your flame. Here are a few strategies to keep your spirit shining.

Beware of Spirit Vampires. Spirit Vampires are people or things that can suck the life out of us. We all know people, friends, and relatives who never have a good thing to say about anything or anyone. They are the "Yeah, but ..." people. I might say how pleasant the weather is today, and they would comment, "Yeah, but it might rain." Twenty-twenty was a year of double negative whammies, pandemic, and politics. To some people, the COVID-19 pandemic was a sign of the end of the world. To others, the presidential elections would be the beginning of the end of our nation. And yet, most of us persevered.

The best way to block the spirit vampires is not garlic. It is to simply avoid them. We have full control to move out of negative conversations. We can replace old negative friends with new positive friends, and we can simply shut off our televisions. Mean-spirited people should not have a place in your life, your mind, or your intellect. It is not a requirement of life to submit your successful spirit to such challenges. Protect your positive successful spirit with your life. Sometimes it will be all you have.

Never Waiver from Your Spirit's GPS. Your successful spirit will drive you and lead you to a future that can be more outstanding than you can ever imagine if your spirit is one of positive thought and success. If it is caring and helping and selfless, then even when your focus isn't as straightforward as it could be, your internal compass will always position and push you towards opportunity and to your vision.

Honor Your Past. I have observed that when people fail, they often fail at things that they have failed at before. I have seen people fail because they did not honor their past and learned nothing from these failures. This constant cycle of failing will quickly kill a weak spirit. One sure way of learning from past mistakes is to listen to those little voices in your head. No, you're not going crazy. We all have them, and I believe that this is our successful spirit talking to us. These "intuitive" thoughts are said to be 95 percent correct if we acknowledge and listen to them.

Another great technique is to KWINK every questionable situation you face. KWINK stands for "knowing what I now know." KWINKing is a way to use past experiences as a resource to help you decide what you should discontinue, reduce, or eliminate in your life. Now you can be optimistic about your past mistakes. Now you can stay positive, draw upon the lessons learned, and honor your past. Just ask yourself the following: *Knowing What I Now Know,*

- *Should I do _____again?*
- *Should I stop doing _____?*
- *Should I continue doing _____?*

It works every time.

Create a Vision and Never Let It Go! A good friend of mine died a few years ago. He was much more than a friend; he was the most influential mentor that I've ever had. He achieved the pinnacle of success in his chosen field, yet he had a white-hot passion for learning. He didn't need to prove anything to anyone at that point of his life but nevertheless, he never let a day go by without study, reflection, and curiosity. When he was asked what had driven him throughout his life, his answer was simple: "I've always believed that there was more." The possibilities in life are endless for those that believe. It starts with having a vision.

I was born and raised in a small farming community in Kansas. When I was in high school, I didn't know much about the world, but I always knew there was more. That spirit voice spoke to me early and pushed me to challenge my comfort zone and continually explore the unknown. I had a rapidly developing vision of what my spirit told me was possible. People who are stuck in a lifestyle rarely have a vision for themselves. Their spirit flame is weak. However, anyone can create a vision for their future. If you already have one, then it should be continuously enhanced and clarified. Here are a few steps you can take to build or improve your vision.

- Set some quiet time aside. Late at night; early in the morning; after work in the quiet of an empty office—wherever it is, find a quiet place that you know will not have any interruptions for an hour.
- Now have some fun and dream. Go crazy. No one will know. Project your thoughts out five years or more. Envision how your perfect personal and professional life could look.
- Dream with no restrictions or constraints.
- Money is not an issue, and anything is possible. Break all barriers.
- Challenge yourself. The question is—how big will you allow yourself to dream if you know you cannot fail?
- Dream with sweet and pure clarity.
  - What will you be doing with your personal life?
  - What level of professional success have you achieved.? How remarkable is your personal life? How spectacular is your house?
  - Record everything on a digital recorder.
  - Do this once and then let it set to come back to and add to later. If it takes a week, that's okay.
- You should now have a clear vision of what your life will look like in the future. Now commit to this vision.

Lock this vision into your mind. Commit to it and believe in it. A solid, clear vision fuels your successful spirit. It also helps in another way. A robust and passionate vision solidifies your belief structure and eliminates the effect of any spirit vampires that will try to invade your mind. The fact is that everybody has both strengths and weaknesses. Feeding your successful spirit drives you to refuse to rationalize, justify, or defend your areas of weakness. Your powerful vision fueled by your energized successful spirit will now allow you to identify any area of liability, set a goal, and create a plan to become very good in each of those areas. Sometimes this opens a new path to achieve your vision and change your life.

Feed the Spirit. It is essential to protect and feed your successful spirit. Just like a muscle, without consistent work, it becomes weak. In *The Shade of My Own Tree*, Sheila Williams said, "The human spirit is tremendously resilient. It can withstand the most horrific of circumstances, whether of human or divine creation … It is not these larger-than-life situations that beat us. It's the little things."

The little things count. The personal and business development legend, Brian Tracy, taught me about the One Tenth of One Percent Success Rule. The rule says, if you do something to improve your thinking quality by one tenth of one percent every day, you grow and improve your thinking by nearly 35 percent over a year. Using compound interest, you grow and improve your thinking by over one thousand percent over five years. Success happens by disciplining yourself to simply upgrade the quality of your thinking by doing the little things.

- Eliminate negative influences.
- Find something or someone to say something nice about.
- Read one more paragraph or page in a motivational book.
- Read just one positive quote.

Whatever you find to do, make it a habit and a discipline. It sounds simple, but it could be the most challenging thing you'll ever learn to do consistently. When you focus on improving your thinking quality, your attitude improves, your intellect grows, and you feed the fire that is your successful spirit.

We've now gone full circle. Remember that your successful spirit shows. People can see it and feel it in your walk, your talk, and your smile. Your successful spirit has everything to do with the perception that people have of you, good or bad. You can generate an aura of success and a positive attitude, and you can profoundly affect those around you. People will feel good just being near you. And, it all starts with a spark. This spark is the spirit that is embedded in your soul, waiting to be fed and nurtured and grown.

I've been an entrepreneur all of my life. I once wondered what the requirements were to become a successful entrepreneur. I considered everything I could think of: education, income, family background, gender, age, location, etc. After thinking about this for a long time, I have concluded that none of these things matter. There is just one thing that makes a difference: at some point, every successful entrepreneur has to have a one thousand percent unquestionable belief in themselves and be willing to step out in faith. They have to have no doubt that what they are doing is right and that the time of planning and wishing and hoping is over. It is time to get after it, blaze a trail, and learn from the successes and failures that are sure to follow.

To paraphrase a classic rock anthem by The Doors—come on, baby, let's light the fire and let our successful spirit shine!

About the Author

Danny P. Creed is the "Super Coach" working with business owners, entrepreneurs, and corporations globally. He is a business, executive, and leadership coach. He is a best-selling author, global keynote and workshop speaker, experienced entrepreneur, and successful business owner. Danny is a Brian Tracy International Certified business coach. He has been involved with 15 successful startup businesses and over 400 business turnaround challenges. Coach Dan is the six-time recipient of the FocalPoint International Brian Tracy Award of Sales Excellence and the 2019 FocalPoint Coaching International Practice of the year.

Danny P. Creed is the published author of *A Life Best Lived: A Story of Life, Death and Second Chances*, *Straight Talk: Thriving in Business*, and *Champions Never Make Cold Calls: High-Impact, Low-Cost Lead Generation*. He also co-authored the bestseller, *The Successful Mind*. His books are available on Amazon.com or at https://www.businesscoachdan.com/books/

Email: dcreed@focalpointcoaching.com
Website: www.realworldbusinesscoach.com
LinkedIn: www.linkedin.com/in/businesscoachdan/

CHAPTER 5

BE STILL

By Dartanyon Crockett
USA Paralympic Medal Winner, Speaker
Denver, Colorado

Do the best you can until you know better. Then
when you know better, do better.
—Maya Angelou

"Be still."

I was surrounded in darkness when those words found their way to me. "Be still." A gentle surrender had fallen over my body. "Be still." I couldn't actually hear those words; however, I could feel them. Then my body responded accordingly. An eerie silence entered the space around me before I was woken up.

"Don't move, or I'll f**king kill you. Now empty your pockets."

These words shook my soul as they brought me to full attention. I was chest down with the left side of my face pressed to the sidewalk. I could tell that I was about one hundred feet away from the house I lived in. Initially, I was not quite sure what was happening. Even still, my body had remembered the wisdom of those words and remained still.

Without a word, my awareness shifted to the full situation. I was pinned beneath the barrel of a gun, with two men standing over me. One straddled my frozen body as he continued to apply his weight to the gun against my head. The other quietly stood over my head keeping watch. I did not have a chance to think as these words left my lips: "I don't have anything, just the food."

Time stopped as I waited for them to respond. When I opened my eyes, the two men were gone. And so was the food. That was okay though, because I was still here.

With my body void of strength, I did my best to stand strong. To just man up and walk home. However, that was not the case. My steps were unsteady. My body was trembling. My emotions were like nuclear bombs going off inside of me. I was not standing strong. I was walking in defeat. I couldn't man up. I was a child. That walk home was the longest walk I've ever taken. With every burdened step, I felt an assault of painful thoughts and emotions that began to tear away pieces of my spirit. I was feeling *all of it* that night. I was angry that I was attacked. I was happy that the event was over. I was afraid because I was 12 and alone. I was disgusted with the world because my dinner for that night was taken from me. I felt a deep shame for being too weak. I was sad because that night, more than any other, I wanted to go home to my mother. I couldn't, however, because she had passed away when I was eight.

I was honestly surprised to still be alive. I was feeling all of these emotions, simultaneously. I had never felt so calm and yet powerfully overwhelmed. Those emotional explosions continued to go off until I reached the back door of my home. As I stepped through the door, there was silence again. All my emotions stopped abruptly, and I felt numb. Completely and utterly numb.

Whenever I think back to this traumatic experience, I am reminded of the Yoruba concept of both/and. It can also be referred to as divine dichotomy. Wherein, two contradicting elements exist simultaneously within the same reality. That experience both destroyed and rebuilt my sense of self. Not over the course of a few months or days even, but on that night. I was no stranger to trauma at that point; however, you could say that the assault was the straw that broke the camel's back. Then replaced that camel with a far stronger and super-fast camel. That encounter is also what sparked my interest in sports.

At first the sports that I joined served as tools to help me survive my environment. I competed on four different sports teams in high school. Each of them served a different purpose for my survival. Powerlifting helped me to become much bigger and stronger than I ever thought possible. Football taught me grit and getting the job done with a team. Track and field led me to cultivate speed and agility, even with my bulky stature. Ultimately, I found my home and family in wrestling. This is where the warrior within me emerged. Over time, the world around me began to change along with my thoughts and perceptions of it. I found that people began to marvel at my physique and were in awe, or intimidated by my abilities.

In time the pursuit of my high school wrestling career opened a splendid opportunity for me—my career as a United States Paralympian in the sport of judo. Like wrestling, judo was a combat sport and grappling was the end all, be all of it. My Paralympic career gave me brilliant gifts in the form of friends, family, and incredible experiences.

Judo has also helped me to tap into a truly valuable skill: the warrior's calm. Just moments before stepping onto the mat before a match and right after a warmup, I learned how to bring my consciousness away from the physical plane of reality. My consciousness would then travel inward to the warrior's calm. There, it was quiet, peaceful, and profoundly invigorating. In this place of power, I would meet with each of my emotions, thoughts, and feelings. We gathered as if we were the knights of Camelot, sitting at the round table. Once we'd all taken our seats at the table, I would open and end each meeting with these words: "My dear friends, welcome. Once again, we head into battle, and I can only take some of you." After the conclusion of each meeting, I felt a gentle surge of adrenaline course through me. I'd feel ready for anything, equipped with everything I needed. No more, no less. I eventually finished my career as a two-time Paralympic bronze medalist and world champion.

My career as a United States Paralympian has been one of the greatest blessings of my life. There are not enough words in the human language to explain how I feel about it. So, I will just leave it at, I am so grateful.

At the same time, my career as a United States Paralympian was an escape and sometimes an excuse to not be focused on me. It was as if I was in a sports car that was traveling down a long stretch of road. The car was on autopilot. After a while, the gas ran out, and I came to a slow, should-a-done-this-sooner halt. When I finally found the nerve to pull myself from the car, I had no idea where I was or what to do next. I didn't think I would ever find another sports car like that either.

Remember that camel, though? You know, the one with the broken back from all that straw? Well, he was there. He too was scared, lonely, lost, angry, confused, shameful, traumatized ... all of it. This time, however, there was no replacing him. There was no getting away from him. I had to face him and sit with him. I was unaware at the time, but there was much that I had forgotten.

The camel, which of course is a representation of my past self, had a lot to say. There was so much he wanted me to remember. But you see, my past was not a place I ever wanted to revisit. I did not want to hear any of it. So, quietly and behind closed doors, I muffled his words with alcohol. Whenever he'd raise his voice, I'd raise another glass. Before long, I recognized this trend in myself.

During this time, I was working toward a degree in social work, and the focal point of my study was substance abuse and mental health. My education was being sponsored by a group of individuals who had watched an ESPN documentary that I was a part of called *Carry On*. They then quickly became family. It is important to me that I mention them because, as a direct result of their help, I was able to pull tools from the education they paid for. Tools that saved my life. The education gave me the tools to construct the courage needed to write this.

Like with my judo career, there are not enough words in the human language to describe what their gift means to me. This is also because that gift showed me that I had seen enough substance abuse in my life to know that I did not understand enough about it. Nor the cause of it. Not even the cure. This education I have, has given me a new language for substance abuse that I never had before. The difference between the two languages was that this new one spoke of treatment and a cure. Prior to my education, I had only perceived the horrors of substance abuse. I could neither imagine a cure nor a treatment. To me, substance abuse in families seemed a dark, painful cycle with no discernable origin. And no end.

When words failed to reach me, my past-self began to weaponize my thoughts, feelings, and emotions. I was back to experiencing those internal explosions again. However, they did not stop this time around. They assaulted my spirit with a mighty vengeance. Overtime, I was nearing my limit of this. My thoughts felt hijacked, my emotions were in total chaos and my body writhed in pain most days. At this point in my life, I began climbing deeper into my studies of mental health. At the same time, I was peeling back layers of a buried and forgotten past.

Eventually, my studies led me to researching childhood trauma. This was great because I was shoulder deep in my own trauma looking for a rope to pull myself out. However, I felt like there was just too much damage, and I was losing my grip on reality.

On a cool May morning in 2019, I woke up with a feeling of defeat in my chest. The first words that left my lips as I opened my eyes that day were "I just can't do today." I also shared these words with my partner at the time.

Her response to me was so tender, so warm, and so genuine. She reminded me that I had been moving incredibly fast without taking any time to look back. Now that I had to slow down, everything caught up with me. She held space for me, she held space for my fears, she held space for my pain, and she held me up while I was leaning over a cliff.

This day was another turning point for me. While I did not experience an overnight shift, I held on to the fact that I was a different kind of fighter than before. I had new skills and tools that served me in ways I could have never foreseen. Her words, they saved me that day. Her words also served as a call to action for me. Just as I pray that my words here will serve as a call to action for you.

As we go through life trying to cultivate our own ideas of success, we tend to encounter a multitude of barriers. This is also true when we find the strength to make a public declaration about ourselves. For example, the year that I declared myself a teacher as I embarked into a new career was 2020. Needless to say, that year, the entire universe sent everything it could to test my resolve on my claim. When we are tested in this way, we tend to panic, especially when we feel lost in the process and no one is answering our calls for help. Know this—teachers are silent during examinations. And this is an open notes test. So, let us revisit the key takeaways that will aid in manifesting the success that lies in each of us.

Three-Part Being

When thinking of cultivating a successful spirit, the first thing that comes to my mind is understanding ourselves as three-part beings: mind, body, and spirit. Also, thoughts, feelings, and emotions. Even id, ego, and superego. All of these words serve as definitions for the pieces that make us who we are. And, at the crux of them all, we are three parts.

This understanding is important because sometimes our three parts can become out of sync. We become stuck in place when this happens. We need to make sure there is alignment with our minds, bodies, and spirits. Do self-checks regularly. Ask, "How is my mind, my body, and my spirit? Where is my mind, my body, and my spirit? And what do each of them need right now?"

Both/And

The Yoruba concept both/and is much easier to put into practice once we perceive ourselves as three-part beings. It becomes more natural to sit with the duality of challenging situations or even people. Ultimately, we come to appreciate the darkness and light in every situation. We will also come to appreciate the fact that light never loses its value either. Both/and reminds us of the duality all around us and teaches us to control only what is within our grasp. With Both/and something can be both difficult AND rewarding, miserable AND necessary, painful AND healing.

The Warrior's Calm

Each of us needs and deserves to have a peaceful space in our minds, our bodies, and within our emotions, where we feel safe and empowered. Remember we are three-part beings; this is just a part of doing the alignment. Internally is where we are able to do the most work on ourselves. It is where we build the foundation that will be strong enough to bear the weight of our success. It's big, it's heavy, and it's worth every ounce. Trust me on this.

In regards to actually cultivating a warrior's calm, meditation is key. With that said, meditate on these words, would you? Observe your own peaceful nature, then live in it. Always. All ways.

Language

Stress, trauma, and mental health are truly topics to be taken seriously, and having the gift in developing a language for what happened to me was vital to my healing.

Language is critical in any kind of communication. Especially the language we use for ourselves. Learn how to speak the language of your pain, your fears, and your anger. Seeing a counselor can also help in developing a language. If insurance is a problem, look up "sliding scale" counselors. If you are someone who needs help, don't let anything be a barrier from you getting it.

Departure

From lying on the pavement with a gun to my head, to winning a Paralympic medal, to escaping through alcohol, to learning how to heal myself and others,

I've had ups and downs in my life. The journey wasn't always easy, but I grasped on to things that would help me through difficult times, including the warrior's calm, the Yoruba concept of both/and, my education, and the words from a loved one. These things helped me move through the challenges of life and spread my wings to enjoy the beauty life has to offer. I imagine my challenges in life are not over, but by paying attention to my mind, body, and successful spirit, I know I'll be fine.

The pursuit of success is a glorious journey, and the most important part of any journey is the start, the departure. Now go forth and manifest your successful spirit. It's yours.

About the Author

Dartanyon Crockett was born in inner-city Cleveland, Ohio. He's had his story shared across the world, thanks to the help of ESPN producer, Lisa Fenn. Dartanyon was blessed in pursuing a career as a US Paralympian in the sport of judo. As a Paralympic athlete, Dartanyon also began to build a career in inspirational speaking. Dartanyon's speaking career has led him to pursue knowledge and insight from the fields of social work, sociology, and education.

While stepping into his new career as a sociologist, serving as a program manager for YESS, Dartanyon has grown to become an expert in the area of recovery and resilience. Dartanyon addresses these concepts by generalizing knowledge from his international experience as an athlete, coach, and speaker, as well as his sociological and trauma-informed research.

Email: Yess.dartanyon@gmail.com

CHAPTER 6
FEEL YOUR SUCCESS

By Barbara Daoust
Business, Performance, and Success Coach
Los Angeles, California

Get into the spirit of the state desired by assuming the feeling that
would be yours were you already the one you want to be.
—Neville Goddard

After years of mindset and peak performance coaching with entrepreneurs, business owners, and professionals, the one truth I know is that success can be taught. There are success principles available to all of us and many highly successful people have followed these principles. There are plenty of programs, books, practices, concepts, tools, exercises, and processes to help people achieve their success, but sadly it remains a fact that only a small percentage of people accomplish their dreams, goals, and desires in life. Getting the right support, mentorship, and accountability can make all the difference in whether or not you can achieve what you desire. One of the benefits of support and mentorship is that trained professionals can often help you ignite your spirit thus creating a strong desire to take action toward your goals and your success.

What I have discovered to be a missing link for most people is their inability to connect to the feelings of having their wish fulfilled. More often than not, most of my clients start out saying that they don't know how to visualize and that they don't know how to feel.

After a few quick processes to help them visualize, they better understand that they are actually visualizing all day long and embedding images into their subconscious mind whether they are aware of them or not. The same goes for when they say they don't know how to feel. Most people are stuck in their logical mind: the conscious mind. They have difficulty dropping into what is considered the emotional mind: the subconscious mind.

When I ask someone if they feel frustrated that they can't feel, they immediately say, "Yes."

To which I reply, "Then why are you lying to yourself? If you feel frustrated, you are having a feeling."

Most people who want to attain greater success, know what they want. They have a burning desire to achieve a big dream, a goal, or a life mission. The biggest challenge that they share is that they are not doing it. They know what to do, but they are not doing it. Yes, they have the information and the knowledge to do it. Yes, they have the strategy and the plan. But they don't realize that their conditioned mindset is responsible for keeping them just where they are: stuck on knowing what they already know. It takes a growth mindset to change results in your life, and most people are justifying, explaining, rationalizing, and making excuses for why they can't have success or why they can't have their dream come true: "I don't have the time," "I don't have the money," or "I don't know if I can leave my job."

One of the first questions I ask everyone is "Are you willing to change?" This question helps me see if the determination of their spirit is aligned with their desire for change. If they are ready to change, then it's time to make a committed decision to create that change. That is when the journey begins. It takes conscious, deliberate effort to create success in life. It takes commitment. It takes desire. It takes clarity, focus, and most of all, it takes a willingness to grow. If you are currently not satisfied with the results in your life or if you are seeking bigger, better, and more in your life, then ask yourself, "What can I do differently? What can I change?"

First and foremost, it helps to understand that success is a journey. It's a journey of becoming a higher version of yourself. It's a result of thoughts, feelings, and actions that are part of creating a new identity. A new identity that is willing to take a journey into the unknown and find the parts of yourself that you haven't yet met. It's who you are being on a daily basis. For example, if you want to be a successful writer, you must first be a writer. Taking daily action to sit down and write aligns you with the truth that you are a writer, not that you are becoming one. As Goethe, the famous German philosopher, once said, "Before you can do something, you must first be something."

When you've made the committed decision to change and to grow your self-awareness, acknowledging that there is more for you to have, that you deserve to live the life you dream of having, it's now time to fantasize. Let yourself ask for more, want for more, and start to build bigger, better fantasies.

Your level of commitment and the intensity of your desire is what is needed to create form out of formless energy. Formless energy involves your dreams, ideas, visions, and intentions. Moving them into physical matter depends on who you are being every day.

Most of the time, we are operating on autopilot. This usually means that our default system goes back to what it already knows in order to avoid any kind of pain, discomfort, or failure. We are not even aware of the limitations we are imposing upon ourselves. Becoming conscious and self-aware is necessary for expansion and fulfillment in your life. When you consistently focus on what is working rather than on what isn't working, you will experience new circumstances, new people, and new opportunities for success.

The only real power that you have is to choose your thoughts. You must become conscious and choose what is best serving you. Get out of autopilot. Build new perspectives, acquire new information, knowledge, insights, and grow your self-worth. Commit to observing your negative self-talk and make a choice to reframe or reach for a better feeling-thought. Ask yourself if your thoughts are 100 percent accurate or if they are lies that you are telling yourself, so you get to continue playing small. Align your feelings with the truth. Be determined. Be diligent. Be devoted to the change that you want to see.

As stated earlier, start becoming the person you want to be by first being the person you want to be. Do you believe that you can have success in your life? How much faith do you have that you can achieve your aim in life? How badly do you want it? Can you feel the feelings of success in your body? Can you internalize these feelings and be the person you have to be in order to achieve the success you want? What are the thoughts, the feelings, and the actions of someone who has success? How does a highly successful person behave? What are their beliefs about having success?

I love this quote from Clarence Smithison, "Faith is the ability to see the invisible and believe in the incredible and that is what enables believers to receive what the masses think is impossible."

Below are some processes and tools that I share with my clients to help them realize that all the power we have is within.

Feelings

Imagination is a mental faculty that everyone is using daily. Everything is created twice. First in the mind, then in the hand. To first see something in physical form, it starts first as a picture in the mind. This is why we say everything is created twice. Again, some people are using their imagination to bring great joy into their lives, and some people are using it to imagine the worst possible thing that could happen in their lives, not only to themselves but to others as well. We all have very powerful imaginations. It's a gift that is given to all of us, and we have the power to focus it on the direction of our dreams. Use it to reach better feeling-thoughts. We can use it to embed the truth about who we are on a deeper emotional level. You will become more empowered, confident, and determined to win at your fantasies as a result.

Close your eyes and think about something that you don't like about yourself, something that you judge as imperfect. Sense the feelings that come to you when you have those thoughts. How does it feel? What would you call this feeling? Is this a supportive feeling? Or is it a bad feeling? Check in with yourself and feel the emotions attached to the thoughts that you are having. Grow aware.

Now shift your attention to having some compassion for yourself. Acknowledge that you don't have to be perfect. Try on a different thought like, "I'm wonderful just as I am. I have so much to offer and so many gifts to share." Allow yourself to feel the feelings that these new thoughts bring you. Sense your spirit rejoicing with the positivity you feel. How would you describe these feelings? Do you feel lighter? More hopeful? Maybe even excited? Can you feel a shift in your energy? Practice this daily and observe how your beliefs about yourself start to shift. Watch as other people start to react or respond to you differently as well.

Beliefs

Most of us are programmed to have beliefs that are not even our own. We believe when other people tell us what we should or should not do, and what we can or cannot do. These beliefs create habits and patterns that affect our choices and actions in our lives. If you want to change, you must change your beliefs. Your beliefs are part of a program that was created during your formative years, otherwise known as programming. You can change your programming. You can change the image you have of yourself. You can change your results.

If you don't believe that you can have something, no matter how much you want or desire it, you will not get closer to having it. You must believe that it is yours to have. If you come from a place of "getting" or "trying to," you will attract more of the same. You will continue to be "getting" and continue to be "trying to" because you are coming from a place of doubt and a place of lack. You must come from a place of believing that you can have what you desire because it already exists and it is yours to have.

It takes practice. It takes awareness. It takes a willingness to let go of the beliefs that are no longer serving you. Again, there are tools and processes to reach the subconscious mind that can help release the beliefs, patterns, doubts, and fears that are holding you in a place of limitation. One of the most important processes to help shift your doubts and fears is the process of visualization.

Visualization

Visualization is a powerful process for change. It helps to inspire us and shifts our energy in ways that support us having our deepest desires fulfilled. When you fuse your desire with images and emotion, your subconscious accepts the pictures and feelings that you think about as if you are in the experience of "having it."

It's important to understand that it's the "feeling place" that enhances and supports your most wanted desires. If you are imagining a beautiful home, and you feel doubt that you will ever have it, then the evidence will continue to show you that you will not have it. Connect with the feelings that you want to experience. It's not the "thing" that we want in the end, it's the feelings that the "thing" brings us.

When you visualize and see certain pictures in your mind's eye, you are actually activating physical responses in your body. You are engaging your five physical senses. The subconscious mind doesn't know the difference between real or imaginary. The same areas in your brain are fired up as though you are experiencing the actual moment. If you visualize exercising, it has been shown that our bodies respond to the pictures as if we are really exercising!

I want you to take a moment and visualize something in your life that brings you great joy. Create that image in your mind's eye in detail. See yourself interacting with others and sharing experiences with others. Let yourself feel it. Think about why you love it, why you appreciate it, why you admire it. Feel the feelings that this image brings you. Feel the joy, the love, the appreciation. Imagine that you are a magnet with magnetic energy as you enhance the feelings in your body. Appreciate and enjoy the feelings as you receive them. What you focus on expands. What you give attention to grows. When you open your eyes, make a conscious effort to notice how you feel in the present moment and continue to build upon it throughout your day.

Acting As If ...

Visualization combined with "acting as if ..." helps to activate your desire by deepening your connection to feeling. It shifts your energy into a feeling of already "having it." It's a wonderful way to help you focus on what you want and declare it as "done." From that feeling place, you can take inspired action and know that you are becoming a congruent match to your desires.

Write down all the details that you are imagining in your mind's eye so that it feels like you can see, taste, touch, hear, and smell everything you are picturing. Write your story "as if" you are living it now. You are the character in your own movie, and you are the creator of the feelings that you want to have. You get to write the script for the life that you want. You can create scenes, scenarios, and events that you would like to have happen in your life. Use your imagination to create the character of the highly successful person you want to be.

Write out a description of this person's attitude, their thoughts, their feelings, and their daily actions. Think of their habits, their self-image, the way they dress, their values, their decisions, and their focus on the solution rather than on the problem. Build the character as if you were an actor in a movie who wanted to receive an academy award. What is the role that you are playing? What are your thoughts about money? How easily do you quit? How do you talk to yourself all day long? What is your attitude toward yourself and toward others? How do you treat the people you meet on a daily basis? Do you treat them with respect as you would want them to treat you? What is your attitude toward life? Your way of being is the causation of your results.

Motor Imaging

Motor imaging is even more powerful than visualizing pictures in your mind's eye. You get to move and express the feelings of being in your dream. It's simulating the experiences that you want to have. For example, if you want to be a keynote speaker, practice your speech as if you were in front of a large audience; wear an outfit you would wear; say your speech out loud; see the people watching you; add a recording of people applauding—do anything to access the feelings of what it would be like if giving a keynote speech were happening in the moment.

When you think of your dream, create a picture in your mind's eye of having your dream. Fill in the details. Start by writing out a list of all your personal wants. Write down all the things that you would love to have in your life. Then write a list of all the professional things you want in your life. Make sure that you really, really want it. After you've written the list, ask yourself which one you want the most. Notice if it excites you, but also notice if it scares you. If you are going after a goal, and it doesn't scare you, you are going in the wrong direction. Once you've decided on your personal goal and your professional goal, it's time to write each one out in detail. Write it out in present tense and include feeling words. An example would be: *I am joyfully committed to growing my consulting practice. I am wholeheartedly helping people change their lives and grow their businesses. My practice is growing abundantly.*

Writing causes thinking. Thinking causes imagery. Imagery causes emotion. Emotion creates action. Action creates reaction. Reaction creates results.

As you own your role and begin to act your way to success, you will create a new identity. A new identity that is passionate about growth and opportunity. A new identity that is obsessed with feeling good, creating win-win situations, and acting from the higher inner knowing that you deserve to achieve your dreams. The best actors who win are the ones who embody the character wholeheartedly and unabashedly. Who is your character? What are you committing to daily? Affirm, align, and proclaim that you deserve to win at your fantasies, making them a reality.

By committing with heartfelt conviction to a new self-image with new empowering beliefs, new productive behaviors, and new positive attitudes, you'll create new patterns and break up with disempowering beliefs, non-productive behaviors, and bad attitudes that have been in the way of your success. It's chemistry. It's science. It's mind over matter.

In summary, remember to access the feeling place. You want to feel the "essence" of the thing that you want. Let your successful spirit shine. Be playful, use your imagination, and have fun. Remember, your subconscious mind doesn't know the difference between real and imaginary. It's about clarity, focus, and purpose. How focused can you be to get what you want?

Place your hand on your heart and say out loud to yourself: "I am willing to change."

Say it again and make sure that you proclaim it. Say it with feeling. Say it with conviction. Sing it from your heart and create a movement or a gesture to support it. Your energy will shift, your spirit will be engaged, and your heart will open. Who do you have to be to win at your fantasies?

Now go out there—see it, feel it, and BE the success you want to be!

About the Author

Barbara Daoust is an acclaimed success coach, business mindset strategist, author, and inspirational speaker. She shows entrepreneurs, business owners, and individuals how to break through their inner ceilings to play a bigger game and achieve outstanding results in their professional and personal lives.

Barbara helps people to rewire their brains and reprogram their minds, so they can say goodbye to procrastination, perfectionism, and self-doubt. She is a certified, "Thinking into Results" consultant with the Proctor Gallagher Institute and the creator of the programs, "Discover Greatness Within" and "Your Genius Code Unlocked."

Barbara spent most of her career in theatre arts, film, and television as a director, acting coach, writer, and producer. She now blends her 25 years of acting, directing, and writing experience inspiring people to connect to the best version of themselves and to be the star of their own movie.

Email: Barbara@BarbaraDaoust.com
Websites:
www.barbaradaoust.thinkingintoresults.com
www.vibrantresults.com

CHAPTER 7

EMBRACING THE DARK

By Brett Elena
US Naval Officer, Ultramarathon Competitor
Portland, Oregon

12FEB21, 0700: It is 12 days after my stepsister's death. I am tired. I have not started counseling. I have not "processed."

But I will.

Because in every moment of my life, personal and professional, I believe in hope, beauty, and healing. I believe in embracing the dark: in working through our most painful, shameful, and difficult stories one breath, one step, and one day at a time to reach the other side.

Before

When Erik initially asked me to be a part of *The Successful Mind*, I told him, no. "I do not have ducks; they are not in a row. I have squirrels, and they are at a rave."

The Successful Spirit though? Now that I can do it, which is how I find myself contemplating darkness on a calm, peaceful snowy morning.

Life has interesting timing. When I originally pitched my chapter idea, I thought that I had completed my trials. I thought that I could write from the clinical perspective of one who has reached the other side, from a place of already-healed scars.

But now the scars are torn open. Jordan is gone. New wounds are revealed, and I find myself wandering through another maze of shadows. Rage, sorrow, regret—they all have homes here, if I don't make the "right" turn.

Do I still have the strength to "Embrace the Dark?" Do I really?

Because real life hurts. But, perhaps, just perhaps, these are all the right turns in and of themselves: each hurt a place to visit before we continue on our journey, changed, yes, but perhaps, just perhaps, softer, kinder, and more empathetic. Elizabeth Lesser writes eloquently of this process in her book, *Broken Open*; Glennon Doyle smashes windows in her more forceful bestseller, *Untamed*.

But I am not Elizabeth Lesser. I am not Glennon Doyle. I am Brett. So, here's a summary of my path:

Step 1: Play by society's (or your family's, your culture's, work's, etc.) rules. Sacrifice everything to achieve their "success."

Step 2: Look in the mirror and no longer recognize your reflection.

Step 3: Decide. Choose. Is this the person you want to be? Is this the life you want to live?

Looking at the resumes of the other contributors to this book, one might wonder how I was selected. No offense taken—much like when my teacher gawked at my perfect chemistry score, wondering if it was rude to express incredulity, I, too, find my inclusion improbable. Full disclosure: I believe it was because Erik liked my military background, but my naval service does not define me.

That's just one part.

I am a poet. I am a writer. I am a daughter, a stepdaughter, a heartbroken sister. I am an athlete, a singer, a friend. I am an unconventional Christian. I am a gay woman, an American. I am a naval officer. I am a stumbler, a maker of mistakes. I am human.

And it's a human story that I offer.

Step 1: I inherited a double dose of competitive perfectionism, compounded by an instilled belief in self-sacrifice for the greater good. It was Spiderman's Uncle Ben on steroids: "with great power comes great responsibility," or the

Bible's "to one whom much is given, much is required" (Luke 12:48). Both are great ideas, but dangerous if left unchecked.

I played sports, I earned my first black belt in karate, and I joined Young Marines (receiving the "Young Marine of the Year" award in an appropriately feminine sundress). I won a scholarship to a prestigious private high school. In my Bible Belt hometown, where Hooters is banned in perpetuity, there was no question of my sexuality—I was straight, of course.

I spent my childhood in a ferocious, one-sided battle to "prove myself" and to earn an appointment to the United States Naval Academy.

Twelve years later, the phrase "Be careful what you wish for" comes to mind. Though my resume appeared "successful," in reality Annapolis' balmy Plebe Summer (boot camp) broke me. My entire body underwent a horrendous psychosomatic response. I was physically limping and mentally shattered, sporting purple skin and a jumpy, shell-shocked constitution. Hindsight insists that this was the signal for my departure, but I was stubborn. In my mind, to be a midshipman was the ONLY way to succeed in life, so I persevered, even after the development center red-flagged me for suicide risk.

Accordingly, I struggled when deciding to commit seven years to service. I was fully aware that the military and I weren't a good fit, but my childhood ideals of perfectionism and sacrifice warred with my self-awareness. I didn't trust and love myself enough to make a decision "for me" alone. I wandered through the memorials of Washington DC, torn: *Our country has been great,* I mused. *And it can be great again. But it's going to require sacrifice.* And I wasn't prepared to ask that sacrifice of others when I wasn't willing to offer the same myself.

Accordingly, a summary of the following six years: a beautiful graduation and commissioning ceremony. Running a marathon for charity just to feel any sense of worth; an almost desperate need to volunteer. Receiving salutes because I was "respected." Teary-eyed phone calls from Japan, enraged beyond reason because my captain "just didn't like me." Gorgeous Facebook posts from Mt. Fuji. A hotel room for one on base, drinking apple pie moonshine while binge eating Fritos. Sleeping on the ship because my house was too far away. Staring at the South China Sea's skyline, wondering what on earth I was doing.

That period was also when I finally had to admit to myself that I wasn't as straight as I had hoped. My first thought? *Well, f**k.*

2017 found me in Bahrain, a tiny island kingdom east of Saudi Arabia. I was finally able to use my hard-earned Arabic ability, but the expat's decadent lifestyle soon drew me in. My alcohol intake greatly increased in terms of quantity and frequency, and I ignored the worried texts from my sisters far away. "You just don't get it," I told them. "This is just how our [the military] life *is*." No matter how dire the circumstances appeared, my competitive spirit, my need to prove myself, and our family's talent for endurance propelled me forward.

By 2019, I had achieved every external measure of professional success. The admiral had hand-selected me to be his aide (personal assistant), the highest honor to which a young lieutenant could aspire. I travelled the region as part of his entourage, staying at exotic, remote locations most could only imagine, i.e., Egypt's Red Sea, Pakistan's Islamabad, and Saudi Arabia's Riyadh.

And yet, when I looked in the mirror, I didn't recognize myself (step 2). We had crossed the continents for a Change of Command ceremony, one attended by numerous admirals and generals. I had brutalized my trademark curls, donned my uniform—set my features to a stoic, contained mask. I looked immaculate, official, and 100% foreign.

I didn't recognize myself in the slightest.

Frankly, it scared the hell out of me. So (step 3): Decide. Choose. Is this the person you want to be? Is this the life you want to live?

Why is this confused, 20-something lieutenant
writing about the "successful spirit"?

Because I chose a different ending. Alcohol, empty eyes, degrees, awards: this was where professional and society's "success" had led me. But I chose my own path home.

The Present—Courage, Compassion, and Honesty

Merriam Webster defines "honesty" as the "adherence to facts." Facts, however, can be difficult, persnickety, and downright troublesome—particularly when they fly in the face of the comfortable(ish) worlds that we have built for ourselves.

And that's why we need courage: to take in the full truth, even when it hurts (because it usually does). And then, even MORE difficult: the courage to *change* when we acknowledge our world is not as we wanted to believe.

Compassion, however, is always the secret ingredient: to allow that soft, squishy, oh-so human side of ourselves to just *be* (Mary Oliver in her poem "Wild Geese": You do not have to be good. / You do not have to walk on your knees / for a hundred miles through the desert repenting).

I needed all three of these ingredients to forgive myself and to walk that journey home, to where I would no longer feel the need to apologize to my afroed eight-year-old self. I had to embrace my own darkness and tear down my own misconceptions in order to heal.

The day in, day out details are unimportant, but for anyone seeking to start that journey, I would offer these thoughts:

1. It takes time. Cliche, annoying, and oh-so true.
2. Embracing the full, ugly truth has to happen. Whether it's a sky-high laundry pile, a festering cut, or horrific childhood trauma, ignoring the discomfort doesn't help anything. We can skip along merrily, bury ourselves in shopping, work, alcohol, TV, or food, but until we face up to and *stay* with reality, everything will only continue to deteriorate.
3. We need mentors. We need friends. We all need rest, empathy, and kind, listening ears. We need people to sit with us in the dark, not to "fix" us or tell us what to do; we already know our answer. They are there to light the candle, to hold that flicker of hope when we are too exhausted to see its flame. These individuals hold space and validate our experiences.
4. Some days are still horrible, no good, very bad days. You could have turned the corner; you could have really thought you "had it," but I'm warning you now, some days are still monsters in the night. Beware. Make plans and ask for help ahead of time. (Mine is texting a friend to remind me: "naan > tequila.")
5. Rituals help. When I was at my worst in Bahrain, I still worked out and played piano daily. These activities did not help me to *improve* mentally, but they helped keep the spark of "me" alive. Sometimes, the ritual is as simple as brushing your teeth. That works. Though they may seem small, these rituals are vitally important.
6. Remember who you are, whatever that means to you. When I was on a gusty plateau in New Zealand, at the highest point of our 150-mile ultramarathon course, I literally growled through my teeth: "This storm will not defeat me." Plebe Summer, USNA Blackbelt, a

tossing destroyer in the storm, an icy Kilimanjaro summit, Nepal's Annapurna, deserts. "I have been through *too much*, and I will *not* give in!"

7. Back to honesty—it *sucks*, especially in cultures that value appearance far more than authenticity. Honesty is scary, and it hurts, and it's *hard* to admit to anything less than perfection. However, perfection is a myth, and that is why I have always liked live poetry. Is it always great? Heck no. Not in the slightest. But it's *honest*. Although I don't necessarily *enjoy* vulnerability, I do believe that by offering my unvarnished truth, it gives permission for someone else to do the same. "Wait, we are allowed to do that? We are allowed to admit that we're human and have insecurities and flaws and imperfect baggage?" Yes. Yes, we are.

8. Nature is awesome. The importance of animals' unconditional love, grounding our unsteady emotions in the natural world, and getting into the woods/out of our heads simply cannot be overstated.

9. Break. Crumble. Absolutely fall apart. I actually wrote this while listening to John Legend's "Never Break," and sometimes those are the words that I need to hear; I need the encouragement to just keep one foot in front of the other. On other occasions, though, compassion dictates that we also need to allow ourselves permission to *not* be the "strong ones." Sometimes we *all* have to tear/fall down before we can rebuild. Perhaps if I had offered myself the grace to follow my body's instinct and quit Plebe Summer, I could have spared myself a whole lot of pain. Perhaps … or perhaps I lived the life I was meant in order to learn and offer my perspective. Who can say?

10. Breathe.

What Comes Next?—Hope, Beauty, and Healing

On some days, the "healing" seems impossible. Bitterness can seem second nature; cynicism, natural.

Rage, rage against the dying of the light. Do not go softly into that good night.

Dylan Thomas' oft-quoted words can mean many things. However, I like to think of them as the fight to hold on to the good, even when everything seems bleak.

The day I learned of Jordan's death, I was in anger, shock, and hurt beyond description.

The night after, however, I pulled out my old bracelets, methodically polishing the tarnished silver. The dirt fell away to reveal their inscriptions: "sanar" (Spanish for 'to heal') and "Hope Is Defiant." Together, they complemented my Arabic tattoo: "the World Is Beautiful."

I donned these bracelets *because I will not go softly into the night.*
I choose to believe in hope, even in pain.
I choose to believe that I will heal. Maybe not today, definitely not tomorrow. But my soul was not made for bitterness.
There is beauty yet, still.

None of this process is easy. To be human, fully human—to embrace the dark, to take in the world as it is, with all of its heartbreaking sorrow, its anger, its tragedy—it's painful.

I find the "successful" spirit an interesting turn of phrase, though. Who defines success? Is it the most pious, the most holy? The one best able to meditate among the trees, or the one able to tap dance along the chakras?

To me, a "successful" spirit is when we are able to keep both eyes open: to not deny the hurt, to admit and work through our imperfections, but to also hold on to the good. To love and not count the cost; to be true to ourselves, and to die without regrets, even in full awareness that we have made our share of mistakes too.

To me, the successful spirit is one gorgeously, heartbreakingly human: yesterday, today, and always.

18FEB21, 1130: I am sober. I have not lost my temper. I am ridiculously proud of these facts as I stare around Marquam Forest, fog creeping through the trees, clinging to the evergreen slopes. Chill hovers and bites at my ankles, even as diverging paths wind through the dark: a maze of stark beauty.

Patches of snow linger on the ground, intermingling with the mud. My dog scampers before me, pouncing on the fallen needles, assaulting the pine cones. Despite everything, her antics still draw a smile.

Life continues, and I pause. I breathe once. I breathe twice, into the stillness, into the chill.
Be here. Stay.

The words, "Jo Bailey," peek from the top of my Converse sneakers, her name decorated with a flourishing pink heart and faint silver lining.

Have I healed? Has the ache disappeared, have I made peace, am I okay that she will not dance at my sister's wedding, that I will never attend hers? No. No, not at all … but I am here. And somewhere, somehow, I know that she is too. And that is enough.

Breathe once. Breathe twice. *Be here. Stay …*

About the Author

Brett Elena is a naval officer who has served in Japan, Bahrain, and Portland, Oregon. Her book, *Of Course it Hurts* (2019), is available on Amazon. She is also an ultramarathon competitor who calls the Blue Ridge Mountains, Oman, and her cockapoo home. When not scribbling, she can be found trail running, tripping over her own feet, studying Arabic, or tormenting her family. She has crossed six continents in her search for delicious ice cream, savors good coffee, and really does want world peace.

Brett can be reached at brettelena21@gmail.com for further pondering, interesting side tangents, or coffee suggestions.

Website: www.b2-adventures.com

CHAPTER 8
YOUR GREATEST COMPETITOR: YOU

By Nathaniel Errez
US National Team, Flatwater Kayaking
San Diego, California

Success comes from knowing that you did your best to become the best that you are capable of becoming.
—John Wooden

Every muscle in my body burned as the familiar sting of lactic acid filled each fiber of my arms and legs. I could clearly make out the finish buoys, but time was running in slow motion as I tried to push the pain out of my head. I knew that if I could just hold on for 150 more meters, I would finish in the top three at the USA National Team trials and qualify for the Pan American Games. When racing in an Olympic-style kayak, you have to find the perfect balance between aggression and calmness. From years of dedication to kayaking, I've been able to find this balance, and now I apply it to all aspects of my life.

Flatwater kayaking in the Olympics works very similarly to rowing in that we race down a flat body of water, usually a lake or canal, in straight lanes with nine boats lined up, side by side. Our sport is a little different from rowing since we face forward in the boats and race half the distance, 1,000 meters versus rowing's 2,000 meters.

These kayaks are very different from the average plastic sit-on-topper that you might have seen in the past. Our boats are made of carbon fiber, weigh about 26 pounds at race standard, and are about 16 feet long and no more than 16 inches wide. Yes, inches. They are very tough to balance, and it takes years before you can really feel comfortable in a K1 or kayak single.

Being an athlete and a full-time graduate student is a lifestyle that requires an immense amount of dedication, time management, and sacrifice. An average day for me over the last five years has looked like this:

5:15 am – Wake up, eat something light, get ready for morning practice

5:50 am – Leave for training

6:00 am – Start land warmup

6:15 am – Get on the water to start water warmup

6:30 am – Start the training session with longer efforts, about 7.5 to 10 miles

8:00 am – Finish training, stretch, head home

8:30 am – Breakfast

9:15 am – Start doing homework

11:00 am to 2:00 pm – Classes

2:30 pm – Leave for afternoon training

3:00 pm - Afternoon session, usually weights, running, or another paddle workout

4:45 pm – Finish afternoon session, head home

5:15 pm – Dinner

6:15 pm – More homework

9:00 pm – Wind down and try to get in bed before 10 pm

One of the concepts that has had a large impact on my life and career has been this idea of "executive capacity." Now, this is a business term that means an employee gets to have more decision-making power within an organization without necessarily being a C-level manager, but I am borrowing it in this context from kayaking legend, Adam Van Koeverdon. In my context, executive capacity means making a conscious effort to pursue the things that are important to me and realizing that I get out what I put in. While I learned the definition of executive capacity while doing my MBA, because of my athletic drive, I was really applying this at the age of 14.

When I was 14 years old, I had been kayaking for two years and decided I wanted to try out for my first national team. In my sport, there is a race called the Olympic Hopes Regatta, which is essentially the highest level of competition worldwide for 15-, 16-, and 17-year-olds. I had my sights set on competing in it, and I set that as my target. The process for being invited entailed getting through the national team trials, where I would have to establish myself as one of the top US competitors in those age categories. This is where I made a critical error: I completely overestimated my chances of qualifying and severely overestimated my own abilities. I trained for an entire season leading up to the qualifier blithely believing that I would make it on the team without needing to really push myself. I was resting on my laurels.

Flash forward to the competition itself. I went out for my race, the junior K1 1,000 meter, which was on the first day of competition. I got to the start line, and we all lined up. Ready. Set. GO! The race started. The guy in the lane to my left shot out from the blocks, as did the guy on my right. With every stroke they pulled further and further away. I looked around, which you should not do while competing, and everyone else was gone. I was in last place. One thousand meters is a long way to go from last. Everyone's wake caught up to me, and I limped down the course to finish about a minute behind the winner, a huge margin in a less-than four-minute race.

I got off the water completely devastated. I was not expecting such a horrible loss. However, I kept my sights high for the next day where we would race 200 meters. As you might have guessed, the 200s went just about as badly as the previous race. Last place. Again. I went home defeated.

When I got back to my home in Seattle, I was ready to give up kayaking completely. I think quitting is a natural reaction to failure, and I was so young it was one of the first times I had set a goal and failed miserably. However, what happened after that changed the entire course of my life. Two of my friends, who had also failed to qualify, told me about a trip that they were taking in the summer to go to Canada, one of the top countries for kayaking, to train with some of their friends there. They offered for me to tag along. My coach said this was a good idea, and my parents were on board. I agreed too. This was a huge step; remember, I was 14 years old and taking my first trip without my parents.

The first couple days in Canada were horrible. I thought I'd made a huge mistake. I was so homesick, I wanted more than anything to just go home where everything was familiar. I was out of my comfort zone.

Luckily, positive things started to happen. I became better friends with the Canadians I was training with, and my surroundings became less intimidating. I began to have a lot of fun, and the training became enjoyable. I was paddling longer distances and training harder than I had before, and I was seeing huge improvements. By the end of my time in Canada, I didn't want to leave, but our own US National Championships were coming up. It was time to compete again. I would be racing all the same guys I had raced at the national team trials four months earlier. This made me nervous, I was still scarred by my last experience competing against them.

When race day came, I went out for the first race. Again, it was a K1 1,000 meters. This time, things went a lot differently. I wasn't getting left behind anymore. Something had changed, and I finished in the top six in my age. I was ecstatic just to have not come last.

You might ask yourself, "What does this story have to do with executive capacity?" This experience tells how I learned, at a very early age, that I was in control of my own destiny. If I had just given up and quit, then I would never have had the chance to come back and prove to myself that I was capable of better. I saw that a whole summer of hard training had paid off big time. It was a classic example of effort and reward. I saw that the work I put in in Canada had actually made me better. This subconsciously unlocked some potential in me that neither I, nor anyone else, thought was there. I learned the value of dedicated preparation.

I learned that the right preparation means tailoring it to your goals. For the next several years, I set my sights only on making it to the US Junior National team without really considering the larger picture. As unfortunate as it might be, the reality is that the US is not a powerhouse in my sport and so just being the best nationally doesn't necessarily mean that your results will carry over internationally. I learned that firsthand when I competed at the Junior World Championships in Minsk, Belarus when I was 17 years old. My entire goal that year was to qualify for the national team, so after that I didn't really adjust my goals. I achieved them, I was satisfied, and more or less rested on my laurels, again.

When the competition came, our event, the K4 1000m, was on the first day and one of the first races. Unlike the K1, there are four of us in the K4 kayak. The world championship level races usually take place over four or five days, so if you race the heats one day you may not race until the next day or two days later. That is, if you progress from the heats.

We went out for our race, did our warmup, and got lined up on the far outside lane. Looking to our right and seeing 17- and 18-year-olds from many Eastern European countries, I thought, "They don't look like 18-year-olds." My nerves were going crazy at this point; there was a huge pit in my stomach. The voice of the starter came on over the speakers. Ready. Set. GO! I got flashbacks to myself at 14 racing the trials. We were already last within the first 250 meters. As I mentioned before, 1,000 meters is a long way to race from last place. With every stroke, the other boys were pulling further and further away. We finished the race about 15 to 20 seconds behind the winner, and I was again overcome with terrible feelings. I just couldn't help but think that I was not good at kayaking and that I was wasting my time. It didn't help that there were another three days of competition where we had to sit on the sidelines. Once again, I felt like giving up. But this time, that wasn't an option. I had just committed to Point Loma Nazarene University where I would be on a kayaking scholarship. Once again, being at the lowest low of my sporting career changed my life.

On the way back from Belarus, I moved straight to San Diego to start classes and start training with my new team. This was the best decision I'd ever made, without consciously knowing it. I had put myself in the right environment to succeed. My new coach, Chris Barlow, would motivate and push me in ways that I needed. The teammates and training partners would become my second family and would drive me to be better every day. And being able to paddle all year round in California gave me extra time each year to get better.

I didn't know it then, but this new place would be where my love and passion for my sport would grow every single year. This was another one of the biggest learning experiences of my life. I learned that sometimes, you just need to put yourself in the right environment to cultivate success from within.

Sometimes, however, the right environment must also be approached with the right expectations. In my sport, one of my favorite aspects is the sense of community that athletes from all around the world share because of kayaking being so niche. This sense of community is what makes it so common for the best athletes around the world to train with each other and collaboratively get better. I've been lucky enough to be able to train with top athletes on the Czech Olympic team on and off for the past couple of years, and this is certainly an environment in which to get better. In this environment, though, I needed to approach it with a particular mentality, or the human instinct of comparison would actually make this environment have the opposite from intended effect. When the fastest guy in the group is one of the best athletes in the world, it becomes tempting to measure the success of a training session on how well you are performing compared to him. This is dangerous. We should never work for anything because we want to be exactly like anyone else, so we have to remind ourselves to be critical of comparing ourselves as a value of self-worth rather than as an inspiration to work harder, to be better.

The best thing about training with guys like those on the Czech team was that it gave the right environment for me to push myself to be the best version of myself, not because I got to rub shoulders with these extremely successful guys. For me, environments where I'm pushed by people, sometimes better than me, are ideal. This is what I want people to take away from this chapter: put yourself in situations where you can be the best version of yourself without being discouraged by someone else's success but rather by being inspired by others' hard work and dedication. Don't compare yourself to anyone in a way that makes you question the value of your own skill, or life. Instead, compare yourself in a fashion that gets you excited to excel in whatever task you're performing.

While healthy comparisons can help us work harder, I believe that comparison can be the root of a lot of problems we face. I learned this the hard way. When I was in my sophomore year in college, I became obsessed with Instagram fitness photos and particularly those of the guys with crazy eight-pack abs, big shoulders, and a tiny waist. In an attempt to be like the men in these photos, I made unhealthy diet decisions, which made my body seem lean and fit, but which actually hindered my kayaking because I was depriving my body of the amount of calories I needed for my training. Since then, I've focused on improving myself to be a better version of me, rather than be closer to some unrealistic standard I set.

Whatever goal you set for yourself, break it down into steps that are self-focused. Ask yourself, "What do I need to do to make me better?" Athlete, businessperson, painter, dancer—whatever it is, make sure both your goals and your actions are true to you rather than anyone or anything else.

So, what does all this have to do with a successful spirit? First of all, you should understand that you always have the capacity to set the direction of your life. Everything you do is driven by your drive, your purpose, your spirit. Put yourself in situations where engaging in the right kind of preparation is the simplest and easiest choice. As human beings we are always inclined to do what brings us the quickest reward. We seek immediate gratification. If you are trying to lose weight, make the unhealthy choices less convenient. If you are trying to practice the guitar, leave the guitar out of the case in a place where you can easily grab it. Make the right choice, the easy one. Also, never compare yourself to anyone to measure your success. This can lead to disappointment. The best way to feel successful and fulfilled is to compare yourself with the person you were yesterday.

I challenge you now to be the best you are capable of being.

About the Author

Nathaniel Errez is a USA National Team Kayak athlete who has competed at the Junior, U23, and Senior World Championships as well as the Pan American Games. He was the first person to graduate with a kayaking scholarship from Point Loma Nazarene University and graduated magna cum laude in 3.5 years. He is currently continuing his studies at the University of California, San Diego, getting his master's in business analytics while training to qualify for the Tokyo Olympic Games. Winning a gold medal at the Olympic Games in Los Angeles in 2028 is Nathaniel's biggest dream. To get in contact with Nathaniel, you can find him on LinkedIn or on Instagram @nate.errez. He would love to hear if his story impacted you.

CHAPTER 9
THE ALCHEMY OF WILL

By Dr. Elena Estanol
High Performance Psychologist, Leadership Trainer
Fort Collins, Colorado

When the fire of your soul ignites the passion within your heart, don't view it as an opportunity for success or failure, view it as an open door for miracles.
—Jennifer Finley Boyland

What Brings About Success?

In a world where success and achievement are overvalued and overprized, everyone is looking for the fastest pathway to success. The newest hack and the most reliable method to create replicable success. In fact, many studies have focused on identifying the traits, characteristics, methods, and tools utilized by successful athletes, performers, speakers, and CEOs to outperform their competition. And while many patterns of success have been identified, we *still* struggle to create success consistently.

Even more important than success is your ability to overcome adversity when it shows up unexpectedly. While you may be able to "succeed" when things are ideal, can you do so when you experience setbacks, challenges, injuries, or heartbreak? The first key to overcome setbacks and achieve success is WILL.

In this chapter, I will:

- Share the number one reason you are struggling to create consistent success in your life and how humans have been set up both biologically, mentally, and environmentally to fail.
- Explore the role of WILL in helping you achieve success and overcome setbacks.
- Share how you can turn things around and reveal the secret to achieving success with ease and flow.

The most powerful weapon on earth is the human soul on fire.
—Ferdinand Foch

I can't count the times I have been called a "willful spirit" or "spirited" by a multitude of people. Being "willful" or "spirited" can be a double-edged sword. It can work for you or against you, and it can be given as a compliment or an insult. I'll weave my story throughout the chapter and illustrate how WILL played a role for me in overcoming an excruciatingly challenging time in my life.

Having been a dancer my whole life, I felt a sense of invincibility in my body. Dance is my first love and a huge part of what makes my spirit sing.

This was shattered early one morning when I fell and suffered a compound fracture and a complete dislocation of my ankle. I underwent surgery that very same day. Yet despite the success of surgery, I didn't heal as the doctors anticipated. I began to fear there was a deeper problem.

PART I: The Problem Mindset

Where attention goes, energy flows.
—James Redfield

One of the biggest issues we have is that we have been socialized, indoctrinated if you will, to have a "problem-solving mindset." Plus, this is something that is unfortunately supported by biology. What I mean by this is that our minds are like Teflon for positive experiences and like Velcro for negative experiences. Biologically speaking this was adaptive, as we needed to remember where the saber-toothed tiger lived more so than where the tasty berries grew. Unfortunately, we have continued to practice this trait and use it in ways that are now extremely maladaptive and conducive to failure rather than success.

The reticular activating system (RAS) in our brain is often used to support whatever assertion we create. This tiny network of neurons located in the brain stem not only acts as a "gatekeeper" but also acts akin to a "locator signaling device" that seeks and locates the information that it has been pre-loaded with. Our brains are wired to find and avoid problems, so they look for problems to solve, and the more they look, the more problems we find. When this becomes the dominant default way of thinking, then everything is a problem to be fixed, including us!

As a society, we have been indoctrinated with a belief that there is something wrong with us, so we need to fix ourselves before we can be successful. This can be dangerous as it can take us down a path where we are constantly looking for problems, and trying to fix things, and seeing ourselves as broken or not good enough.

And guess what?

This problem orientation just creates more problems. Not more success. This creates a particular "belief structure" that keeps us stuck. The good news is that knowing about our RAS is an important part of the puzzle because we can retrain our brain by aligning our subconscious and conscious thoughts to create the reality we desire.

When I wasn't healing, I delved into research to find every possible reason. I discovered an underlying auto-immune condition, and soon after, I discovered I had developed compartment syndrome, a condition that impacts circulation of the lower legs, causing swelling, pain, and can lead to amputation.

Yet, the more I searched for answers, the more problems I found. I was working with nine practitioners, and nothing was helping me. I felt demoralized and hopeless. I spent three years completely disabled. The solution was surgery on both of my legs. Yet, I didn't know whether I'd come out with both legs (and hopefully regain my ability to walk), or with just one and face a lifetime of disability.

There was a part of me that, despite the nightmare I was living, felt there was a deeper reason why I was going through this experience. As you continue reading, you will understand how I went from feeling hopeless to believing I could walk again.

The surgery was scheduled a day before my birthday. My partner at the time asked me what I wanted for my birthday. After some thought, I shared I wanted a new pair of sneakers. He looked at me in disbelief. And I said, "I know what you are thinking. Don't say it! That's what I want, and it's my intention that I WILL wear BOTH shoes eventually!"

And at some level, despite the fact that I had already been unable to walk for over a year and a half and that the doctors had told me I may not be able to walk again, *I decided that not only would I walk again, but I would dance again!*

Was this just plain stubbornness? Perseverance? Faith? Or WILL?

PART II: What Is "Will" Exactly?

The Wikipedia definition of "will" is "a quality of the mind that selects, decides, brings about a choice and enables deliberate action." Other ways in which WILL has been defined include the APA's definition, "The ability to delay gratification, resist short-term temptations, the conscious, effortful regulation of the self, and the capacity to override an unwanted thought, feeling, or impulse." So "will" has been defined as a "quality of mind" (or a human quality) by most of the literature and research.

And yet … I believe these definitions are missing half of the equation. You are a spiritual being having a human experience, so for every quality of mind-body, there exists a complimentary, corresponding quality in spirit. Meaning that in order for your human self to demonstrate a particular quality or trait, like WILL, it would need to begin at the spiritual level and be brought down through your mind, heart, and body. In essence, as a human being, you are an embodiment of your spiritual qualities.

"Spirit" has been defined as "the nonphysical part of a person which is the seat of character" or "the animating or vital principle that gives life to an organism." This is a mixture of creativity, courage, energy, and determination. In other words, it has been defined as "the fire that animates the body;" an activating essence that initiates action.

There are great similarities between these definitions. Therefore, I maintain that WILL is a type of "invisible spiritual force" that comes to us as inspiration.

The word "inspiration" stems from the Latin word *inspirare*, which basically means "to breathe in" or "to inhale." So, whenever we are inspired, we can say that we are "in-spirit" or that we are "breathing the Creator's spiritual force into our body." This is why when we get inspired, we often get a sudden surge of energy seemingly out of nowhere, or an overflow of epiphanies and creative ideas.

You can feel this when you are moved, inspired, or prompted to take some action. For example, you do something, talk to someone, or engage in some kind of activity, and you don't even know why, but you almost feel "compelled" to do so!

Spiritual Will (SW)

Spiritual will (SW) or spiritual fire is a higher order "inspiration" you receive that compels you to do sometimes seemingly crazy things. From falling in love, to changing careers, to moving across the country, you may not have a rational explanation for your behavior; you just have an inner knowing. It's something you must do. While these messages often come from an intuitive channel, it is the fiery spirit that is communicating its WILL to us.

I believe WILL is a spiritual quality that we are all endowed with; however, we get to choose whether we want to use it or develop it. Similar to an app on our phone, we get to choose whether we want to use the app or not.

Listening to our intuition and our spiritual will is one thing. Having the courage to follow it is quite another.

During the time I was disabled, I began receiving strong intuitive messages that I needed to teach what I had learned worldwide. This was terrifying to me. I was receiving strong messages and images of my soul mission, yet I didn't feel worthy or prepared to do such a thing. All I really wanted was to be able to dance again and experience the freedom of moving along with music, and express myself that way.

I resisted those messages and made rationalizations against them, so I simply continued to focus on ways I would be able to regain my physical ability.

How Is Spiritual Will Different from Motivation?

We also have HUMAN WILL (HW).

If you are INSPIRED, with SW, you don't need MOTIVATION. Motivation comes from HW not SW. It's the thing you need to "get yourself" to do things that you don't really want to do, such as cleaning toilets. I have yet to meet anyone that loves cleaning toilets! We "motivate" ourselves and others to do the things we don't really want to do or the things we are NOT INSPIRED to do.

Human Will, therefore, is a quality that allows us to make choices, set goals, achieve things, meet challenges, and overcome setbacks. *HW is the quality that FUELS MOTIVATION. It can work WITH your Spiritual Will, or AGAINST it.*

HW is synonymous with motivation because we are using "external" forces to motivate ourselves or others to do things we may not be so keen on doing.

I was motivated to go to physical therapy and change my eating, only because I believed it would aid my healing and allow me to walk and dance again. Yet no amount of HW was helping me overcome the dark nights of the soul when I would lose faith that I would ever walk again.

Can Spiritual Will and Human Will Play Together?

As above, so below, as within, so without, as the universe, so the soul…
—Hermes Trismegistus

As you may have experienced, body, mind, and spirit are inextricably linked. What you experience in one, you experience in all three planes. Have you ever met anyone with a fiery spirit who gave up easily? No, and that is what this book is about, a fiery, successful spirit that doesn't give up.

I mentioned before that being "willful" could work for you or against you. The distinguishing factor has to do with your ability to *align* your spiritual will with your human will. If you have ever had the frustrating experience of working very hard to accomplish a goal but it seemed that everything was going against you, then you have experienced the *resistance* that is created when you are trying to exert your HW upon your SW. It doesn't work. And it usually leaves you feeling exhausted, demoralized, and powerless.

Learning to recognize this resistance will allow you to shift your energy and get realigned. Which means that, at times, you may need to let go of something that your human ego very much desires but is not in line with your spiritual goals.

When you are able to create alignment between both of these qualities, you enter a state of *flow*, or easy manifestation, and you experience yourself as the innate creator you are. You experience your genius and your power. *It feels like magic! It's the alchemy of aligning with your spiritual will.*

Ultimately, learning to align your HW and co-create with your SW are the keys to creating success with ease and flow. When your HW and your SW align, then you'll become almost invincible, able to beat the odds and achieve what might seem impossible. The problem is that most of us don't know how to do this, or we resist the promptings of our SW and consequently are in resistance or in opposition to our SW. This is when we struggle.

PART III: Creating a Successful Structure

Ultimately, aligning your HW and your SW for success is based on the structure that you create (unconsciously). Therefore, success is not personal. It is based on the structure. There are four types of structures:

- Stuck
- Oscillating
- Scattered
- Flowing

All high achievers like to be in and experience a *flowing* structure, yet this is ONLY achieved when our SW and our HW are completely in alignment. In order for this to happen, we need to know HOW to connect to our intuition and how to align our HW with our SW.

Most people tend to be in either a stuck or oscillating structure. If you can't move your life forward, then you are in a stuck structure. However, what I see most commonly in my practice is an oscillating structure, in which you make some progress forward, and then you take steps back. You keep going back and forth in this manner. Or a scattered structure in which you seem to be moving in circles, fleeting about, or completely suspended due to confusion. I was in a combination of an oscillating and scattered structures. I was making progress, my bones did heal, I addressed my auto-immune condition, but I was still not walking or dancing.

The structure you set up is the interplay of SW and HW, and how it shows up in your life and each of your choices.

Usually what creates a non-flow structure is *inner resistance* from misalignment of your HW and SW. While you may or may not be aware of it, it's this resistance that gets in the way of your ultimate success.

We often forget that we are already powerful creators and success is within our ability.

You Are Whole and Complete Now

To create the success we desire in our lives, we simply need to shed all of the limiting beliefs, stored emotional baggage, and resistance that has been created by old wounds that are responsible for our maladaptive patterns. It's like scrubbing off all the dirt and mud we have accumulated that has clouded the brilliance that is already within us.

Because many of these patterns are run by our unconscious mind, we are not completely aware of our power to create success. Until we have supportive guidance to uncover our resistance and align our HW with our SW, it can be difficult to attain and maintain success. One of the most satisfying components of my coaching is helping people identify and release all the resistance in order to move into the alignment of HW and SW, and experience flow.

I spent two years in complete resistance. I didn't understand how committing to teaching others had anything to do with my healing. When things got dark enough, I finally surrendered.

What I heard my intuition say was "If you want to stay in anonymity, you will stay as you are (disabled), but if you are willing to step into your mission, you will be supported in healing your body."

The Alchemy of Our Will

Once I cleared the resistance, fear, and negative beliefs holding me back, and I *aligned* my HW with my SW, I began to heal my body and move out of the impasse. I committed to learning and stretching myself in order to reach people worldwide and teach what I had learned. I not only regained my ability to walk, but also to dance. I practice aerial silks, aerial hoop, modern dance, and ballroom dance. I now help my students and clients access the alchemy of their WILL to attain lasting success in the same way I was able to do. To me, a successful spirit is one example of aligning human will and spiritual will in a way that allows for positivity to radiate in your life.

Whatever you do and wherever you are, whether you are in a great place or a difficult place in life, you can change your structure, release resistance, and become a powerful creator. Defy the ordinary, become extraordinary.

About the Author

Elena Estanol, PhD, MFA, is a bestselling author, high performance psychologist, and intuitive leadership, ADHD, and NLP coach, trainer, and speaker. Leaders, coaches, athletes, and high achievers hire her to enhance performance, productivity, communication, and emotional intelligence while also enhancing connection, joy, and play to create deeper meaning, success, and impact in their lives. She is a sought-after expert in leadership, ADHD, energy psychology, healing, NLP, dream, and spiritual coaching. Her work with teams and companies focuses on enhancing communication, emotional intelligence, leadership, and developing high-performing teams.

Dr. Estanol thrives in facilitating teams and individuals to overcome core negative beliefs, release resistance, and achieve greater alignment to enhance success and flow. She has several self-paced courses in meditation, intuition, and self-confidence, among others. If you would like to access a free meditation to connect you to your higher self and intuition, visit www.tinyurl.com/diamond-self.

Websites:
www.intuitivebusinessmastery.com
www.synapsecounseling.com

CHAPTER 10

26.2 MILES OF DOUBT, TRUTH, AND IDENTITY

By Dr. Jen Faber
Mindset and Performance Coach, Athlete
Park City, Utah

"Do you think you can keep going?"

Sweaty and relieved to be under the tent of the aid station, I managed to say this in between breaths, "It's my first marathon. All I want to do is finish."

I was three minutes over the deadline for the checkpoint, the final checkpoint before all racers were allowed to continue. Ahead of me were 14.2 more miles of trails. Behind me was the greatest distance I'd ever covered as a runner.

The race staff member evaluated my physical condition, making sure my stamina was just as certain as my conviction. He was deciding my fate at that very moment.

Will he let me go?

Will he make me quit?

No! I don't want to be driven to the finish line.

I don't want to stop now.

All I could do was channel the voice in my head to him. I just kept saying over and over, "I've got this. I can do this!"

Then I heard him say the best words I'd heard all day, "Okay, you're lucky. Everyone else behind you will be told to stop. You're a few minutes past the cutoff, but you can keep going."

I grabbed a Coke from the aid station, downed it, and started running as fast as I could, just in case he changed his mind.

Two weeks prior to the marathon, I was casually strolling along Main Street of Park City, Utah, off the heels of an epic adventure, hiking through the Canadian Rockies. My body was in rest-and-recovery mode, and I planned to be in that mode for a while. I was happily sipping a coffee, with my partner's hand in mine. We were enjoying a leisurely morning when a bright yellow sign in a shop window stopped me in my tracks.

"The Mid Mountain Marathon is a true trail runner's marathon and is the final stage of the Triple Trail Challenge. Voted best trail marathon in Utah!"

I was like a moth to a flame. I fixated on the words, reading them over and over.

I felt an impulse shoot through me, like a compulsion of fire and lightning. It was a deeper voice that said, "DO IT."

"If you can hike 20 miles in a day, then you can run 26.2," I said to myself.

Instantly another voice, this time a bit louder, started yelling at me, "Are you nuts? You've never done a marathon! The most you've ever run is a 5K, and that was playing around in mud and obstacles!"

But it didn't matter. That sign was like a bell that could not be unrung, and that voice came from deep within me. Not in my thinking brain. Not in my heart. It came from my core. I was being called to do something I'd never done, and I was never more sure that I had to do it. Just like that, the wheels were in motion. A leisurely stroll turned into excitement, planning, and anticipation, thinking about how to maximize the two weeks I had in front of me.

I knew that the window for physical training was past. Most marathoners would say this is the time to taper and rest. So, instead, I knew I had to train my mind even more than my body. I had to take a bold idea of doing a marathon with absolutely no training and cross the finish line. I had to adopt the identity of the runner. Deeper yet, I had to adopt the identity of an endurance athlete. Even deeper, I had to keep listening to that voice within me.

Marathons can act as a metaphor for everything we face in life. Every challenge, every obstacle, every goal can be broken down the same way. Mile by mile, checkpoint by checkpoint, pushing, slogging, doubting, and persevering all the way to the finish line.

As I reflect on the marathon, I want to open windows into my mind including the struggles and breakthroughs. This one race was the key to unlocking my own spirit, and I invite you to think about what you can learn every mile of the way, so you can unlock your own.

Race Prep

I've always hated running. I was the pudgy kid in phys ed who dreaded fitness tests. I was the last girl to cross the line when doing sprints in basketball practice. I was the one you put in the slow heat for the 1,500 meter in track and field. I was the one the coaches loved to point out and ridicule. I was the epitome of slow, and these experiences defined me. They created limits and built up doubt.

Deep down, I always wanted to be an athlete. But in truth, I allowed myself to be the accumulation of what people thought of me over a lifetime. Over the years, I slowly started to crack down those beliefs. I found a love of mountains, which turned to a love of hiking. Then I found a love of hiking longer. Three-mile scenic walks turned to 15-mile journeys up summits, which turned to multi-day circuits.

I started to find my confidence, and I discovered that I had a rare superpower—*The longer I go, the stronger I get.*

That truth revealed itself time and time again, whether I was on the final push to a peak or in the middle of a four-hour row, I became the Energizer Bunny because I could just keep going and going and going.

I built my belief as an athlete, but running was my Achilles heel. It was my anchor to a past, insecure self. And that is why I knew I had to do this race.

I had to adopt the mantra: *The longer I go, the stronger I get. The longer I go, the stronger I get.*

MILE 0: In Over My Head

The two buses jam-packed with eager racers pulled up to the event parking lot. There were race signs everywhere, guiding us to the start line.

The journey ahead would cross through 26.2 miles (or what I learned later was actually over 27 miles) of mountain terrain. Aspen groves, ski runs, and vista views would accompany me the entire way.

As I whisked myself to a comfortable spot among my fellow racers, I couldn't help but notice the air of ease and confidence that my companions had. The most elite of them, who seemed more like gazelles than humans, were casually clocking three miles as their warmups, performing their well-rehearsed stretches, and organizing brightly-colored goos and tablets in their hydration packs.

I felt doomed.

What do you think you're doing here? You're not a runner. Look at these people. You're not anything like them. Stop kidding yourself.

What happened to all that excitement and buzz from two weeks ago? Where was that deep impulse of spiritual knowing?

It was nowhere to be found and covered by a brick wall of doubt. I felt like a fool, a phony. I fantasized about sneaking stealthily back to the bus, thinking about what the driver would think as I pleaded to him, "Please take me with you!"

But even though my ego desperately wanted to escape, my heart didn't. If I didn't finish, no one else would notice, or let alone care, but I would.

Just hang at the end of the pack, Jen, you'll feel better. You can do your own thing back there. Let the gazelles get so far ahead of you that you won't even sense the dust kicked up from their feet.

Before I knew it, the start gun went off. This was it. This was the choice to forge ahead or turn back. I had no choice but to start running … and I did.

MILE 5: The Honeymoon Phase

I pass a sign that says, "Mile 5."

Wait, I'm ALREADY at mile 5?!? This is easy! I can do this!

Five down. Twenty-one point five to go. I had found my stride. I had started to settle into the journey. People would pass. I would pass others. I would hang and pace with others. We were in this together. With every step, my confidence started to build like a wave that was slowly gaining more and more strength. Mile five becomes six, then seven, then nine. I was breaking pace to take selfies. Posting pics to my family and friends to share progress. I had this in the bag. I was in total bliss. Maybe this was the runner's high that everyone talked about. Maybe being a runner could actually feel this easy.

Oh, Jen, there it is, your sweet naivete as a marathon newbie.

Like all honeymoons, this feeling naturally didn't last. It would take work and conscious effort after it passed, which I was about to quickly learn.

MILE 11: Reality Check

Just as I was starting to really feel in the zone, I felt a shock wave of pain through my shins. It was agonizing. I looked down at my legs, covered in compression stockings and Kinesio tape that I'd put on hours ago, thinking they would shield me from pain. Now they were just colorful accessories trying to mask my body screaming at me to stop. I adjusted my shoes. I took a break and hydrated. I tweaked my gait. Hoping that something would ease the pain, but it didn't. Every step was a bolt of lightning. The pain increased with every step. Teasing me. Making me question how long I could bear it. Was it really worth it?

Now the miles started to drag out right when my pacing was so critical because the key checkpoint was just two miles away.

Talk about irony. As I hit my stride, I had to slow myself down to a walk. That's the test of momentum. As you start to master your stride, you are faced with a challenge to test it before you can keep going.

MILE 13: The Ultimate Checkpoint

Now reality was sinking in. I was in pain, feeling completely gassed, and I was only halfway there. Rather than thinking about the distance I'd covered, I thought about the looming distance ahead of me.

I saw the race tent of the critical checkpoint. I had to make it in time or I was out, and it was a taunting mirage. I saw race volunteers, and they started cheering me on, waving electrolytes, energy bars, and bells. They were my beacons of rest, reprieve, and perhaps my fate.

I bet those gazelles are already at the finish line, celebrating and pounding food before making their way to an ice bath and a warm bed. Stop it, Jen, that's not helping.

This was it. I could easily make my own choice to call it a day and stop now. It wouldn't be a defeat ... technically. I would have run longer than I ever had. That was enough of a win, right? I could just settle and throw in the towel. That would be the safe choice. There was a comfy couch waiting for me at home.

It would also be the easy way out. I didn't sign up for this race to play it safe. And I definitely didn't sign up searching for an easy way out.

As I approached the tent, I knew I was a few minutes past the cutoff. Maybe the choice was already made for me. But, even with the pain, I still felt that deeper fire that wanted me to keep going. Once I heard the words, "You're a few minutes past the cutoff, but you can keep going," I did.

MILE 20: The Tortoise and the Mirror

Now this was a matter of just one foot in front of the other. There was no hare in this race. Just me, the tortoise. The slow, methodical, practically walking me who was in agony versus my ultimate opponent—myself.

But something was changing inside. After I passed the checkpoint and the sugar high faded away, I saw clarity in the agony. I saw the mirror reflecting back. I was choosing the pain. I was choosing to continue. Now there were no mile markers or checkpoints or aid stations waiting for me. The only thing waiting for me was the finish line, and the only pace I had to make was my own.

At that moment, I was never more happy to be the tortoise, hanging out in last place.

After a lifetime of chasing goals and perfection and approval, pushing myself to the point of my own demise, there was no one else around me whom I had to prove myself to. I was surrounded by the serenity of the mountains, and I think they wanted to echo that same serenity back to me.

It was just me and my own thoughts running our own race.

MILE 25: My Truth in Sight

After miles of solitude, I saw Olympic Park below. That was the final destination. Somewhere 1,500 feet below was the finish line. A wave of relief washed over me as I thought about all of the distance I'd covered. The pure sight of it almost took me to my knees. Then I felt that deeper superpower kicking in.

The longer I go, the stronger I get. The longer I go, the stronger I get.

There it was. My mantra. My truth. It had been with me all along. Through every goal, hike, and summit. And here it was, with me now to carry me to the end.

The trail started to do what it hadn't done in 26 miles: go downhill. It was like my spirit aligned with the course. Now that I saw myself clearly, the race felt steady, easy, and freeing. I was just minutes away from crossing that finish line, and once I did, I'd always be a marathon runner. No matter what I did for the rest of my life, no one could take that away from me.

I am a runner. This is my truth.

MILE 26.2: Finish for Me

Out of the final grove of aspens, I reached a clearing. I heard music. I saw the words I'd been wanting to see since that wishful, doubtful moment at the start.

"FINISH LINE"

And it was beautiful. I was sprinting. I was actually sprinting towards the finish line. *How was I sprinting?* Somewhere in the same place where the deep voice spoke to me two weeks ago, I found a reservoir of energy. I felt my power and my speed as my legs moved faster and faster. I crossed that finish line in a blur of elation, exhaustion, and relief.

As the race director put the medal around my neck, I realized that this was what true fulfillment felt like. There were no other racers. It was just me. There were no massive crowds cheering. Just a few spectators hanging on till the end.

I wasn't doing this for anyone else. I was only doing this for me.

*

We are all in our own marathon. We all have our mile markers, meltdowns, and moments that define us.

The marathon you are on doesn't define you, but the choices you make do. Your life, your identity, and your happiness all come down to a string of choices tied together, mile by mile. The pure choice of doing something bold creates action. Once you start going, you'll hit your stride. Just as you get comfortable, you'll hit a roadblock. Every checkpoint offers a chance to stop, to quit, or to accept defeat. People will question whether you can continue, making you ultimately question yourself. So you have to find that power deep within yourself. Only you can bust past old stories and limits.

To reveal your truth.

The ultimate choice that you will always have is—do you stop pushing, take the easy way down, and regret it later, knowing you could have pushed yourself more?

Or—do you keep up the pace, dig to see how deep your confidence goes, and stay the course to your finish line?

It's not really a question because your spirit knows. It knows exactly which choice to make. It may not be the easiest path. It may not be the most comfortable. But in the end, you must choose to shatter the walls holding you in and keep running. It is what your spirit is calling you to do.

The longer you go, the stronger you'll be.

About the Author

Dr. Jen Faber is a mindset and performance coach, outdoor athlete, and fierce advocate to building a life on your terms. Known as the "identity whisperer," Dr. Jen has coached people all over the globe on how to create bold and epic lives. She has helped transform the confidence and mindsets of executives, Olympians, CrossFit champions, and elite endurance athletes.

Named as one of the "Top Ten Wellness Leaders to Watch," Dr. Jen is the author of *The 90 Day Life: How to Live More in 3 Months Than You Have in 3 Years* and founder of Expedition, a self-mastery program designed to help high performers achieve the one epic dream they've been putting off.

Dr. Jen is an avid mountain athlete and has her eyes set on completing the Seven Summits by 2030.

Email: coach@drjenfaber.com
Website: www.drjenfaber.com

CHAPTER 11
CULTIVATING A SUCCESSFUL, JOYFUL SPIRIT

By Jory Hingson Fisher
Coach, Trainer, Community Builder
Harford County, Maryland

*I am not a human being enjoying a spiritual life; I
am a spiritual being enjoying a human life.*
—Pierre Teilhard de Chardin

A Human Life

We'd wondered if my "brain earthquake," as I called it, was caused by TMJ, a joint and muscle disorder in the jaw. When his treatment didn't diminish the eerie sensations, my dentist recommended I see a neurologist.

"It feels like Thing, from *The Addams Family,* is massaging my head," I told the doctor—and anyone else who would listen. "Like tectonic plates are shifting inside my brain. It's been plaguing me for weeks! *What is it?*"

The first neurologist asked me a host of questions designed to test my memory, including this one: "Now say the names of all the presidents in your lifetime, going backwards in order."

"Sure. Trump, Bush, Obama, Bush, Reagan, Ford, Nixon, Kennedy, Eisenhower... Dammit. That's not right, is it?"

"No."

I was mortified. "Who'd I forget?"

"Clinton, Carter ..."

Silence. The sound of embarrassment.

That was the first day I heard the words, "You might have MS. I'll order MRIs of your brain and spine, with and without contrast."

What?

I have a friend who's grappled bravely with multiple sclerosis for four decades ... in a wheelchair since 1980. *That* is MS, I thought—not missing a couple of presidents on a stupid memory test. Right?

Skeptical, I chose to get a second opinion. Neurologist #2 put me through a battery of assessments and scans. Six months later, #2 referred me to a third neurologist, Dr. Daniel Becker, as he was unable to "call it" for sure. Dr. Becker specializes in multiple sclerosis and is the founder of the International Neurorehabilitation Institute in Baltimore, Maryland. I knew I was in good hands as soon as I met him.

Fifteen *more* months and several blood tests and MRIs later, Dr. Becker confirmed what I had already begun to accept: "Jory, we've ruled out everything else. You have MS as expected." He, my husband, and I proceeded to explore options for managing a disease which, as of 2021, is incurable.

I received my official diagnosis of relapsing-remitting multiple sclerosis (RRMS) in March 2018, two weeks after my 65th birthday. That "brain earthquake" experience was part of a relapse evidently. Ah.

The first obvious symptoms appeared twenty years ago when I was a practicing attorney and law professor in Lynchburg, Virginia. Little did I know those symptoms were MS-related. Little did I know I'd need to cultivate a successful, joyful spirit to the *max* if I wanted to fulfill my divine purpose as a human being on this planet.

You've noticed how each event in life serves as a building block (or perhaps a wrecking ball)? The more we learn, the better equipped we are for whatever happens down the road. Building block upon building block, we need to lay a firm foundation if we want to live life to the fullest on planet earth.

Ten years before my MS symptoms appeared, I found out serendipitously that I had two holes in my heart—an ASD (atrial septal defect) and a PFO (patent foramen ovale). According to both of my cardiologists, I should NOT have made it to 55, statistically speaking. It was a miracle I'd lived so long, they said, *and* that my body had been able to do so much, e.g., giving birth to three healthy daughters including twins.

Pediatric cardiologist D. Scott Lim, MD, at the University of Virginia Medical Center, prolonged my life by repairing those holes before they wreaked irreversible (fatal) damage. I'm forever grateful to him not only for his skill and knowledge, but also for his guidance and support while I was in his care. He helped me turn a traumatic, wrecking ball discovery into a positive, building-block experience. He helped me continue to enjoy this human life, so I can continue to share my life and calling with family, friends, colleagues, and acquaintances. With you!

Many people in the world have health journeys far more taxing than mine. I've lost friends and family members to cancer, accidents, ALS, suicide, and drug overdose. Like you, I have friends and family members who currently battle chronic fatigue syndrome, Lyme disease, depression, anxiety, solitude, marital strife, domestic abuse. Even while we do what we can to encourage and support others who are going through trials and challenges, we must do what we can to encourage and support *ourselves.*

We must do whatever we can to cultivate a successful, joyful spirit that will sustain us in all circumstances.

But how?

A Human Life as a Spiritual Being

Jesus is my Lord and Savior and best friend. I can't write about cultivating a successful, joyful spirit without bringing Him into the discussion. Raised in a Christian family, I grew up going to church, studying the Bible, and participating in groups like Young Life and Youth for Christ (YFC). I knew God was with me, loving me unconditionally, even when I was focused on secular pursuits far from the shelter of my communities. Even when I felt ashamed.

Love your neighbor as yourself is an instruction that appears throughout the Bible (Leviticus 19:18 and Mark 12:31, for example). Sometimes we seem to forget the "as yourself" part, don't we? Yet, how *can* I love someone fully if I don't fully love—*me*?

Jesus uses a story, the Parable of the Good Samaritan (Luke 10:25–37), to define "neighbor" for a sly, inquiring teacher of the law. He shows us that being a good neighbor means being merciful. We need to show mercy to others, absolutely, *and* we need to show mercy to ourselves!

To cultivate a successful, joyful spirit,
love others as you love yourself.
To cultivate a successful, joyful spirit,
show mercy to others as you show mercy to yourself.

If you have a health challenge, or any kind of challenge for that matter, do it—show mercy to yourself. Love yourself. Be kind to yourself. Give yourself GRACE!

I've learned to laugh when I can't remember a word, name, or face; when I mean to type one thing but type something else instead; when I learn a new skill one day but forget how to do it the next.

Those nerve misfires (as I call them) are simply a reflection of how MS affects my thought process, not a reflection of who I am at my core.

Loving myself, showing mercy to myself, means chuckling at the crazy things I do rather than getting upset. I am a spiritual being intent on enjoying this human life to the *max*!

But what about those times when we *can't* just laugh it off? I speak from experience of course. Loving myself, showing mercy to myself, enjoying this human life isn't always easy, is it?

Take, for example, pain. You'd think I'd know how to deal with it by now after lo these many years. But I don't. Not very well anyway. Ask my chiropractor. Or my physical therapist. Or my husband! I hate pain—especially in the middle of the night when I can't sleep because of the aches in my arms, legs, hips, ankles, feet that terrorize my slumber.

Moreover, when I don't rest well, like most people, I don't function well the next day. I'm grumpy and tired and stiff and achy. It's hard to muster up JOY when we hurt.

Yet, if I'm to give grace and love and mercy to others, regardless of who they are and what they say or do, I must give grace and love and mercy to ME even when, *especially* when, I'm not functioning at my best. I need to be a good neighbor to myself.

What else will help us cultivate a successful, joyful spirit?

If you haven't read *The Four Agreements* by contemporary Mexican author and spiritual teacher Don Miguel Ruiz, do it. If you have read it, read it again and *integrate* each agreement into all areas of your life.

- First Agreement: Be impeccable with your word.
- Second Agreement: Don't take anything personally.
- Third Agreement: Don't make assumptions.
- Fourth Agreement: Always do your best.

Imagine how your spirit will soar!

I know you've heard of IQ, aka, intelligence quotient. IQ is a measure of our ability to think, reason, and solve problems. Whether a person can increase their IQ over time is debatable. You've also heard of EQ, aka emotional quotient or emotional intelligence. EQ is defined as the ability to understand and manage our emotions in positive ways to relieve stress, communicate effectively, empathize with others, overcome challenges, and defuse conflict. Note: our EQ *can* be increased.

If we wish to cultivate a successful, joyful spirit, increasing our EQ is more important than increasing our IQ. Increasing our *spiritual* intelligence (SQ) is more important still!

Let's say level ten is the highest score possible. Having level ten spiritual intelligence means:

- We have defined our life purpose.
- We make decisions based on our divine calling.
- We recognize the impact our divine calling has on generations to come.
- We're making a significant difference in the world.

The benefits of achieving level ten spiritual intelligence include:

- Increased compassion for humanity
- Increased harmony in relationships
- Increased peace and joy (knowing you're in alignment with your divine gifts and calling)
- Increased fulfillment (e.g., having a purpose-guided, mission-driven, *profitable* business that makes a positive difference in the lives of others
- Increased capacity to love others

When you're leading a life full of compassion, harmony, peace, joy, and love, you're sharing your successful, joyful spirit with a world that needs it. Now.

If we're not at a level ten spiritual intelligence, how do we get there?

I know from personal and professional experience that finding and working toward fulfillment of our divine purpose increases our spiritual intelligence—and JOY.

If you're not living at level ten spiritual intelligence, then work with a mission-minded, purpose-guided coach, pastor, and/or other spiritual advisor to get the clarity you seek and the support you need. (Reaching level ten spiritual intelligence without a guide to help you is a daunting task.)

> *Joy is the infallible sign of the presence of God.*
> —Pierre Teilhard de Chardin
> French Theologian, Philosopher, and Scientist (1881–1955)

Core Values of a Human Life as a Spiritual Being

When I was in college, one of my best friends created a colorful needlepoint for me that says, "The joy of the Lord is your strength." Nehemiah 8:10 has guided me throughout the decades—I'm gazing at Christy's gift to me right now.

Another verse, Romans 12:12, is brightly highlighted in my Bible: "Be joyful in hope, patient in affliction, faithful in prayer." Also highlighted is 1 Thessalonians 5:18: "Give thanks in all circumstances; for this is God's will for you in Christ Jesus."

Joy. Hope. Patience. Faith. Gratitude. Integrating positive values, attributes, and practices into our *human* life helps us remain true to our calling as a spiritual being who flourishes in the presence of God.

I know without a shadow of a doubt that I am more than my experiences, more than my years on planet earth, more than my bio, more than my multiple sclerosis. Perhaps that's why the song "You Are More" by Tenth Avenue North speaks to me so powerfully. Reflect on the refrain and be blessed:

But don't you know who you are?
You are more than the choices that you've made,
You are more than the sum of your past mistakes,
You are more than the problems you create,
You've been remade.

I've messed up over and over again; yet our almighty, ever-patient, ever-faithful, ever-loving, ever-present God has sustained me and encouraged me throughout my human experience.

I am grateful.

Throughout the Bible, we're told to be "strong and courageous," for God is with us and *for* us (e.g., Deuteronomy 31:6, Joshua 1:9, 1 Corinthians 16:13). We're en**cour**aged (heartened) to be **cour**ageous (have brave hearts), regardless of circumstances.

Yes. I'm concerned about how the next few decades will play out as my body ages and MS fights like hell to progress. But!

1. The joy of the Lord is my courage and my strength.
2. I'm blessed with a husband, brother, and daughters who keep me laughing; seven grown, productive children and stepchildren who make me proud; lots of loyal, loving friends; and a puppy dog and guinea pig that crack me up.
3. I love the work I'm called to do.
4. I keep my mind and body as healthy as possible through diet, supplements, exercise, medical care, chiropractic care, massage, and physical therapy.
5. I love life.

So ... I'm good! I'm a spiritual being who continues to enjoy this, my human experience. Thanks be to God.

About the Author

Jory Hingson Fisher helps entrepreneurs build positive relationships and profitable businesses through networking, masterminding, and personality science. She owns and operates a Network In Action franchise in Harford County, MD.

As an attorney in Virginia, she specialized in juvenile delinquency, criminal law, child abuse and neglect, and domestic relations. She also served as a founding faculty member and associate dean of Liberty University School of Law and as a faculty member of the Virginia State Bar's Mandatory Course on Professionalism.

In 2008 Jory launched her coaching business. She now serves as a coach, trainer, and community builder for small business owners and entrepreneurs.

Her credentials include Certified Business Coach & Startup Expert, Certified B.A.N.K.® IOS Coach, Certified B.A.N.K.® Trainer, Certified Business Networker, and Master Certified Christian Coach.

Jory graduated Phi Beta Kappa, *summa cum laude* from Southern Methodist University and holds graduate degrees from Middlebury College and the University of Virginia. Her awards include Alignable Local Business Person of the Year for Bel Air, MD (2020-21 & 2018-19); Codebreaker Technologies Power Team Award (2021), which she shares with her daughter Jana Beeson; ACHI Magazine Woman of Achievement Award (2019); the DAR Award for Women in American History (2008); and the Women's History Month Award presented by the University of Virginia School of Law (2006).

Email: jory@joryfisher.com
Website: www.joryfisher.com

CHAPTER 12

BALANCING LIFE AND THE THREE DS

By Fabian Florant, MBA
Olympic Athlete in Triple Jump, International Banker
The Hague, Netherlands

*Successful people do what unsuccessful people are not willing
to do. Don't wish it were easier; wish you were better.*
—Jim Rohn

Foundations of a Successful Spirit

In order to have a successful spirit, you must have a successful balance of life. A good balance will help stimulate positivity and that will help guide you to a successful spirit. I will elaborate. At a very young age, I realized that being happy and successful in one aspect of my life wasn't sufficient. This meant, being happy or successful in only sport or school or work simply wasn't enough. My spirit always felt like something was missing, so I always felt some emptiness. Therefore, I started to explore the necessities in achieving a solid foundation to a successful spirit. This gave birth to balance in my life and inspired me to focus on three things that I could share with others as a way to help them find balance. I call them the 3 Ds—determination, drive, and discipline.

The 3 Ds Cycle

The utilization of the 3 Ds is something I developed over the years as an All-American athlete and eventually as a professional athlete. Let's look at the 3 Ds—determination, drive, and discipline.

Determination: You have to be determined to be a successful person. For me, it was simple. I was determined to be one of the best triple jumpers in the world. I saw determination as part of my planning. I was determined to achieve all my athletic goals and work towards being successful. With this determination, I also worked hard on having a spiritual balance. I am determined to pray in the morning, before meals, and before bed to be thankful for all my blessings, thankful that I'm able to fulfill my goals. I'm also determined to find my inner peace. I did this by allocating time in the week, usually over the weekend, where I can, in absolute quietness, relax mentally; no phones or technology, only me and nature. I usually find a park, forest, or even a quiet back yard where I can connect spiritually. I was determined to win, physically, mentally, and spiritually.

Drive: After being determined, you need the drive to keep going. Drive pushes determination. You need to drive the determination towards your target. When I prepare for training on a daily basis, I am determined to go to practice and have a solid training. Mentally and spiritually, I am ready. I am ready to perform to the best of my ability. I utilize my drive during training to push myself to perform at the highest level possible during every single exercise. My drive on that day is what builds the momentum for the next days, weeks, and months leading to my competitions. The drive pushes me to beat my competitors, beat my personal records, and beat the standards for the major international competitions, like the Diamond League, European Championships, and Olympics. When the drive is present and optimal, you can imagine it, you can see it, you can feel it, and you can hear it as a clear indication that you are continuously giving your all. From a spiritual perspective, training with drive is mentally pushing yourself, and as you do this, you will develop a spirit that will push you to your limits and beyond.

Discipline: Discipline will ensure that you will not give up on your determination and drive, no matter what happens. Discipline is obeying the efforts you have made to achieve your goals as long as it takes. This sets the positive tone for your spirit. You will feel more accomplished on a daily basis with a disciplined mindset.

Some goals are long-term goals; therefore, they need to be broken down in small incremental deliveries. When this is done, you will be, on a daily basis, providing a successful momentum to your spirit, which will help give you that utopian-spiritual feeling. As you attempt to achieve many milestones you have set in your life, you will fail along the path, and it's the discipline you have that will determine if you will become successful or not. In fact, you might fail more than you succeed, but how do you continue?

I will give you an example. As an Olympic athlete, we might fail more than we succeed, but when we do succeed, it makes up for all the failure we experience. In fact, without discipline, a person simply cannot make it to the Olympics! I have to train in the rain, cold, snow, and extreme heat. These are all conditions that are not suitable for optimal performance, but I mentally prepare myself to never give up no matter the circumstances.

I started preparing for the 2012 London Olympic Games in fall of 2007, coming off one year since I won my NCAA Division 1 All-American title and school record. That's a solid five years to ensure I would become the first Dutch triple jumper since 1932 to make it to the Olympics. I started working with my first processional coach, learning all the best practices on how to mentally and physically prepare for the highest stage in athletics.

However, the year of the Olympics, despite achieving the highest lifetime world ranking (top fifth longest indoor triple jump in the world, February 2012 at University of Arkansas-Tyson Invitational), I endured a lower calf injury that haunted me all the way to the Olympic qualification deadline. This injury significantly reduced my chances of qualifying, and I didn't make it.

I was devastated, my spirit was also injured, and I was at an all-time low in mental capacity to continue. Not only did it affect me but also my family, for my father had paraded me as the son who would make it to the Olympics to all his friends and relatives, and it did not happen. At that point, I had to make a decision: retire from professional sports or kick in my second gear of discipline and fight for one more shot at my lifetime dream of being an Olympian. To achieve this, I had to positively rejuvenate my spirit, so I could have the determination, drive, and discipline to try again for another four years, which I did, and I did it better than I could ever imagine.

Balance of Life: Feeding Your Spirit

Feeding your mind, body, and soul with adequate food will help play its part to a successful spirit. Food will ultimately be happiness. Prioritizing the aspect of your life that needs to be fed is something you have to plan, prepare for, and figure out. For me, it was, and still is, being successful in school/work, sports/health, and family. I needed to have these three aspects of my life equally successful or at least work in progress; otherwise I would feel unaccomplished or some form of imbalance. It's become a never-ending cycle of fighting to ensure all of these three aspects are satisfied.

The two steps to the balance of life are *spiritual beliefs* (believing in something or someone), and feeding the spirit (multiple types of happiness). Let's look more into these.

I found a link between my religious beliefs and my spiritual successfulness. As a born Catholic, praying and thanking God for life and all my successes is part of living a balanced life. I pray in the morning, thanking God for life, I pray before I eat, and I pray before bed. The more successful I become, the more I pray to thank God for all my blessings. I very rarely ask for anything, but when I do, God delivers.

Even if you are not religious, believing in something or someone gives you some hope and spiritual stability to carry your momentum. I'm not necessarily saying you have to be a Christian or someone with strong religious beliefs in order to achieve a successful spirit, but there has to be spiritual beliefs in some form to achieve this balance. The way I feel when fulfilling my religious obligations is the same way you might feel if you donate money or give a helping hand to someone in need. In this case, you would believe in doing something good and that will make you spiritually happy.

When I was in high school, being the best track and field athlete fed my spirit, but I also had to make sure my grades were good, so my parents could be happy, so I did. Years later, my high school targets turned into college targets. At that point, I was focused on completing my bachelors in finance, doing a banking internship, while working on being a conference triple jump champion and NCAA All-American, which I did. That made my parents happy. This mentality and structure rolled over to my life after college. Now, I'm a full-time international banker who completed his master's in business and sports management climbing up the corporate ladder, while simultaneously pursuing my Olympic dream, which I accomplished. Naturally my family is happy as my success rolls over to their happiness in life. This gave me a super human feeling, but like most addictions, it continually stimulated me to want more.

When I was 16 years old, I made a comprehensive plan to reach the highest possible achievement in every aspect of my life. And at that time, it was getting the highest level of education, highest level of track and field, and highest level of work possible. I knew that my athletic ability was limited, so I needed to avoid sacrificing any other aspects of life that I would need to carry my balance of successfulness; in other words, I should "not put all my eggs in one basket." This became the one biggest rule I set for myself, which ultimately guided me throughout my life.

Life is about balance. We all have and will always have multiple challenges to manage simultaneously, so why wait? The easier you can prepare and plan, the better. Don't overload yourself but practice proper time management instead of being afraid to take on multiple important challenges that already exist. Create your 3 Ds, work on your balance, and just try to take it on and make it happen.

Now that you have the formula, focus on maintaining the successful spirit, which is all about keeping a continuous cycle at the foundation to use as a guide to achieve a successful spirit. For me, as previously mentioned, that's maintaining the 3 Ds—determination, drive, and discipline—and keeping a balance of life, which healthily feeds my spirit. Once these requirements are met, I can always continue to utilize this approach for all aspects of my life, and so can you!

About the Author

Fabian Florant is the best triple jump athlete in the history of the Netherlands. He is a European Teams and Clubs triple jump champion and an Olympian (2016 Rio Olympic Games). He holds the Dutch indoor and outdoor triple jump records, and is undefeated in triple jump.

He attended Lindenwood University in St. Charles, Missouri, and during his freshman and sophomore years, he was a four-time All-American and two-time NAIA National Triple Jump Champion. He then transferred to Missouri State University in Springfield, Missouri, where he became a three-time Missouri Valley Conference Champion and a two-time NCAA Division 1 All-American.

He completed his bachelor of science in finance and master of science in business and sports management. Currently he is pursuing his PhD in business-organizational leadership.

He is a lifetime master in balancing life, i.e., sports, school, work, and family, using the 3 Ds—discipline, drive, and determination. In addition to being an Olympic athlete, Fabian has over 15 years of business and banking experience, and is currently a banking senior program manager focusing on digital transformation with one of the largest banks in Europe.

Fabian is devoting his post-professional track and field career to writing books that contain the formula to a successful balance of life and to fulfilling multiple non-profit projects throughout the Netherlands, the US, and his birth country of Dominica.

Email: fabian.florant@olympian.org

CHAPTER 13
FEEL YOUR CHANGE

By Mandi Freger, MEd, DCEP, LBS, LPC
Licensed Counselor and Behavior Specialist
Pittsburgh, Pennsylvania

"What's in it for me?"

One of my colleagues a while back suggested that this appeared to be a theme amongst some of our other colleagues. As I gained momentum in being more heavily rooted in a behaviorist frame of mind, this became a key concept with respect to motivation with those whom I serve. I find myself applying my roots in energy psychology and applied behavior analysis in my framework of a "thera-coaching" approach.

Motivation is a key component for many of the people with whom I work (if not everyone), which directly ties into happiness and a successful feeling of spirit. Spoiler alert—most often, this comes down to being anchored into bigger picture thinking.

Let me start with basic tips for self-care that I find myself repeating frequently with clients during sessions which greatly affect thinking, emotions, emotional regulation, contentment, and then happiness.

Media. Media. Media.

What does the media tell us about how to engage in self-care? Demand "me time." Try this tool and then that one. Quick fixes. Spiritual retreats. These can all be a result of or lead to overdoing it. It is a belief, in my world of behavior modification, that one must evidence a "stick-with-it-ness" or consistent practice for someone to find lasting change. There is no single shortcut to squelch bad feelings and to be "happy." Media messages can cause us to jump on the pendulum of "What do I do? Or what should I believe?" swinging from opposite poles of overactive or underactive initiative with respect to self-care.

The overactive side of self-care can come across as entitled independence such as "me time" or "It's time for all you to work around me."

The underactive side may be where "I need to have fulfilling relationships to fill me up." If you are familiar with energy work, you can imagine how one or more chakra centers must be expressing themselves behaviorally and emotionally with this type of imbalance. This secret "error" at the poles of this pendulum swing relates to a framework of "other people," when in fact the framework really needs to be within yourself.

We live in a world that tells us as humans, we need other people. From my radical behaviorist lens and from my years of working with those diagnosed with autism spectrum disorders, *needing* other people and feeling unfulfilled without them is a *choice*. We live in a modern world, not like that of the times of our grandparents or ancestors. For example, today marriages are no longer contracts for resources and survival. Some may argue that this is still in our biology, but this somewhat contradicts modern neuroplasticity research. Media sells to us by playing on our emotions, but we have the responsibility to keep it in check. You need to be your own best friend with honest and personal accountability to yourself and others.

Self-Fulfillment and Attachment

Self-fulfillment lies in self-love. So, we need to jump off the pendulum that references others and look toward self-love through mindful isolation. Not for just a few weeks, a few months, or in between relationships, but could you sustain *happily* alone? If not, what are your fears? This is what makes me a radical behaviorist, in part. This is so contrary to what many of my colleagues would suggest with the more mainstream belief that our social biology requires us to need other people. When I approach therapy from this lens, it changes much for me as a practitioner and how I empathize with a person. I am also not a therapist overfocused on processing feelings but on actions taken. Actions to change the targeted unwelcome feelings and to feel better.

Another concept that goes hand in hand with how we define ourselves in relationship to others is attachment. Just because we need to learn healthy bonding as infants, doesn't mean that ongoing development remains the same in form. Good parents teach their children to be independent across many levels. The majority work toward behavioral independence, but emotional, moral, ethical, spiritual, and philosophical independence are areas that can become parcellated. Sadly, relationships with others can quickly be molded by self-referencing the question, "What's in it for me?" If the answer has something to do with validation, this is something that you may want to explore.

When considering spiritual leaders, many who stood with their convictions were not popular. For many of them, I believe that is part of their messages and teachings. You've got to master *you* before successfully assimilating new people in your life. You may outgrow people. Let it be. You may make passing connections. Let it be. Why should you have to demand "me time"? What did you sign up for, or what were your old behaviors that led to this point? Even though the media tries to sell us on "You can have it all," loving yourself takes considerable work and reflection. So you may need to let go of things that are cluttering up your life. When you choose to spend time working on these things, you will change. As a result, like gears that are interconnected, energetically, things will fall in and out of alignment.

Are you too reliant on others for your happiness? Here may be a modern construct which may support why that is. Think about how much access we have to others growing up, the way that our schools are designed. You may have recognized this access, or the lack of, when schools went remote during the COVID-19 pandemic. Pair this with children gaining access to others through their electronics, and it is a formula that encourages high connection, possibly to the point of addiction, through the college years.

When friends start to drift apart as people approach young adulthood, this becomes a crisis for many people. After all, you were conditioned with ease of access to peers for perhaps more than 12 or 16 years. That is quite a long time to maintain a behavior with such a heavily embedded pattern and then to try to suddenly change it. Some people cope with this crisis by jumping into romantic relationships.

If any of this resonates with you, some questions you might ask yourself are: What did I emotionally sign up for and *why*? Am I afraid to be alone? Did I make an assumption about an expectation of another person and their responsibility toward me? Do I expect another person to fill me up with love?

If we redirect ruminating energy that we channel into a few relationships to humanitarian causes, the world's problems could potentially be lessened. We, as a collective, and each of us as individuals, need to start with finding a better balance within ourselves.

Are We Trying to Do Too Much?

Our media smashes us with bigger, better, faster, stronger—you've got to do it all, and do it now. I have seen countless people's spirits broken when they have a "plan" for life and it doesn't happen, or they are living with ridiculous anxiety levels to have the plan play out. What kind of quality of life is that? Is having a rigid plan necessary? We need to stop letting society over-program us and not place much stock in the illusions that social media platforms mostly let us show the world, i.e., our best selves only. Unless you have a strong ego state to neutralize some of these messages and think independently and realistically, you may let maladaptive feelings take over.

Additionally, life has become too fast-paced. Consider how much you are doing. Is it healthy? For example, take filling your or your family's evenings up with activities after work or school most nights of the week. This keeps our minds and bodies programmed to believe we *need* to keep going. This not only can keep us in activated states that turn to more pervasive anxiety, but also it can create a psychological panic if we *don't* have anything to do or don't have others around us. In turn, this exacerbates the aforementioned thinking that we need other things or people to fill us up. This is one of the biggest issues for modern-day Americans I see consistently in my practice.

We need to slow down as a society and make time for mindful individual reflection and self-care. Perhaps for many of us, the COVID-19 pandemic contained a great message for us to slow our pace.

What Is Your Bigger Picture?

I've given some tips to fuel your introspection, but the broader tool for feeling motivated and successful really is connected with what you believe happens after you die and what you were conditioned to believe. This shapes your day-to-day existence through choices, whether or not you are actively aware of it. I tell people, if you believe nothing happens after we die and consciousness is gone, then you will never know or remember anything about this life. So, do the best you can, focusing on your own values and don't over-focus on regrets or things that can't be changed. Keep moving forward, making the most of the present. If you believe in a heaven-like afterlife where "things are better," then perhaps the struggles in this life are really what the concept of "hell" might represent, and this time here on earth is a minute fragment of what an afterlife has to offer. So, do the best you can, focusing on your values and don't over-focus on regrets or things that can't be changed. Keep moving forward, making the most of the present, because remember, you believe there is way more good stuff to come in the afterlife. If you believe that consciousness reincarnates in another body or form, then you have every chance to do what you didn't again! So, do the best you can, focusing on your values and don't over-focus on regrets or things that can't be changed. Keep moving forward, making the most of the present, because remember, you believe there is way more good stuff. You may not have to master it all, only this body. Therefore, you may have gotten the picture that spirituality (not necessarily indoctrinated religions) and/or morals and values should be explored and reflected upon daily to create motivation and sustain purpose, drive, and a happy spirit.

Think Like a Subtle Energy Practitioner

As an energy therapist, I subscribe to Dr. William Tiller's work that maintains that a person can have science *and* spirit—that they don't have to be opponents. I suspect that modern science will support more of this as our technological resources grow. Our thoughts have an electromagnetic charge, and Tiller's work shows us how our thoughts extend outside of us to create a field—a principle that most of us energy therapists have been using for years as an underlying concept in our work. Most energy therapists also harness the idea that the highest state of feeling vibration is love. That is the *feeling* that we strive to help our clients attain.

One of the things I hear many times from my clients is how they have tried to use the law of attraction. There seems to be a common thread in people, amongst those I work with anyway, who overfocus on a thought but neglect co-creating the loving vibration *feeling* surrounding the thought or intention. This takes a lot of practice to successfully pair the two and sustain it. This is what energy psychology tools, specifically, do with tremendous speed and efficacy—extinguish the not helpful feelings stuck in the body connected to specific thoughts or events, neutralize those feelings, and then make new connections for desired behaviors paired with loving feelings.

No matter where you are in your self-development spiritual journey or performance levels, these tools can be individualized for you by a seasoned practitioner. It is amazing when you can change the feeling in your body about something, and your thoughts about it completely shift. As an energy therapist, I am essentially a behaviorist—healing one disruption at a time, so a person can feel better and engage in more helpful behaviors, which creates a happier spirit. This is also available to you. Focus on first changing your feelings about things, and see your thoughts follow with positivity and joy, allowing you to live the successful life you deserve.

About the Author

Mandi Freger is not your typical counselor. Throughout her career, she has served in multiple roles within many service lines of behavioral health treatment, including acting as a supervisor in both outpatient and residential settings. In providing decades of psychotherapeutic treatment to various populations, she has gained extensive experience with those with autism spectrum disorders. Mandi was one of the initial candidates to obtain the behavior specialist license, as well as status as a certified trainer in functional behavioral assessment in Pennsylvania with an emphasis on autism spectrum disorder treatment planning. She is also a licensed professional counselor in Pennsylvania.

Originally trained in energy psychology techniques (EMDR and TFT Test Dx^{TM}) to treat trauma, mood and pain disorders, and learning challenges, Mandi has been using a variety of energy-based modalities with children, adolescents, adults, and staff. Mandi holds diplomat status in comprehensive energy psychology.

Email: mandi@mandifreger.com
Website: www.mandifreger.com

CHAPTER 14
FOCUS ON YOUR WHY

By Susanne Grainger
Olympic Athlete in Rowing
Victoria, Canada

Fearlessness is not the absence of fear. It's the mastery of fear.
It's about getting up one more time than we fall down.
—Arianna Huffington

Six to seven days of training per week, 25-plus-hour training weeks, two to three sessions per day. This lifestyle of a national team athlete is exhausting and impossible without a determined spirit. It is one thing to make it onto the national team, but remaining on the national team and sustaining the lifestyle of an elite athlete is something different altogether. I have been rowing for 17 years, ten of which I have spent training and competing with the Canadian National Rowing Team. My ultimate goal is to win a gold medal at the Olympic Games. So how have I remained at the top of my sport for so long?

The Why

Every journey has difficult days and, on these days, doubt creeps in. It is on these difficult days where a spirit of focus, drive, and determination is most needed. On hard days, I question myself: "Why am I getting out of bed at 6:30 am on a Saturday to train outside in the pouring rain? Why am I still rowing after 17 years? Why do I row at all?" On the tough days, it doesn't matter what the question is. What matters is having an answer. That answer is the why.

To achieve my goal of winning an Olympic gold, one element of my why is about striving to be the best possible rowing version of myself. Rowing is something I excel at because I know I am capable of the hard work it requires. At each level of competition, I have been able to prove that I have a place in the next level of competition. The more I accomplish, the more compelling the next opportunity becomes. I want to, and I will, see this journey through. While the competition only gets harder, what was true in my first high school regatta holds true at the Olympic level: "Someone has to win, so why can't it be me?"

The second element of my why is about choosing freedom from regret. I have given 17 years to my rowing career. The idea of getting to the end of this career and not achieving my Olympic goal is terrifying. However, this fear pales in comparison to the nightmare of having the opportunity to achieve my goal and knowing that I didn't give it my all. On the days that I want to quit, I stop and think about how I want to remember this journey. I want to be 100 percent proud of both my training and my final performance as an Olympic rower, even if that doesn't result in a medal. I don't want to look back and remember that I quit when it got hard. I refuse to walk away from the opportunity to achieve my dream simply because things become challenging. Quitting will never be a part of my life story. The fighting spirit in me won't let quitting be my story.

Whether in athletics or elsewhere, the lifestyle associated with high performance is hard. Thinking about quitting does not make you a quitter. On the really tough days, it's normal to think about walking away. That's why it's important to know exactly why I won't. As long as I have my why when the alarm goes off at 6:30 am on a Saturday, I will fight through.

The How

Wanting something is important, but simply wanting is not enough. If the why justifies the journey and keeps you going, the how is what actually gets you there. Throughout my athletic career, I have found four things that, when done consistently, help me maintain the high intensity required to stay at the top of my sport. Together, these make up my how:

1. Set small goals and celebrate wins along the way.
Given that my ultimate goal is an Olympic gold, the opportunity to achieve my goal occurs only once every four years. Setting smaller objectives along the way helps to make my everyday efforts manageable and purposeful. I get ahead of myself all the time. I'm always thinking of what's next, which is important, but not when I forget to recognize what I've accomplished along the way. If I don't remember to celebrate the small goals, I find myself feeling unsatisfied and impatient with my progress. Setting small goals helps keep me in a healthy headspace. Sometimes the goal is as small as remembering to pack my bag the night before practice.

I set daily goals to help create purpose and a path for progress. Before going out for a row, we decide as a team, or I decide individually, what I am to work on, even if that is a one percent better row for that day. One percent may not seem like a lot, but if I am able to see one percent progress every day in a row for a week, the improvement adds up very quickly. Not every day is going to be a step forward, but I lead with this mindset.

I set monthly goals to give myself benchmarks, check my progress, or test whether I've actually made and maintained my positive improvement. Every couple of months, we go through individual lactate and VO_2 max testing to check our fitness levels, see whether our training is working, and look for areas of improvement. I like to look at the results from my previous tests every few weeks to remind myself where I am with my fitness and how I can get better. I set goals for what I want to achieve on the testing we complete. It helps me strive to push past my limits and set new ones.

Yearly, I set goals with my teammates to give us specific achievements to push towards each racing season. Every year of the quadrennial, we have an international summer racing season with three to four races. As a team, we set goals for our own internal performance as a crew at each race. We know what we are capable of, but we are unable to control what other crews are doing or how they have trained. We set goals to help us achieve our best possible performance as a boat, no matter what is going on around us. Standing on the podium is always a goal of ours, but we want to be proud of the performances we lay down as a team in every race, regardless of the ranking.

My ultimate goal is to win an Olympic gold medal, but my athletic career will not be defined by whether I achieve that one goal. I set a variety of goals for myself throughout the quadrennial and celebrate every small success on the journey. It's important to set small goals along the way to see and celebrate progress, so at the end of the journey, you can walk away, no matter the result, knowing that you could not have done anything more.

2. Stay humble and hungry.

"Stay humble and hungry" is something that my university rowing coach, Kevin Sauer, used to say to our team when we were training for NCAAs. This was his way of reminding us to celebrate progress, but always remain driven, strive to better yourself, and learn from leaders around you. In 2010, my university rowing team won its first NCAA championship. We celebrated this success, but we didn't let this win make us complacent. We trained hard as a team, and, in 2012, we won the overall NCAA championship title a second time and won the varsity eight championship race for the first time in the university's history. It's important to celebrate what you've accomplished, but not become content.

I strive to remain humble and hungry now, in my second Olympic quadrennial. In training, if we are out for a row and something in the boat doesn't feel quite right, I try not to blame those around me. I always try to point the finger at myself first. I think, "What can I do better?" I may be an Olympian, but I do not row the perfect stroke. I do not allow myself to feel like I've "made it" or that I can stop pushing. I am always looking for ways to improve.

However, there is a fine line between staying humble and hungry and living in perpetual dissatisfaction. This is why the goal setting I mentioned earlier is so important to create balance. Setting goals helps you take a moment to celebrate and acknowledge what you have achieved before looking to the next goal. Take pride in your accomplishments, but always strive for more and continue to push for better.

3. Accept failure on the path to success.

The journey to success is not a straight line. Resilience and perseverance are key to pushing forward with confidence and sticking to goals when things get tough. After joining the Senior National Rowing Team in 2013, I trained hard and was lucky enough to stand on multiple World Cup and World Championship podiums with my teammates leading up to the 2016 Olympic Games. I earned my spot on the Olympic team and achieved my goal of becoming an Olympian.

Everything was falling into place. We had had such a successful quadrennial. Then our Olympic Games final happened. We were favoured to stand on the podium, and, in that last race, we placed fifth. While fifth in the world is still an incredible accomplishment, it absolutely devastated me. In my eyes, we did not live up to what we were capable of and did not race our best as a crew. We had worked so hard, seen so much progress, and I really believed that it was going to all come together for us in the Olympic final. We had it in us to stand on that podium, but it was not our day. In this challenging moment, I had to persevere.

At the time, this felt like a failure. When we placed fifth, I could have stopped. I could have walked away and accepted that moment as the failure that I saw it as. But choosing this failure was unpalatable. Instead, I had to find a way to turn devastation into a fire to fuel my drive, dust myself off, and try again. Finding a way to grow and learn from these tough situations made me stronger.

I train every day to make sure that failure is not truly failure, for if I have trained as hard as I can, prepared as best I can, and raced my best race, I will have succeeded, regardless of outcome. I aim to do everything in my power to minimize regret, so when I close the book on my rowing career, I can walk away knowing that I put my all into being the best I could be and couldn't have done anything more. That is something to be proud of.

4. Have an identity outside your ambition.
My goals are not just sport-focused. It is helpful to have focuses and goals outside of your core ambition. When I first joined the Senior National Team, my goal outside of rowing was to complete my master's degree. Currently, I have a baking side-gig, I am taking some university courses, and I have a part-time job with a charity called CAN Fund.

Each of these things plays an important role in my life. Baking is a way to turn my mind off—I find it stress-relieving and a way to express creativity. Taking courses, learning something new, and working are ways to use my brain in a completely different way than I do when I'm rowing. When training feels monotonous, I love to sit down in front of new information and learn. In order to do so, I have to completely shut my "rowing mind" off, and it's nice to take a break from that world and learn something new.

I absolutely love working part-time with CAN Fund because I love to help people. Working for a charity that supports athletes, like myself, and being able to help others creates a sense of fulfillment and joy in my soul. Having these other things to focus on outside of sport provides a much-needed mental break from rowing.

There are times when sport disappoints me. That's life—things happen and the journey to success is not linear. It's important to keep sports in perspective. On the days that sport disappoints me, or practice does not go well, I have my other goals and aspects of life to focus on. If all I had was sport, when I had bad days or something did not go well in training, what would I use to keep my spirits up? My baking, education, and charity work keep me from developing an unhealthy, hyper-focused relationship with rowing. It's important to have variety and balance in life. Given that I am training for the Olympics, rowing has to be a lot of my life, if I want to succeed. It is my priority right now, so the balance may tip heavily to sport, but it's not the only thing on the scale.

Many athletes identify solely with their sport. Many careerists identify solely with their work. This can make it difficult to take a mental break and refresh on days when things are difficult. It can also make the transition out of a sport or a specific job even that much more tough. If an athlete solely identifies with their sport, when it comes time to retire, they have then retired their identity.

I know that transitioning out of sport will be hard, but I try to set goals and focal interests outside of sport to not only keep myself balanced and provide a mental break from training, but to also help me prepare for life after rowing. As long as my focal interests and goals outside of sport are providing me with a mental break from rowing and not taking away from my ability to train well and recover, they are important for helping me to maintain a healthy sport/ life balance.

*

The lifestyle of an elite athlete is tough and exhausting, but with the help of goal setting, a determined spirit, resilience, my why, and my how, it is also incredibly rewarding. Being able to see progress in myself, even after 17 years of rowing—ten at the elite level—keeps me driving for more. I am so grateful that rowing has given me the opportunity to push myself and put myself up against the best in the world.

However, the competition season is quite short, and the Olympics only come around once every four years, so it's the work that you put in on the tough days in between that makes all the difference. On the tough days, I think about my why—I want to be able to walk away from rowing knowing that I have trained as hard as I could, had the best performance I am capable of, and that I couldn't have done anything more.

One day, I may be asked why I rowed for so long. I will say, "If someone told you that you had a real chance to win a gold medal—a small chance, but a chance—would you walk away before discovering the outcome?" I want to be able to confidently say that I did everything in my power to achieve my ultimate goal of winning Olympic gold. If I train as hard as I can, become the best possible rowing version of myself, and have the best performance I am capable of, I can walk away proud, regardless of the outcome. Naturally, the same applies to you. with all you've built and all you've been given, give it your all.

About the Author

Susanne Grainger, now Susanne Wereley, is an Olympic rower originally from London, Ontario, Canada. She started rowing in grade eight at the age of thirteen. While attending the University of Virginia on an athletic scholarship, Susanne rowed in the varsity eight, winning the NCAA championships in 2012. During her university summers, she competed for Team Canada at the U23 World Championships in the eight and the four, winning gold in both 2011 and again in 2012. After graduating, Susanne moved back to Canada to train with the Canadian Senior National Team and complete a master's degree at Western University. In 2016, she competed at the Rio Olympics to a fifth-place finish. Susanne has competed in 22 international regattas, medaling in 16 of them. Susanne is currently training with the National Team in British Columbia with the aim of competing in the Tokyo 2021 Olympics.

Email: susannesmindset@gmail.com

CHAPTER 15

EMBRACE THE SUCK: TO ENDURE OR TO GROW

By Drs. Annemieke Griffin, RT SV
Clinical Performance Psychologist, Coach
Austin, Texas

*Sometimes, struggles are exactly what we need in our life. If we were
to go through our life without any obstacles, we would be crippled.
We would not be as strong as what we could have been.*
—Friedrich Nietzsche

I have been working as a performance psychologist for ten years now, and when
we reach a milestone, like the ten-year mark, we start reflecting. When I reflect
on my career and the field I am working in, I conclude that the concept of
mental toughness is as much misunderstood now as it was ten years ago. It's
a painful, eye-opening realization because despite my hard work, few strides
have been made when it comes to a general understanding of mental toughness.

If something is bothering you and sticks with you, you must do something
about it. My motto in my daily practice is "If you want to fly, you got to give
up the shit that weighs you down." Excuse my language, but most of the time,
that's what the things that are holding us back are, am I right? Having this
motto in my head, I should not just talk the talk, but walk the walk.

The small strides that have been made when it comes to an accurate understanding of mental toughness over the years bother me. So here I am now,

writing this, excited, even passionate, to explain what mental toughness is about. I'm passionate because mental toughness is a powerful concept. When you understand what mental toughness is and how you can use it to your advantage, you hold your own key to success.

My workdays are mostly spent in the areas of professional sports and the military. I am fortunate to work with experts from all over the world who understand the type of determined spirit needed for success. When I ask the experts about the importance of mental toughness, as it relates to peak performance, there is 99 percent consensus that mental toughness is crucial when it comes to the ability to reach peak performance. It is great that mental toughness is seen as foundational to achievement.

It is the answer, however, to the next question that worries me. When I asked the experts what they do in their day-to-day practice to train this crucial component, my question is often met with silence. More often than not, they do not train it at all; or they train it now and then; or, in many cases, experts think they train mental toughness while in fact they do not.

I cannot blame them. The people I work with are all experts in peak performance, but this discipline lacks a workable definition of mental toughness. Plus, the research that has been done on mental toughness is largely untranslated into trainable pieces. A misunderstanding I have seen in the military is that mental toughness is about the ability to endure. When things get hard, you just suck it up, you endure it. The tough endure! While mental toughness entails an aspect of enduring, mental toughness is much more than just enduring.

Mental toughness is a true component of human growth. You are capable of enduring because you know why you are doing the things you do. You do not endure because you go blank and wait until the storm passes; you endure because you know that by doing the right things, you will be stronger after you work through the hardship. It is important to shed the old school perspective of mental toughness—the strong endure—and hold on to a more accurate perspective of mental toughness—the smart create the environment to grow. You see that the old concept is stagnant while true mental toughness is an active building block to success. You are the creator.

It has been difficult to get rid of the passive concept of enduring, especially in the military, in which passively enduring is still perceived as a medal of honor. A better understanding of mental toughness leads to the needed shift in perception.

After my ten-year anniversary, my reflection, and the hard realization of the little strides that have been made, I knew I had to share my knowledge about what mental toughness is, so that my clients could start training and using it in the right way, in a way that would help them.

The readers of this book are all people who are interested in bettering themselves, and I commend you for that. I will share with you the building blocks of mental toughness. When you start incorporating these into your day-to-day practice, you will get stronger and more functional every day. Let me take you on my journey of sharing knowledge with military personnel that I coach. How I taught them not to passively endure, but to actively grow.

Mental Toughness as Active Growth: The 4 Cs Model

I am a true believer in simplicity. I like to use simple models when it comes to sharing knowledge. I have noticed that this way of sharing knowledge leads to the best results. I often think of a quote by Albert Einstein, which states, "If you can't explain it simply, you don't understand it well enough." Having this in mind, visualize mental toughness as a big pie cut up into four pieces. Each piece is the same size and is an equally important piece of the pie. The four parts are all made from different components and together make the whole pie. The four parts of mental toughness include the following:

- Commitment
- Challenge
- Control
- Confidence

We call this the 4 Cs model of mental toughness. You might think, "That makes sense. I can understand that these parts are important contributors to peak performance, but now what?" We have reached the point where usually the true understanding of mental toughness breaks. We see the words—commitment, challenge, control, and confidence—and the words make sense, but it stops right then and there. When it comes to mental toughness, it is vital to translate these parts into concrete, usable knowledge.

That was my main mission in working with military personnel, to teach them how to use the 4 Cs of mental toughness and train others in the military to apply them as well. I am calling it my "mission" because passively enduring comes with a price. The human spirit is like a sponge. Similar to how a sponge holds on to water, our spirit holds on to experiences. The more emotions and stress linked to an experience, the more our spirit holds on to them. If you endure hardship without a strategy, it will start weighing you down. It can lead to a form of learned helplessness and can lead to feelings of depression, anxiety, and psychosomatic problems. Problems which are present above average within the military population. The exposure to stressful situations, which is common for our military personnel, in combination with just passively enduring these problems, sucks the person up and can lead to extreme damage to their spirit, body, and mind. So let's look at mental toughness through the new lens of the 4 Cs.

First C: Commitment

The first C of mental toughness is the C of commitment. During my observations of many training events, I have seen the following way of training:

Soldier A: I need you to dig in your machinegun at location B no later than 1800 hours to be ready to cover squad C's movement to the objective. Do you understand, and are you able to do so?

From this, you might think Soldier A is a good leader, asking the additional questions about whether the other soldier understands their task and if they think they are able to execute the task. Pretty thorough communication, right? I agree because in many cases the latter questions of understanding the tasks and the ability to execute the task are enough.

But when it comes to the ability to perform at a peak level, to which mental toughness is a crucial component, the most important question is lacking. When you want to transform passive enduring into actively growing, the most important question when it comes to task execution is "Are you going to do it; are you truly in?" Perhaps this question seems like an open door? I might agree with you when it is smooth sailing, and the sun is out. But I can tell you, when things are getting tough, and the bullets start flying, only the committed ones will be able to execute their tasks. It is not about doing your job; it is about still doing your job when things are hard and the situation is difficult.

The C of commitment is about "Are you in?" Are you willing to leave everything behind and be fully committed to the task at hand? In good and, even more importantly, in bad times? If the answer is no, you might want to go back and look at your goal. If your goal is not worth committing yourself to, you do not have the right goal.

As a leader, never leave this last question out. I encounter too much frustration with leaders when it comes to the task execution of their soldiers. Too little of what they have been taught and told is seen in their performance. They do not understand why this is the case. They explain to the soldiers what to do and the soldiers have the skills to do it, so why is so much of what the soldiers were told missing from their performance? The soldiers understand what to do, and they have the ability to do it, but are they truly going to follow through when things are tough? When you want efficient task execution, ask for commitment, ask your soldiers (or your employees or colleagues) if they are in. If not, create a situation in which they are. Give them more ownership and responsibilities. Ask them for input and let them create solutions.

One tool that we use to create commitment is the powerful history of the US military—the many soldiers who have died wearing the same uniform as the current soldiers are wearing now. Wearing the uniform has a meaning; it holds value, and you should give it honor.

There are many powerful stories you can use to form a strong sense of commitment. An important psychological mechanism to understand when it comes to commitment is the more you make a person a part of something, the more they will commit to it. If a soldier lacks commitment, I recommend the leader to make the soldier a bigger part of the task, to ask for input, to let the soldier problem solve, and to give them ownership. These are all big parts of commitment.

Second C: Challenge

The second C of the 4 Cs model of mental toughness is the C of Challenge. The C of challenge is linked to what we call the "layer of perception." Our perception is a powerful system when it comes to the level on which we operate. When we are faced with a demand, our perception generally goes in one of two directions: we perceive the demand as a threat, or we perceive the demand as a challenge.

Our perception is powerful because it determines our behavioral outcome, our level of performance. If we perceive a demand as a threat—"I can never do this"—we will experience distress and our performance declines. If we perceive a demand as a challenge—"I am well trained, and this demand gives me an opportunity to show my ability and grow even stronger"—we will experience eustress, meaning beneficial stress, and our performance increases.

If you notice that under stress your performance or that of your soldiers, employees, colleagues, or teammates declines, check the layer of perception. It is likely that the demand they are facing threatens them. You will notice negative self-talk: "I will fail, I don't have what it takes, I will never get it." It is important to reframe the perspective of a threat into a challenge.

Every demand you are facing is an opportunity to grow, to learn, to become stronger. You do the best that you can do in the moment, you take responsibility, and you learn and move on stronger. You can imagine that if you are able to see the challenge in hardship and you can trust all the experiences that are inside you, enduring becomes growing.

I am thankful for my struggles because without them, I wouldn't have built my strengths.

Third C: Control

The third C of the 4 Cs model of mental toughness is the C of control, which is linked to the ability to stay in control over your thoughts and emotions. When it comes to human behavior, we must understand that we have more control over our behavior than we often give ourselves credit for. When we do not perform as well as we can, we all like to make excuses: "It was the weather, or we didn't sleep well." Let's be honest, we are all guilty of making these excuses, and we are all eager to believe them. For this reason, I like to state that we are highly in control over our behavior and, therefore, our level of performance.

It is important to focus our attention on the right things—the steps that we need to take to reach our goal. A mechanism that we must understand is that there is a connection between our emotions, thoughts, and behavior. They influence each other. The way we think determines the way we feel and behave, and the way we behave influences the way that we feel and think. When we notice our performance is declining, we must check where our attention is at. Are you overthinking or are you feeling emotions, and are your thoughts and emotions negatively charged? To make a quick and functional change that puts you back in the moment, focus on taking action. Take the steps that make you better, and your thinking and emotions will follow your actions and neutralize quickly. By doing this, you get out of your head, and you place yourself back in the moment.

If you notice, as a leader, that the performance of your soldier, employee, teammate is declining, check where the attention is placed. In many cases, negative thinking is the cause of a performance decline. Provide your soldier with basic and concrete steps that build their performance and will help them take control over their attention. You can say, "When you notice that you get inside your head, start placing your feet sturdy on the ground, start moving, ask input from your colleagues, and tell yourself, 'I am going to do this.'" Acting is the best remedy against negative thinking or intrusive emotions. Keep it simple and basic. The more complex your tasks, the greater the decline in performance you will encounter under stress unless you control the stress in advance.

Fourth C: Confidence

The last C of the 4 Cs model of mental toughness is the C of confidence, and it is a difficult one for many. Confidence is often perceived as a mythical force. It is either there or it is not. If you are lucky, it will be there, but if you are not lucky, it will not. Let me tell you here and now, confidence is inside of you; you are your confidence. You determine if your confidence will be there or if it will not.

Confidence is highly linked to the ability to problem solve. If you know that you have the solution for every obstacle that you could encounter, you have nothing to fear, so you can be confident. It is useful to practice a diversity of situations, to train adaptability, but in the end, you can only practice so many ways. You must train the skills to problem solve. As a leader you must create a psychologically safe environment, in which soldiers and employees can fail, retry, and refine their approach. Too many times I see that whenever a mistake is made, we highlight the mistake and tell the soldier how exactly to do it next time. Highlighting a mistake makes most people very self-aware, which can lead to avoidant behavior. Nobody likes to make a mistake, and in most cases, we know that our approach wasn't the best. To have mistakes highlighted can make us more self-aware, and we try to avoid getting in this situation again. We start playing it safe to avoid making more mistakes.

Playing it safe and reaching your peak performance are not compatible. To be the best that you can be, you must grow by trial and error. If you want to develop confident soldiers, employees, and teammates, let them problem solve.

Let them develop the best approach by trial and error. Give them a goal and the freedom to maneuver to get to that best approach. Let their spirits be free to fly. This way you develop confident soldiers who are adaptable and able to capture success in whatever they do.

As I expressed in the quote earlier, if you are committed, challenged, in control, and confident, you can be thankful for all your struggles. Your successes do not determine who you are, but your struggles do. The way you go about them. You can passively endure and eventually get defeated, or you can actively use them and grow stronger. Let the 4 Cs model of mental toughness guide you.

About the Author

Dr. Annemieke Griffin is a clinical psychologist and founder of StatuMentis, a peak performance consulting firm. Annemieke's expertise started in grief psychology where she took part in global research projects but found her true passion in performance psychology by helping motivated people achieve their full potential. Annemieke works globally with elite athletes, teams, coaches, military personnel, and business professionals.

Annemieke's work has translated into players once riding the bench being selected for national teams and military officers advancing into nominative positions. With Annemieke's research background, she is continuously immersed in the newest studies to integrate and shape the way StatuMentis meets the demands of clients. She is also dedicated to helping expand mental health and peak performance knowledge to everyone regardless of status or position. With this at heart, Annemieke is a central figure in the development of the StatuMentis Academy where the key component is the sharing of knowledge.

Email: annemieke@statumentis.com
Website: www.statumentis.com

CHAPTER 16

DEVELOP A STRONG FOUNDATION FOR YOUR SUCCESSFUL SPIRIT

By Jeroen Keymolen
Performance Psychologist, Coach
Bruges, Belgium

The energy of the mind is the essence of life.
—Aristotle

The spirit, materialized through our brain, is wonderous.

Our brain in itself is a peculiar organ. The weight is rather light, in average not much more than two percent of our total body weight. It's productivity, however, is enormous, with scientists estimating it to produce 70,000 to 120,000 thoughts, feelings, etc., per day. Our brain is always active; there is no "pause" or "stop" button. Needless to say, this requires an enormous amount of energy. Here, research estimates that our brain uses between 20 to 30 percent of our total available energy. The only other systems in our body that require such amounts of energy include our digestion and immune systems.

When we look at these figures showing how much energy our brain uses, we quickly realize that mindset is very much affected by our energy levels. It is much easier to focus on your goals, as well as to make conscious and successful decisions, when you are full of energy. It is much more challenging when we feel tired and lack energy. When we experience mental fatigue, we often give in to excuses and procrastination much more easily, and our goals suddenly might seem less important. This is where our ongoing internal dialogues come in. These internal dialogues originate from the most primitive part of our brain, often referred to as the reptile brain, which is composed of the brainstem and cerebellum. Unfortunately, these internal dialogues do not always help us to achieve our goals. They are focused on comfort and are by definition change-avoidant. Our goals, however, are commonly composed of desired changes and are constructed in the rational parts of our brain, the cerebral cortex.

The cerebral cortex is the part of the brain that needs the most energy. When this energy is available, the rational brain mostly succeeds in controlling our internal dialogues, reorienting them to a positive direction when necessary. When the energy is lacking, however, for instance, due to long or complex mental and/or physical activity, the rational brain doesn't succeed as effectively in controlling the wild primitive brain. This is where internal dialogues often become more negative or destructive, acting as saboteurs. They are strong and forceful in attacking our winner's mindset. How many of us had to fight not to give up during a challenging goal because we felt tired and deprived of energy only to be unable to understand what really went wrong with our thinking upon completing the challenge and were refueled with energy? Although it might have been difficult to continue, our cerebral cortex was able to redirect our negative thoughts of quitting long enough to finish.

If you look at it from an opposite angle, you see that a successful spirit also delivers a lot of energy. Here, I refer to energy in the form of neurotransmitters in the brain. These are substances in the brain that are often linked to feelings. Amongst them are dopamine, characterized by that happy and powerful feeling when we achieve goals; serotonin linked to happiness and wellbeing; oxytocin when we are cuddling or in love. Someone who experiences success will experience more of these positive feelings and will be more likely to look for situations where they can relive these emotions, hence creating new opportunities for success. But neurotransmitters are not only linked to feelings, but also to focus, concentration, dealing with pain, expression of emotions, memory, and relaxation—all skills that the winning mind uses effectively.

Therefore, someone who wants to continuously demonstrate a successful spirit in their performance, whether it is in sports, business, or another area, should manage their personal energy to the maximum. Increasing your energy capacity to the maximum, while keeping unnecessary energy loss to a minimum, allows you to deliver your maximum energy when performing and striving towards goals. A winning mindset is easier to develop and maintain when your energy foundation has a strong base.

My key advice is to make sure that your brain is fully energized by creating habits that optimize your energy system on a daily basis. And, in the process of creating these habits, you'll inevitably develop your mindset, even as your internal dialogue will try to seduce you back into your old habits. If you manage to strengthen your energy fundamentals, however, you win twice: once by freeing up all the energy you need to develop a strong mind, and secondly by developing the mental toughness you can later use when faced with other challenges. By focusing on everyday energy gains, you will propel yourself into a positive cycle: more energy creates room for a successful mindset, and your successful mindset will create positive energy and confidence. If you succeed in maintaining this, you will become a person who is trained and ready to achieve challenging goals.

Five Energy Fundamentals

Here, we turn to discuss five energy fundamentals: sleep, breathing, movement, nutrition, and social support. While all five of them influence both body and mind, with respect to the topic of this book, I will mostly discuss how they affect our mindset.

Sleep—let's start with sleep. There are still many things that scientists don't yet know about sleep, but one thing is for sure: sleep is crucial for all mammals in recovery of both mind and body. Because sleep cleanses and refreshes the brain, it is key during periods when we are learning or experiencing high levels of stress. Similarly, recovery from muscle damage, bone fractures, or abrasions takes place especially during our periods of deep sleep. This is why top athletes take great care of their sleep, often sleeping up to 12 hours per day. In a business environment, on the other hand, top managers often brag about the small amount of sleep they need, working long hours without recovery and neglecting time zones when traveling between continents. You could question if this helps the winner's mindset and if it really helps them with top performance in the long run. The key to a healthy sleeping pattern is regularity: develop a pre-sleep routine and make sure that you get up each morning around the same time, which will automatically trigger you to go to bed every evening around the same time.

Breathing—next to sleep, our breathing is key in regulating our energy. Breathing happens automatically. Luckily, we don't have to think about it. On the other hand, our breathing signals us how we feel. We breathe more heavily when we are confronted with danger, tension, or stress. We breathe more calmly when we feel at ease. In addition, if we try it, we discover that our mind likes to focus consciously on our breathing.

Controlling our breathing is one of the easiest and quickest ways to gain control over our mind. Breathe consciously and slowly for several minutes per day, on different occasions throughout the day, and you will notice that your overall stress level will decrease and that your capacity to deal with adversity and challenges will increase. In sports, all top performers use breathing techniques to achieve results under high pressure conditions. In business or other performance areas, simple breathing exercises in the morning, afternoon, and evening could help to decrease stress levels, which allows you to bring your A-game throughout the entire day.

Movement—when moving, you provide oxygen to your organs, including the brain and body cells. People who move regularly have a better oxygen transport system and are able to free up more energy for mental activity. Secondly, movement in combination with recovery enhances memory and feelings of happiness by releasing the neurotransmitter dopamine in the brain. Thirdly, movement helps to calm the brain, as well as helping you to put things in perspective. Sometimes you literally feel ideas falling into place during a walk, run, or bike ride.

Nutrition—the science of nutrition is still evolving on a daily basis with ongoing examples of new diets and theories about eating. Of course nutrition is crucial to providing energy and fuel to the body, and there is a difference in the amount of energy that nutritional elements provide. When investigating the link between nutrition and our brain performance, scientists are only at the beginning of their understanding. Interestingly, recent research has revealed that there is a clear link between our bowel system and our mind. Disturbances in our bowel system are correlated with negative feelings and emotions. A recent study also showed that people with depression miss two important gut bacteria, namely Faecalibacterium and Coprococcus. Some doctors even argue that depression can be treated by adapting nutrition or by injecting feces of a "healthy" person into a depressed person.

There is more and more research that links nutrition to the aforementioned good-feeling neurotransmitters, dopamine and serotonin. This is logical, as the building blocks of neurotransmitters are enzymes provided by what we eat. For instance, nutritional sources that help to build dopamine are fish, meat, eggs, milk, nuts, seeds, legumes, etc. Serotonin, as another example, needs tryptophan, which is provided by brown rice, bananas, pumpkin seeds, sesame seeds, sunflower seeds, etc.

Finally, the amount you eat and what you eat will definitely influence your digestion and the amount of energy that is lost for the brain. For instance, fatty foods require much more energy to digest. Therefore, it is not advised to consume a too heavy or fatty lunch when you're planning complex brain activity immediately afterwards.

Social support—last, but surely not least, there is social support as a crucial energy fundamental. We all know that successful people are often surrounded by other successful people. But which is the chicken and which is the egg? Success definitely attracts others, but people who are able to build a strong social network are also more likely to develop success. And this is logical: we are mammals, and if it weren't for our social skills, we wouldn't have evolved to the point we have. Other people may stimulate us, they might challenge us, but they also help to put things in perspective, to relativize and support us when we need it.

Successful people also dare to make choices in the people they deal with. They will focus on people who bring them positive energy, and they will avoid or disinvest in people who bring them negative energy. Also, they will make sure that there is balance and reciprocity in their relationships. When giving or helping, they do not immediately ask something back. Rather, they trust that in the long run the favor will be returned. And if it isn't, they accept that as well. They do not blame or finger point others when they act negatively. Rather, they lead by example and trust that by consequently adhering to their own strong personal values, others will follow in the end.

To conclude, no doubt you will find a lot of inspiration and practical tips to develop mental toughness and a successful spirit throughout the different chapters in this book. If you want to enable yourself to benefit from them to the fullest of your potential, then my advice is to start with the basics: create the best possible conditions for your spirit and the organ that allows us to conceptualize your spirit—your brain. Focus on the five energy fundamentals each day through small but conscious choices. These small choices are themselves little successes, and if you add them all up, they will provide you with a broad foundation while developing your successful spirit.

About the Author

Jeroen Keymolen is a Belgian organizational and performance psychologist. He started his career as a career coach and subsequently developed his executive coaching skills further on an international business level. He has worked in several consulting firms, as a sounding board, trainer, and coach of human relations and business leaders. Later on, he progressed into internal talent and HR-management roles, developing and working with C-level leaders, as well as shaping organizational cultures towards high performance. In 2017 Jeroen started to coach high performers in sports, focusing on the mental aspect of their performance. Today, Jeroen is still active in both sports and business, integrating theories, models, techniques, and experiences from both worlds. Jeroen is co-owner of PeakLevel, a multidisciplinary team that supports athletes to achieve their goals. In September 2020 he co-founded Kokoro Business. Kokoro Business enhances mental, physical, and business fitness of individuals and organizations in order to enable them to achieve results with high energy and enjoyment.

Email: jeroen@kokorobusiness.com
Website: www.kokorobusiness.com

CHAPTER 17

THE THREE PERMISSIONS OF PERSONAL EMPOWERMENT

By Dr. Tarryn MacCarthy
Prosperity Coach, CEO of The Business of Happiness Podcast
Cumberland County, Maine

Dream and give yourself permission to envision a You that you choose to be.
—Joy Page

It was February 18, 2008 when I pulled out my husband's front tooth. It was the right thing to do, but it was the wrong time. At the height of stress and fear about my teetering orthodontic business, an historic economic recession, and two babies in diapers, I made it worse, adding one more crisis to the list, another one I couldn't run from. I had decided to align Killian's smile and to start him down a two-year journey of braces on the inside of his teeth. The braces would end up cutting his tongue daily, limiting his speech, and testing his self-esteem as a newly graduated oral surgeon with a missing front tooth. It was a poorly focused action piled onto a multiplicity of fear-based reactions and impulsive decisions made from a place of panic.

I was spinning out of control. In the mirror, I saw a highly functional, high-achieving wreck of a human, stripped of all sense of self-worth and joy, incapable of empowered decision-making. I was terrified. I was living the life I had sacrificed my twenties for. I was a professional boss lady and mom. I was a mansion owner, driving a fancy car, living in a wealthy suburb, but "successful" was not how I saw myself. I was straddling a razor thin line of life and death, home-owning and bankrupt, married mom and run-away, capable business owner and professional failure.

For as long as I can remember, I have searched for significance. I love serving others, I love art and creativity, and I have always been proud of my hard work and commitment. I dedicated my life to studying dentistry in pursuit of a lucrative career combining medicine and art. I buried my head and my heart in studying to become an orthodontist and then to buy an orthodontic practice. When my hard work to build a financially successful career wasn't fulfilling, I reached for the next thing society promised in the success algorithm—motherhood. I struggled to conceive and dedicated my early thirties to undoing the damage I had done from ignoring my body for decades.

In my pursuit of "success" I was blind to the fact that every promised result, after labored intensity, was stripping me of myself along the way. What I thought would feel like success turned into an unwieldy beast of my own creation and one I couldn't control. I felt like a failure, unable to stabilize the house of cards I had built. I was balancing a fast-paced career, supporting a team of employees relying on me for their income, two babies, and $1.5 million of debt. Even sound decisions, like extracting a tooth in my husband's too crowded mouth, felt like a noose pulling tighter, threatening my breath.

It was time to breathe. It was time to give myself permission to find me.

What I know to be true is that within each of us, we have the power and the ability to achieve greatness. I now know that we are capable of so much more than we give ourselves credit for. I never knew that I could ask for happiness—I always thought it had to be earned. The secret is that our greatness and our happiness is dependent solely on our own version of success and that borrowing someone else's version of success will eat us alive. I have learned that we can run from our lives, from our businesses, and from our marriages, but that we can never run from ourselves.

I now know that the only permission we need to redefine success is permission from ourselves. Before I could even begin to feel successful, I would have to unlearn everything I had been told about achievement and fulfillment. I would have to learn that what I value is unique and that no one else can offer me the formula to my own success. As I walked this journey of self-discovery, I learned that true success asks that we honor three things in ourselves. I made a promise to myself and to my children that I would share these permissions with my high-achieving, success-seeking colleagues whom I saw suffering all around me. I made it my life's mission to empower others to realize and redefine their own version of success. Let me share with you now the three permissions.

Permission #1—The Permission to Dream

In front of the Lincoln Memorial in Washington, DC, on a hot day in August, 1963, Dr. Martin Luther King shared his dream and painted a portrait of a new reality. His dream was one that, at the time, seemed insurmountable and took enormous courage to imagine, let alone to share. Dr. King taught us the first step in cultivating a successful spirit. It is giving ourselves the permission to imagine something different, better, ground-breaking, or simply more fulfilling. It is recognizing an inner calling for and a vision that is all our own. Sometimes this vision sparks a revolution, and sometimes it can save a life.

Watching my daughter at the age of nine, her world is full of big dreams. She has no limitations to her fantasy. She has not yet been marred by society's limitations or rules or impressions of her. Most importantly, she has not yet learned to limit herself. Somewhere along the line, during adulthood, so many of us stop this magical dreaming. We stop reimagining our vision of success. We stop acknowledging that what we dreamed of when we were 15 or 20 years old can change. We choose to settle, to compromise our inner yearnings, and we call it honorable and dedicated.

There is nothing in our man-made world, no invention or creation, that didn't first live in someone's imagination. It is this brilliance within us that adds the spark of success. The critical first step is giving ourselves the permission to dream. All too often we find ourselves settling for what is. How often have you heard the saying, "I made my bed; now I have to sleep in it"? It is a restrictive mentality to accept what looks like the facts and to just live with it or muscle through. The spirit of true success is to honor the spark of inspiration and the vision for what could be. It is the courage to ask ourselves, "If not this, then what would be better?" This is the reason why great leaders are called visionaries—because they dare to DREAM.

Permission #2—The Permission to Honor Your Own Values

When I first realized how unsuccessful my success was, I got scared. I left it all and ran away. I gave in and gave up on my dreams. Not surprisingly, running away didn't solve anything. In order to build myself back up again, I would have to learn to love and to know MYSELF. I realized that I had been reaching for a prototype of achievement that someone else had designed for me.

As I studied and worked and plowed toward my goal, I had ignored the most important piece of the puzzle—me. Before I could move forward, I had to come to terms with what mattered most to ME. I had to redefine success for myself and stop killing myself to live the circumscribed idea of success that society had fed to me. I had to face my own intrinsic values, own them, love them, act on them, live them.

Honoring your own values is the core of pouring passion into your work or life ventures. When you know WHY something matters to you and when you can identify your intrinsic core values, then you can create alignment in your life and find your purpose. Blending your vision with a passion that speaks to your core values creates a powerful force that few can dissuade you from and that no circumstance can perturb.

Values are funny things; we all think we have high values. But have you ever stopped to write them down? Do you know what your core values are? Because no one but you can know what they are. Only you can know what matters most to you. And as a result, only you can define what success will look like to you.

Permission #3—The Permission to Pursue

The final permission is the permission to take massive, consistent action toward your dream. This, in and of itself, is rewarding. It is in human nature to do, to build, to create. Fueled with the vision of something greater than what is, with the passion of speaking to your core values, the only thing standing in your way is your own permission.

Integral in this permission to pursue is the acceptance of the inevitability of failure, of stumbling and making mistakes. This final permission gives us the strength to stand back up and pursue again and again and again. Also, intrinsic in the permission to pursue is the imperative stripping away of self-judgment. There is no room for doubting your new definition of success when it is your dream fueled by your values—there is only the permission to pursue—your own permission.

Keegan is my three-year-old niece. She is brilliant. Watching her play and hearing her intricate speech, there is no doubt in my mind that she will be successful. She is the epitome of creativity; she has a spark of life in her and a sense of adventure that is hard to beat. Her dreams are all her own. She doesn't yet care what anyone says about the world she is creating in her head, and she doesn't need anyone else's permission to keep dreaming. We all know a Keegan in our own lives. We say, "The world is your oyster," and we mean it. Funny how when we feel this way about our own children, we excuse it as having bias. Honestly, my own three children are truly brilliant. Each one is totally unique and has different skill sets, but all three possess a spirit of unparalleled potential. Success is inevitable.

This boasting of the intelligence and future potential of my family is meant to remind you of a moment when you have seen that untamed spark of life and adventure in children in your life. When you were blown away by a nugget of brilliance that seemed impossible for a child to possess. That is the spirit of success.

Here's the secret. You were once that child. You once blew the adults in your world away. You were once that harbinger of brilliance and possessed the miracle of infinite potential and, yes, success. Even if you were never told that you were gifted, you had an idea that you were unique. And therein lies the spirit we are reaching for.

The light of achievement and of success is still within you. Nothing changed with time. You never lost the brilliance. Age didn't wash it away. You simply covered it up. You muddied and marred the mirror with dust and smudges. But she is still there. The imperative mindset is the permission to acknowledge who she is at her core. I know because I did the same thing. I was living a life that was not my own, a life I created, a version of success that I had designed, but it was not mine. I woke up to stare at a face I didn't recognize and didn't like.

It wasn't until I started to wipe that mirror clean that I came to see that brilliant being inside of me that had been there all along. I am still learning to see her. This is a story of how I found my inner success, how I rediscovered my spirit and the enormity of abundance that flowed into my life when I did. Once I was able to tap into my own happiness, my own definition of success I could create a business model and a daily life-model that spoke to me. The magic that followed was that my business took off in ways that I could never have imagined. My relationship with the man I loved took off in ways I could never have imagined. My newly defined idea of success for my business allowed others to see me that way and allowed me to stand in my truth with every business decision I made. Instead of just being good at what I did I saw a greatness that blossomed into real dollars and cents and recognition in my field. My newly defined success in my marriage and in my family translated into a deeper understanding and respect for one another than I ever could have imagined. We finally learned to play and to enjoy this life with less expectation and more adventure and appreciation.

The integral magic within each of us is asking us to offer ourselves the permission to shine with our own personal success and to own the leader within each of us. The true spirit of success is not outside of ourselves but uniquely within.

About the Author

Dr. Tarryn MacCarthy is an orthodontist, motivational speaker, Business Prosperity Coach and host of *The Business of Happiness Podcast*, empowering business leaders and leaders of their own dreams to strive for inner fulfilment. "In the first decade of my career I reveled in culturally recognizable success and drowned myself in personal turmoil and depression. I have since embarked on a quest for greater purpose and joy in business and in life, and I am committed to even greater contribution."

Dr. MacCarthy is co-owner of Mbrace Orthodontics in Maine. Using the techniques she teaches, Mbrace grew from a scratch start to the top one percent Invisalign Provider in the country within four years. Dr. MacCarthy coaches business owners across the globe on empowering their teams to be ambassadors of their dreams and how to redefine success to find happiness in work and, ultimately, in their lives.

Email: tarryn@thebizofhappiness.com
Website: www.thebizofhappiness.com
Instagram: https://www.instagram.com/thebizofhappiness/
Facebook: https://www.facebook.com/thebusinessofhappiness
Linked In: https://www.linkedin.com/in/dr-tarryn-maccarthy-2b401b123/

CHAPTER 18
CLIMBING MOUNT EVEREST

By Tim Wayne Medvetz (Interview by Erik Seversen)
Climber: Mt. Everest, Discovery Channel's *Beyond the Limit*
Hollywood, California

When I called Tim Medvetz about writing a chapter for *The Successful Spirit*, he was literally on his way to climb a mountain in Russia. Always able to find a way, we agreed to an interview chapter. Below is the edited version of my (Erik Seversen, ES) conversation with Tim Medvetz (TM) on February 23, 2021.

We make the impossible a reality by empowering our injured community through physical and emotional training, allowing them to explore the farthest reaches of themselves and the world they live in.
—The Heroes Project

ES: Let's start with The Heroes Project. I've been happy to support The Heroes Project for many years and see the wonderful effect you've had on seriously wounded veterans. Can you describe exactly what The Heroes project is?

TM: Well we're definitely not your typical nonprofit charity. We don't adhere to a lot of rules and regulations and policies that most organizations do.

For me, I had a really bad motorcycle accident. I remember back to that day, and I broke pretty much every bone in my body and was in a wheelchair for six months. And I was asking, "Why is this all happening?"

I was a 280-pound guy in an outlaw motorcycle club, the Hells Angels, and I felt I had everything in control. I'd been a bouncer in New York City for ten years. I lived in Brazil for two years and trained with the Gracie brothers, learning the art of Brazilian Jiu Jitsu, so I was, like, your typical tough guy. Then, next thing you know, there I was in a hospital. I got this nurse wiping my ass, and I was literally being pushed around the hallway in a wheelchair. The most demeaning part was to have another adult wipe my ass. It was traumatizing, and I felt like I was losing a part of me. I couldn't do what I used to be able to do when I was that big, tough guy. I wasn't on top of the world.

When I finally started getting out of the wheelchair, and I started the recovery process and was going to physical therapy, it was like, "Okay, sir, squeeze the ball ten times for three sets." When I looked around the room, I saw old people with diabetes and guys who had hurt their back on the job. I found myself looking around thinking, "What am I doing here?"

So, I walked out, which led to me spiraling out of control with drugs and alcohol. I basically went into this yearlong self-destructive phase consuming anything I could get my hands on to numb the pain and make me feel tough again. One afternoon I was drunk and high as a kite, wallowing in my shit, wondering what I was going to do with my life. It was in this moment that I finally accepted that I was never going to be the same again; I was damaged. I remember this moment clearly because the light shined through the window lighting up my book shelf, and their it was—Jon Krakauer's book *Into Thin Air*. I stumbled over to the shelf and grabbed it, never putting it down until I was finished reading it. That was it. I knew what to do. I sold everything in my apartment in Hollywood. I got on a plane with a one-way ticket to Nepal. I was on a quest to go find Mount Everest and stand on the summit.

I lived in Nepal for a year, completely off the grid—no cellphone, no electricity, no Wi-Fi. Completely off the grid. Just myself. I started climbing new peaks and saturated myself in that world. I thought, "If I'm going to climb the biggest, baddest mountain in the world, I'd better train with the biggest, baddest climbers in the world...the Sherpas." That was my theory. It was the same thing with the motorcycle club: "If I'm going to join a motorcycle club, I'm going to join the biggest, baddest motorcycle club in the world." And with jiu jitsu, "If I'm going to train to be a UFC fighter, I want to train with the best fighters in the world—the Gracie family in Brazil." This has been my mentality my whole life.

So, after training in Nepal for a year and perfecting my climbing skills for the next three years, I summited Everest. The mountain is what rehabilitated my life.

When I returned to the USA, I found myself wondering, "What's next?" I'd shocked the world. I'd proved all the doctor's wrong. I had just done the impossible. I'd just climbed Everest. With metal all throughout my body from the motorcycle wreck to a wheelchair, I climbed Mount Everest. So afterwards it was like—so what's next?

I found myself at a Naval hospital in San Diego. I was sitting in a court-yard, watching guy after guy. Soldiers. Marine after Marine. Most with missing limbs going by me in wheelchairs. A light bulb went off on in my head, "Oh, shit, I just proved to myself how to get back and find my way back!" As I saw it, a lot of these Marines had similar stories as me—big, tough guys with a platoon of guys under their command, trained badasses. When they're back home in the US, they walk into a bar and girls swoon over them. These guys have that classic buzz cut hair. They're big, badass Marines. But, the next thing you know—*BAM!*—an IED goes off and the guy loses both his legs. Now he's in a wheelchair and people are holding the door open for him and wiping his ass. That's the part that I related to.

I'm not comparing my injuries by any means to what these guys have gone through, but I can definitely relate to the journey from the hospital bed to get-ting out of the wheelchair and getting my life back. So, I wanted to show these guys how I did it. But how I recovered wasn't through flyfishing or through modified skiing, golfing, or surfing. What worked for me was I literally had to put myself back in harm's way. And I felt like, with these soldiers, when you are such a big, tough guy, a Marine or a Green Beret, something told me that going and dropping a fishing line into the water really wasn't going to get them back to the Marine that they were. However, after putting them back in actual harm's way on a serious mountain, basically a different type of battlefield, a difference could be made. That's what I knew for myself—I had to put myself in front of death.

The reason I'm telling you all this is because you asked me to explain The Heroes Project, and I want you to understand that we are definitely not your normal nonprofit for soldiers. Every mountain we've brought a guy to, people have died on. We have witnessed death on most every mountain we been on.

We've seen people in bags being carried off the mountain. While deaths like this are terrible, it also acts as the best way to get somebody back to where they were, especially with these soldiers. We basically put them back on the battlefield. Hence, The Heroes Project was born.

We started out just helping one guy, which turned into more. The emails started coming in, and it started this whole thing. The next thing you know, we're on *60 Minutes* and all the news channels and in the *New York Times*, and it became a whole village behind us, like you Erik. It's because we have one cause—to get these guys back. To get them back to be the Marines and the tough guys that they were before having a leg or an arm blown off.

ES: What do you look for in getting veterans to join your program?

TM: I've never actually picked anybody. They find us. There's a guy with no legs, and we help him to get up the mountain. Then he tells his buddy because the wounded soldier community is a very tight knit community.

ES: I remember one of your support climbs on Mt. Baldy. I was hiking with my own group of people, going towards camp three. I heard some people behind us complaining about how tired they were, and then we came upon one of The Heroes Project climbers who was going up to the same camp. He was a double amputee above the knees. It was a part of the trail like a goat track, and we were in a single file, so I was right behind him. Every single step he took seemed like the biggest amount of energy he could muster in a day, pushing with his forearm crutches, and he just kept going up and up. It made me choked up as I watched him, not just because the struggle but because of what a wonderful thing he was doing. What do you get out of The Heroes Project?

TM: I have so much metal in my body because my whole body has been patched, pinned, and rebuilt. I've got so many implants in my body, it is tough. My body hurts and I'm constantly in pain. And doing The Heroes Project is what saves me. I get more out of The Heroes Project than the guys in it because there are many moments in life, like when those people behind you on a climb were complaining, and then you see these guys with no legs climbing up the mountain, and it puts everything in perspective for you.

When I'm hurting, and I see those guys, I say to myself, "Really, Tim? Shut up. What do you have to complain about? This guy's climbing a mountain with no legs. Okay? You got nothing to complain about. Watching them take those last 100 steps to the summit and throwing their arms up in the air victorious is a powerful moment in life, especially when it's not you.

I learned everything there is to know about climbing mountains before I attempted Mt. Everest. One of the most important things in the world of climbing is that the mountain isn't going anywhere. It's always going to be there next year. Getting to the summit is optional. Getting down is mandatory. It is an important thing to remember that the summit is only halfway. A lot of people don't realize that, and I realized that on my first attempt on Everest in 2006. When you get so close to the summit, you just don't realize that you better have some fuel in your tank to get back down.

Coming down is the hardest part. You have to have that in the back of your head. You have to think two steps ahead of the things you know. So, yes, you have this successful spirit that is driving you up that mountain. It's driving you up to get to the summit, but you also have to be smart enough to know that you have to get back down. If you have that spirit inside of you, and it's strong enough inside you. then it doesn't matter if you fail —you'll come back, and you will never stop doing what you have to do while you walk this planet until you have achieved your goal.

That's exactly what happened to me because the first time I attempted Everest, I missed the summit by 300 feet. I easily could have made it. Easily. But I would have run out of oxygen coming down, and I probably wouldn't have had enough fuel to get down.

On Everest, there are frozen bodies everywhere, and you're walking past them. The majority of those guys, probably 99 percent of them, made the summit but didn't have the strength to get back down. That mentality inside of them wouldn't let them turn around when they needed to. They weren't able to just tell that spirit inside, "We'll come back next year."

Having a successful spirit is one thing, but it's equally important to have the smarts to realize that sometimes you have to regroup, get back to camp, and figure out a new plan to achieve success no matter what goal you're trying to reach.

ES: What's it like above 26,000 feet where people call it the "death zone?"

TM: It's pretty simple. The best way to explain it: take a plastic bag, wrap it around your head, tie it off around your neck with a few rubber bands, and then run up and down the stairs in your house. And that is pretty much what it's like above 26,000 feet.

Your body is essentially dying at that altitude. The human body only has a short window of time that it can survive at that altitude. We're climbing in a place where you fly from New York to Los Angeles. It's the same altitude, but you're not in a pressurized plane. The body is not meant to survive there. We do have a small window, but everything is in slow motion. Even the simple task of tying your shoes, you have to think about it. Your brain function slows down; your motor function slows down; your digestive tract slows down. Your lungs are slowly filling with water. Your brain is swelling, and if you stay in that zone for too long, you start suffering from pulmonary edema or cerebral edema and eventually you lay down and die.

You hear all the stories, and I've witnessed it firsthand. Guys start stripping off their clothes. It's 50 below zero, the wind's ripping at 50 miles an hour, you're on a summit ridge at 28,000 feet, and a guy's literally taking his jacket off and ripping his gloves off. The brain just stops working, so you really have to manage your health and your mentality when you're climbing at that altitude. It's a really scary, scary place, and something keeps me going back for more. I read in a book by a famous rock climber that we all just need to "feed the rat." We need to satisfy the drive to do extraordinary things by pushing ourselves to the limit.

I've been back to Everest five times already. Three summits out of five expeditions. For me to "feed the rat," I have to push myself to the brink. At least once a year on a big mountain where I put myself into a position where I'm going to run out of food. Where I'll be starving. Where I'll be sleepless and completely exhausted with no fuel in the tank. I just really push myself to the brink. How do I really know what I'm capable of if I don't do this? In everyday society today, men and women have become soft, so I feel it's really important that everybody get out there to feed the rat once a year to see what they are truly capable of. Whether you have legs or you don't have legs—or whatever your injury is—and everybody's Everest is different. It doesn't mean you have to try to climb Mt. Everest, but you can go on a three or five-day hike into the back country. Go do something that's completely out of your box at least once a year, and see what you are truly capable of because, as human beings, we're capable of so much.

For some of the earlier Everest expeditions, the guys wore primitive heavy gear, and it would take them six months of hiking just to get to the base camp. Now we do it in in eight days. When you think you know the successful spirit, just think—the spirit that they had back a hundred years ago is a lot different than the spirit that we have now. But it doesn't mean that those earlier rugged and powerful spirits went anywhere. It is still there. I've seen it. I'm always trying to tap it into it.

Even though I live in Hollywood, California, I can drive an hour, and I'm at a 10,000-foot mountain with big horn sheep up there. I've got an ice axe in my hand, crampons on my boots, and a rope tied to my body. In this way, I'm tapping into that ancestral spirit.

I feel like everybody needs to tap into that spirit. As I see it, you can only be successful in a business, or anything, if you're actually getting in touch with your body, and only your inner spirit can do that.

I have a very strict no cell phone policy on any of The Heroes Projects climbs with our veterans. You see, when you're off the grid, away from the cellphone, and away from Wi-Fi and all that, you have to connect with your inner spirit. If you're spending time looking at your cell phone in the mountains, even scrolling through pictures or old texts, it takes you off the mountain and brings you back to your life back home, back to your city life...Leave the damn phone in the car.

Wounded soldiers must be completely removed, so true healing is possible. It doesn't mean you have to have a serious injury to heal. We all need to heal, and that's why I have that "no cellphone" rule for Heroes Project climbers.

It's a good idea for everyday citizens to challenge themselves. Put the cell phone away, and get out to see what you're capable of doing. See where your spirit drives you. Everyone's brink is different, and few people even know how far they are able to push themselves.

About the Author

Tim Wayne Medvetz has always sought adventure. He realized early in life that he wanted to see the world. In 1998, he rode his chopper across the country to Los Angeles and became a member of the Hells Angels motorcycle club. On September 10, 2001, Tim was racing his motorcycle through the San Fernando Valley when he was hit by a truck in a catastrophic accident that left him physically devastated, partially paralyzed, and fighting for his life. His injuries required eight surgeries to save his leg, two metal plates and 20 screws to repair his cracked skull, a titanium cage for his shattered back, and a rebuilt fake knee. He was not expected to walk again or to fully recover.

For six months Tim struggled to regain the use of his legs, work through excruciating pain, and find some meaning in his life. He was adrift and not accepting the loss of his old body and his old life. One day, after a yearlong self-destructive binge sitting in his apartment in Hollywood, he looked up at his bookshelf and saw Jon Krakauer's *Into Thin Air*. After finishing the book, he vowed to climb Mount Everest. Thirty days later he gave up his apartment and booked a one-way ticket to Nepal where he began to put his body and his life back together, and after years of training, he summited Mt. Everest.

After returning to Los Angeles, Tim once again found himself at a cross-roads. Summiting Mount Everest on May 21, 2007 was about his own personal recovery, but he felt he needed a reason to continue—a purpose beyond his own personal satisfaction. His goal was to take a wounded veteran with him on his next climb. He realized that if he could renew his faith in himself on the summit of a mountain, he could help others do so as well. This led to the creation of The Heroes Project, which trains and supports wounded veterans on climbs of the highest mountains in the world. To date, The Heroes Project has helped amputee veterans reach the summit of Mount Everest and all of the seven summits, the highest peaks on each continent. The Heroes Project continues to support work with veterans through climbing mountains.

Email: Tim@TheHeroesProject.org
Website: https://theheroesproject.org/

CHAPTER 19

THE POWER OF FAILURE

By Stephen Miller, MBE
Six-Time Paralympic Medalist
Cramlington, England, United Kingdom

A gem cannot be polished without friction, nor a man perfected without trials.
—Seneca

Success is in the eye of the beholder; like with beauty and all the other things in life that rely on perspective and imagination. To achieve success, we must understand what it means to us and why it's important to strive for it.

As a professional athlete who has competed for over 25 years at the highest level of my sport, I've learned that a successful spirit isn't simply about winning or getting what you want. For me, success is about having the intention to progress each day, by taking on challenges and enjoying the daily process of improvement.

A big part of happiness is fulfilment. Nothing gives us a greater sense of this than when we learn, understand, and master something new. Each day is filled with opportunities to reward our urge to be fulfilled; we just need to have the courage to maximise these opportunities through action and focus.

Success is often acquired from failing, then coming back better and stronger. You could say that it is impossible to succeed without failure. If you are not willing to fail, you cannot learn, and you won't improve. In its absence, the feeling of succeeding will always be something that other people experience, but not you.

Here, I will explore the power of failure.

Embracing Failure

In a book about success—developing and harnessing a successful spirit that will lead to desirable health and happiness—why am I focusing on failure? Failure is its opposite, right? That's what we are led to believe. Indeed, that is the definition of the word "failure" on Wikipedia.

We often grow up thinking that it is a bad thing to fail. Something to be avoided, a step in the wrong direction. But who decides what is right or wrong? Good or bad? The truth is that everybody does, and nobody does. The truth is that these things—these ideas and conceptions—do not exist other than in our minds; they are whatever we believe them to be. The same can be said for other shared human ideas and beliefs such as language, money, organisations, nations, dare I say religions, and many more. The ideas and beliefs we carry around with us can shape our perceptions and thoughts of the world. Ultimately, they determine the kind of person we are and what we do in life.

To see failure as negative or bad, and the opposite to success, is to reject it, avoid it, and fear it. This can hold us back and stop us from doing what we want to do; stop us from striving to fulfil our potential, which is where true happiness and contentment lie.

The good news is that we do not have to fall into this way of thinking. We have the power to choose which thoughts we hold on to. To realise that good can come from any situation in life. As the stoic philosopher Epictetus said, "You cannot control what happens to you, but you can control how you react." I have experienced how failure can be your catalyst for positive change. How it can help you to find a new direction, a better direction. And how it can be the springboard that propels you forward.

I reference stoicism a lot. I aspire to be a better stoic each day. To approach challenges gratefully and maintain a balanced approach towards life. This is something that helps me to continually strive for progress, looking for ways to improve and learn. I believe this is where enjoyment and contentment live: in embracing the process of improvement. Failure is very much part of this. Stoicism will not be for everyone, but we must have belief mechanisms that help us to build and support positive daily habits and that encourage routines geared towards progressing. After all, life does not stop until it ends, so why not make the most of it?

The Failure Spark

You could say I have been surrounded by failure my whole life. I even failed at birth. I started my life with a bang, arriving late and feet first, which is typical for me the more I think about it, seeing as I have never been great at time management, and I often jump into things a bit hastily. I guess I must have decided to jump into life. "What's the worst that could happen?" I imagine myself thinking, if unborn babies could rationally think.

The worst that could happen turned out to be that my head got stuck (I must have had a big ego even back then). I was suffocating. It's scary to think that my life nearly ended right there and then. The amazing staff at the Princess Mary Maternity Hospital, in Newcastle Upon Tyne, reacted quickly and courageously. They saved my life. However, I did sustain a small dent in my skull, the size of a Ping-Pong ball. This dent eventually popped out of its own accord. When my parents eventually took me home, they were relieved and excited, believing they had a fully healthy baby boy—albeit with ginger hair, but you can't have everything I suppose.

In the weeks and months that followed, it became apparent that something wasn't right. I was not developing in the expected way. I was not moving properly. I started trying to crawl around awkwardly on my back. I was soon diagnosed with cerebral palsy, a neurological condition caused, in my case, by brain damage sustained at birth. So that moment at the very beginning of my life—which I had no control over—would end up affecting the rest of my life.

This was my failure spark or to paraphrase Marcus Aurelius—the impediment to action that advanced action. In other words, when things go wrong, and not the way we expect; when we get stopped in our tracks and experience a setback—this impediment, this injustice, this obstacle, this failure—it gives us the energy and the spark to move on and succeed differently. We can start an exciting new journey on a different path, if we react in the right way.

You could say I was born a failure—broken, damaged, defective, abnormal. The result of an accident. However, as I look back on my life—on what I have achieved and continue to achieve; on the person I've become and experiences I've had—I am excited by what I see. As I reflect, I think that moment when my head got stuck as I was born, that caused me to sustain irreversible brain damage, was one of the best moments in my life. Sure, there have been many times in my life I've bemoaned and begrudged it; wished it hadn't happened; and felt bitterness and frustration towards it. But it ultimately provided a spark within me. It helped me find solutions to problems; to become vigilant, but also resilient; and not to give up when things get tough.

From being a skinny, ginger kid with cerebral palsy, I went on to become a Paralympic champion three times in a row. Winning my first gold medal at age 16, I held a world record for 11 years, graduated from university, worked as a web developer in the NHS for 16 years, published a book, and am now enjoying a career as a mindset coach. Failure provided the spark in me and continues to do so.

To make progress, there must be somewhere to start from and something to push against. Failure provides that. It provides the opportunity to stake stock, gain a different perspective, and move forward in a new direction. Ultimately, failure provides that impetus to change and learn. Failure is powerful, but you must use that power in the right way.

There are lots of good and bad examples of how to use the power of failure. If we stick within the field of sport, we can look to the "greatest," Muhammad Ali. Throughout his career as a boxer and in his life, he came back from failure stronger and better, using defeats and adversity as tools for learning and motivation; improving and getting stronger. Alex Ferguson, the most successful British football manager of modern times, failed at first when he became manager of Manchester United. He almost got relegated and sacked in his first season. However, he continually changed and adapted his approach, using failure as the fuel for future success. Most notably in the 2012 to 2013 season, his team lost the Premier League title on goal difference to archrivals Manchester City, in the last minute of the last game of the season. He used the pain of that failure to spark a reaction, sustaining the motivation to go on and win the title back at the next attempt.

Of course, there are ways that failure can spark a downward spiral if you are not prepared to react positively. If you don't change your ways; don't learn any lessons; or don't challenge your beliefs and perspectives, then you can just continue to fail. Crucially, you will fail to get better or make any progress. This can happen when we become obsessed with the outcome, focusing on simply avoiding more failure and forgetting about the process of improving through learning and adapting. As Albert Einstein said, "Doing the same thing over and over but expecting a different outcome is a sign of insanity."

Take the Cleveland Browns American Football team that became only the third team in NFL history to lose all 16 regular season games in 2017. Their fear of failure just led to more failure. They have since adapted, and this year, 2021, they made it to the playoffs for the first time since 2002.

So what then allows one person or team to take on a positive go-get-'em mindset after a failure while another doesn't? For me, it was my parents who were a huge inspiration and who influenced my positive mindset towards life. I think back to how they reacted to me when I came into their world. How they embraced the adversity and the challenges that followed, changing and adapting to support me day by day. They gave me the confidence and encouragement to constantly challenge my abilities and limits and to strive to learn and improve.

What I advocate as the way to engage failure as an opportunity is this: accept failure for what it is—an opportunity to change, to learn, and to begin a new journey. Take failure as a chance to embrace new challenges and to strive towards future aspirations, without the past weighing you down.

Failing Forward

Whatever you aspire to in life, you can only get there through taking action and risks. Whether you want to be an Olympic or Paralympic champion, get a job, earn a promotion, start a business, write a book, or simply try something new—you cannot achieve anything without doing something to make it happen.

Marcus Aurelius said the universe is changing. I learned from a young age that nothing in life lasts forever, everything is temporary, and you have to work on yourself every day to get the real rewards in life.

I started school at the age of two, attending the now unthinkably named Percy Hedley Special School for Spastics, words that may well have some readers' heads spinning around. But I have never been one to get overly offended by words. If anything, growing up I found the stigmatism of medical descriptive words both humorous and sad. I think this may have been helped by the supportive nature of my parents. They always encouraged me to embrace my vulnerabilities and perceived weaknesses; not to be ashamed of them or try to hide them. I learned to accept what made me different and use it positively to make me stronger. If you can truly accept who you are and what makes you different and vulnerable, then you can start to put yourself out there. This allows you to embrace challenges, without being worried about what you may look like or what others might say.

At school I did conductive education, also referred to as "Petó" after Hungarian Professor András Petó. His work with people who had neurological motor disorders in the 1940s pioneered conductive education therapy. The foundations of conductive education lie in repetition—doing basic movements over and over, getting a little bit better with each effort, and developing coordination and balance gradually over time. It's based on a simple idea that applies to every single person on this planet—all humans are capable of learning and developing regardless of their starting point or ability. I have taken this attitude with me throughout my whole life, and strive to apply these principles to everything I do.

John C. Maxwell coined the term "failing forward." He produced the quote, "Fail early, fail often, but always fail forward." I have embraced this notion of using failure as a tool to constantly progress and learn. Failure is the heart and soul of striving to succeed. Failure is an integral part of a successful spirit.

From a young age, I constantly failed. I failed at crawling, standing, walking, talking, getting dressed, feeding myself, getting washed. I was surrounded by failure. I was not special because all infants learn through failure. It is when we get older that we start to avoid failure for fear of embarrassment or feeling bad. When we stop failing, progress halts, and the fuel gets taken away.

As an athlete, my training is geared around failing forward. Constantly pressing against my boundaries and limitations, never giving up, and refining and adapting constantly through repetition. I aim to take heart in slight improvements along the way, all the while knowing that big breakthroughs will happen eventually if given time. Progression does not always go in a linear fashion. You can have periods of next to no progression or even regression, but eventually something will click. It's like chipping away at a rock: you can hit the rock 100 times with no impression; then on the 101st hit, the rock cracks. The cumulative effect is what breaks the rock.

It takes time and effort to get the great rewards in life, and progress is the greatest reward.

How to Fail Better

Samuel Beckett told us, "Try again. Fail again. Fail better." Often in life, though, we have an idea of where we want to get to, but not of how we are going to get there. Even if you know you need to fail in order to get better and are prepared to do so—how do you know what you need to fail at?

We could look to what others are doing or to what has been done in the past. This can give us an idea of what actions we need to focus on in order to fail forward and work towards success.

However, the answer isn't always in copying others or looking to the past. We are all unique, and the best solutions are often discovered when we embrace uncertainty, stay curious, experiment, and advance through trial and error.

I was about ten years old when I started doing the club throw, the event in which I would eventually become Paralympic champion. This sport is the Paralympic equivalent of the javelin for my classification group, which is probably a good thing because if I tried to throw a javelin, I would end up killing myself. I wasn't brilliant when I started doing this sport. Even though I enjoyed doing it, I could not throw the club very far. I was trying to throw forward like other athletes, applying the most popular and common technique. While it made sense to try doing it that way, it did not work for me. I couldn't throw over seven meters whilst a lot of my friends at school and others my age could throw well over ten meters.

The coach at my after-school sports club was a Paralympian. He could see I was struggling to throw forward and that I was not getting anywhere or making much progress, no matter how much I tried. One day, he suggested I try something different; that I throw the club backwards. This sounded crazy and a bit scary if I am honest. But as soon as I gave it a go, I knew that was the way I was meant to throw the club. The rest is history.

The takeaway: we shouldn't try to conform to some idea of normality or do things based on known prior knowledge. We learn more effectively and creatively through experimenting, finding out what works and doesn't work.

Discover through trial and error how to fail better. If progress stalls, ask yourself if you are failing enough. Are you adapting? Are you learning? Are you asking the right questions? Are you challenging your perspectives and beliefs? Are you getting enough help and support? Are you measuring and tracking effectively? Do you need to give it more time?

Our world is what we make it, how we see it, and how we approach it every day. Use failure to spark your journey. Discover how to fail forward. And use the power of failing better to relentlessly pursue your aspirations.

Making It Up
In the weeks and months to come,
will you reflect on the things you've done
since when you were young.
So often,
the world feels like it's on fire
and life seems to conspire
against our hopes and dreams.
Drying up our streams,
polluting our means.
With an infinity of time ahead,
who can say what will happen
and what does matter?
Block out the chatter,
ignore the chitter-chatter.
Every breath is a scoop from life's lake,
how many are left is anyone's take.
Savour each breath you hold in your chest,
without worrying about what comes next.
—Stephen Miller

About the Author

Stephen James Miller, MBE, is a British Paralympic athlete. He has competed at six Paralympic games, winning six Paralympic medals, including three consecutive Paralympic gold medals in the sport of club throw, a sport in which he held the world record between 1997 and 2008. He has represented Great Britain for over 25 years, and is one of the longest-serving Paralympic athletes, winning 34 international medals in a career spanning four decades.

Stephen is a qualified athletics coach and mindset coach, and has a degree in business information systems. He is an experienced speaker, tutor, and facilitator. Stephen delivers experiences in-person and online, relating to various themes including positive thinking, performing under pressure, aligning values and beliefs, developing resilience, achieving goals, managing change, and embracing stoicism.

In 2013, Stephen founded the charity SMILE Through Sport, an organisation with a mission to create opportunities for disabled people to take part in sport. This charity has helped thousands of disabled people of all ages and abilities to gain access to sport.

Contact Information:
stephen@smilethroughsport.com
stephenjamesmiller.co.uk
airbnb.co.uk/thinkpositive
smilethroughsport.com
facebook.com/StephenMillerMBE
@hailfabio (Twitter)
@hailfabio1 (Instagram)

CHAPTER 20

THE POWER OF ATTITUDE AND MIND

By Dr. Emmanuel K. Nartey, PhD, LLM, MSc
Olympic Athlete, Three World Cup Golds
Bath, England, United Kingdom

Success.

What is the meaning? Can it be defined?

According to Cambridge Dictionary, success is "the achieving of desired results, or someone or something that achieves positive results." Perhaps it is true that success is achieving a desired result or positive outcomes. If so, then humans have dug irrecoverable graves for themselves.

On the other hand, perhaps this definition is not the case because success is part of creation and creation is entanglement. The true meaning of success is a web of creation and manifestation, whatever that be. Success is an experience that starts at the conscious level of being, and being means living in the present and not passively existing. When we live in the present, we can say success is a behaviour that is cultivated through the mindset of an individual.

With that said, when we talk about success, the first thing we need to try to demystify is the human brain. What is the role of the human brain in cultivating success? How do we turn our internal thoughts and desires to creation and success? In this chapter of *The Successful Spirit*, I explain the composition of success, how it is created, what success means to me, and why a successful mind is the collective responsibility of every human being on planet Earth.

The journey of success starts from the heart to the mind, to the external world that we call reality. So, it means that success is an internal driving force that can be projected by the brain to the external world. What this means to human beings and creation is that our success starts from our thoughts and to our brains.

Our brain controls every aspect of success in the physical world. However, to succeed in life requires us to connect with our mind and creation. Within us, we have the tools to recreate and the tools to destroy ourselves in the blink of an eye. That blink of an eye is what drove me to write this chapter. It is what moves toward the unknown. The unknown is my point of belief, my point of success, and my point of creation. This is because, for me, to become somebody, first I must accept both in thoughts and mind that I am nothing, but I am also everything. Through this, my success becomes my mindset, something I cultivated as a young child on the street of Accra in Ghana, West Africa.

Some say all roads lead to the same destination. I say, all life leads to the same destination, but the only difference is the planning and what experience you gather along the way. Your ability to navigate the road of life requires an internal intuition but not validation. I do not rely on validation in my walk of life, but I seek inspiration, knowledge, and understanding.

My life experience started on the streets of Accra. I was born into a family of eight. Life was a struggle and poverty was real. Poverty in my world feels like someone has put a knife in your heart and threatens to rip your living soul out. What to eat is a problem, what to wear is a problem, education is a luxury. This is the story of someone born with nothing, but this is also a story of someone born with big thoughts, a powerful mindset, and a fighting spirit.

I was poor. I could have been a criminal, and I could have died on the street like some of my peers, but the difference between us was my mindset and belief. As a child, I have always seen the bigger picture. I have also believed in the unknown. I have always believed in bigger things in life and changing the world. Dreaming is bigger than reality because when you dream, you programme your mind to believe that its ideas are truly happening and that things will play out as you dream them.

One of the ways I dreamed about a better life as a child was to use my imagination. I remember our parents used to live in a wooden house not far from the airport. Each day I walked to the airport to see the planes coming and going, people flying in and out of the country. Rich people, but while they were coming and going, I was also coming and going within. Sometimes

I would sit at the roadside at the airport with my dirty clothes on and watch the planes till sunset. I do not know why I kept staring at the planes and the sky, but one thing I understood was that if I could dream inside my mind, I could create my future.

Today as I write to you, I have been to 146 countries and five continents. This is the collapsing of all possibility to possibility. My dynamics and my journey were ingrained in the observer's point of creation. What I mean is that I used my mind to co-create with the higher authority; therefore, I collapsed all possibilities and created new dreams and new realities from the unknown.

Our existence might be a composition of many factors, but our success is determined by our state of mind and our spirit. In my hopeless situation at the age of nine, I knew my success was my state of mind and my spirit. It was about believing, it was motivation, it was determination, but it was also about knowing that the universe would guide me in my walk of life. Hence, if I ever feel lost, the sun will always guide me home. If the universe would not guide me in my walk of life, then the light would guide me home because I believe I am light, and I shall always return as light, not matter.

These are the views I have always lived by since I was a young boy. Perhaps the reason for my views is that every human being is a hero, we are born to be heroes, we are born to enjoy these experiences we call life. Through these experiences, we are able to draw the hero within us, to make changes in our lives and the world.

My walk to grace and glory is a walk of bravery and tears, but it is also the walk that brought joy and happiness to the environment I was born in. I remember walking back home, tired and thirsty. I walked to people's houses to ask for water to drink before continuing my walk home. The sun was very hot, the ground was hot too, but so was my mind. To succeed in life is about being an exception, it is about doing the good things that others will not do. It is about helping others when they need help. It is about looking for energy from the sun to inspire you. It is about understanding the negativity and positivity in life and learning to love all that exists in the moment and in our journey.

My journey, along with my fighting spirit and my understanding of the world and how I interact with the world, is what led me to this very moment of writing. You must die, but it does not mean you will not rise again. Falling and staying down is dying. Transcendence is not dying, it is liberation. Dying is falling down and watching your dreams disappear with you.

When we change our views of life, we change our path with the belief that things will be better, and they will. For those who may not understand or see the light, they may think the world is full of darkness. I encourage people who do not see the light to consider this: perhaps the world is full of life, and perhaps you are creating your own darkness through your thoughts and mind.

When I was young, I refused to curse my own future with my thoughts. After all, I had nothing to lose, so what worse could happen? We struggled to eat, we slept on the floor without beds, and when it rained the floor was flooded and we could not sleep. Everything was against us, but that sparkling light called the mind never switched off. It was my spirit, and it was always working for a better life. Hope is part of success; determination is hunger and aspiration, and is part of collective responsibility. If you put hope, determination, and aspiration together, you will create a positive future for yourself and others too.

There is only a thin line between success and failure. There is also a thin line between my winning the Judo World Cup gold in Samoa in 2009 and losing my first match. It is not that difficult to become a winner, and it is not that difficult to be a loser either. What is difficult is understanding and believing that you are born a winner; therefore, you are a winner already. It is difficult for many people to understand and to accept this believing and achieving mindset, but this is the trick to being a winner and becoming successful in life.

At a young age, I understood that for me to come out of poverty, I must believe I was a winner. I must believe I was born to be great, but I must also believe I needed to be humble, be compassionate, love others, love nature, and help others. In this belief, I started building my unseen castle. I remember at the age of ten, every single day, I'd get up at 5:00 am to go for a run with the senior judo practitioners. I hated it when I'd come in last in the run, but I had no motivation to give up either.

Life, for me, was, and is, about going forward, about shining my light so that others may see themselves through me, so that others can believe in themselves. This is what I call success as a collective responsibility.

When you embark on a journey of achievement, you must also embark on a journey of goodness, inspiration, and kindness. This is the secret of my successful sports career. I knew that my journey to glory was not about myself. It was about the future of Ghana judo and the future of judo in my country. For this, I would fight and compete. With this motivation, I became the first Ghanian judoka to take Ghana to the Senior World Judo Championship in

2005 and also the first Ghana judoka to take Ghana to the Olympics Games. Looking back, for some people, it might be an extraordinary achievement, but if someone asks me, it is normal. We are created equal, and I am not special, but where most will give up, I will stand and fight. This is the difference between others and me.

The spirit of success means engaging with all reality at the same time. Let me call it synchronicity and resonance of mind and matter. This is the moment where spirit and success unite with matter in a stage of progression in the physical world. In this stage, you become fearless, you accept the shifts of life in the universe, and you return to the source to seek a path of understanding. Returning to the source was very important to me at the age of nine. Perhaps it is because I had nothing in this world. Perhaps it is because my life was hopeless and the only meaning and purpose I could find in my life came from asking the questions, "Who am I? Why am I here? Where do I come from? Where am I going?"

To some people, this purpose is very stupid, it is the dream of the fool. If you do not have food to eat but are dreaming of inspiring others, this could be the most ridiculous thing a child could ever dream. Many very poor children may concentrate their thoughts on getting food, but as a child, I thought of the world and why I was in it. I thought of others. I thought of my mother. How I could help her. I never thought much about my father, but my mother was central to my complex thoughts and daily communication with myself.

We must always live and die for something, right? Therefore, regardless of where I am now, I must reach that ultimate goal in life. That is dying for something, right? After all, what do you have to lose when the universe plays you lousy music? Do you stop dancing and put up a fight that you will lose? I do not think so. No one has won a battle against the universe because pure consciousness we came from and to pure consciousness we shall return. I dance to the music of the universe, regardless of how painful it. This is the spirit of success.

For me, life is a journey, and success is a journey. It is a journey that is determined by my attitude and my understanding of the power within me. Like a judoka, in life, you lose more than you win, but in the end, it does not matter how many fights you lost. What matters is you were there to compete; you went through it all and can understand the pain. Through the pain, you build your resilience and courage to win because you fought all battles, and there is nothing left to fight anymore. At this moment, you become your own conqueror and winner.

People forget quickly. They forget pain. They forget the journey. I never forget my journey because my journey defines who I am. It reminds me of the world, and it tells me the power I have within myself.

As I conclude this chapter, my simple message to you is to dream big, fight bravely, fight with your heart and soul. Fight with hope and inspiration. Fight for others. Bring out the hero in others because success is the collective responsibility of all humankind. For me, this is the true spirit of success, and this is what creates noble men and women who become immortal.

About the Author

Dr. Emmanuel Nartey holds a PhD in international law and human rights law, and is director of the International Youth Court and CEO of Mary Nartey Foundation. He has also served as Head of the Research Integrity and Research Ethics Committees at the International Women's Initiative. He is the author of the book *My Olympic Dream*. His research focuses on the human brain, behaviour, international law and human rights, environmental law, public and civil law, tort law, and criminal law, among others.

Email: maninartey@gmail.com
Website: https://maninartey.wixsite.com/emmanuelknartey
LinkedIn: https://www.linkedin.com/in/dr-emmanuel-kojo-nartey-phd-llm-msc-mcmi-maps-oly-and-ba-b75b27102/

CHAPTER 21

NINE KEY PRINCIPLES OF HIGH PERFORMANCE

By Tom Perrin, PhD
CEO, Perrin & Associates, Former NCAA Basketball Coach
Charlottesville, Virginia

Emily Perrin
CEO, Perrin Wellness and Performance
Raleigh, North Carolina

Achieving and sustaining top performance in any field, and certainly in highly competitive sport, doesn't just happen. It's a process that involves high level, very committed thinking, preparation and hard work over time.
—Geno Auriemma, Head Women's Basketball Coach, UConn

To achieve and sustain high performance in any field requires a high level of detailed preparation. High-performing people don't just show up and play. They prepare at a very high level. People who achieve high levels of sustained success demonstrate higher levels of sustained preparation. This evolves over time. From our work in highly competitive business and sport settings, we see preparation as a complex and sophisticated process that involves mental, physical, and emotional aspects. It requires high-quality thinking.

This chapter's purpose is to outline a set of principles that reflect this level of preparation. These principles represent our experience in working with people who have achieved and sustained high performance in a multitude of fields or endeavors. These principles have emerged through our years of work with top-performing people. In our work, performance occurs in competitive settings where there are outcomes, expectations, and results to be achieved. High-performing people are always competing with themselves. But they may also be competing with another individual, an external standard, or against another organization or team.

As we observed, listened to, asked questions of, coached, counseled, and advised individuals in a wide variety of performance settings, we've identified nine principles that emerged among them. These principles are not specific to a field or industry. We work with performance in business environments and highly competitive sport settings. It could be manufacturing, banking, healthcare, higher education or construction. It could be basketball, baseball, lacrosse, or soccer. These principles apply to anyone who is trying to be highly successful at what they do. To make this chapter relevant to a broader range of readers, we define performance as, "whatever it is you do," and we allow you to set the context, because, regardless of the context, the principles discussed here are foundational to a spirit of balanced preparation leading to success.

To clarify, these principles are not a guarantee of success. There are many other factors that play a role. For example, achieving top performance in highly competitive sports requires physical talent and ability. A person cannot simply "think their way to high performance." As evident by these principles, the preparation needed for high-level success in any field is both mental and physical.

The challenge here is space. Each one of these principles could be a chapter in itself. After all, whole books have been written on character alone.

To accommodate our space constraints, we will describe each principle, talk briefly about why the principle is important, and highlight what difference it makes. We will not go into depth. The value to the reader is that this outline can serve as a guide for identifying the key elements needed in preparation and provide direction for further exploration. This outline will be useful if you are trying to achieve high performance yourself or for those of you in roles where you are coaching, counseling, or advising someone else in their pursuit of greater success.

Generally speaking, we do not, as a matter of practice, tell people what to do to be successful. We guide people and equip them with the fundamentals that they will need. There are idiosyncratic differences, nuances, adjustments, and adaptations that go into successful performance. There is tremendous complexity when it comes to "what makes people tick" and in the interaction between "who a person is" and the context in which they perform. It is a mistake to think that there can be a single recipe that would fit everyone. High performance is not a one-size-fits-all approach. These principles are the basic building blocks for high performance, inside of which, you will need to find what works uniquely for you.

Principle 1—Be a Person of High Character and Integrity

The first and most important principle to achieving and sustaining high performance in any field is character and integrity. You must be a high-character person. This means you have high moral and ethical standards for how you will conduct yourself in this world. These are standards and expectations to which you hold yourself, standards that you live up to every day, and they are standards you hold others to as well.

Notice, we did not say that this principle is about "bringing" high character and integrity to what you do. It's not about "putting something on" in order to perform. It's not about wearing a persona for the occasion. It's about "who you are" as a person, which is very different from adopting a demeanor, disposition, or temperament for an activity, task, or purpose.

Character drives behavior. Character is the underlying driver of what we see people do with their lives. This is why this principle is the starting place and the foundation for the other nine principles. A person who lacks high character and integrity will not be honest with themselves. This makes it impossible to accurately assess, evaluate, and come to terms with what they need to do in regard to their performance in order to make it better. High-character people demonstrate consistency in the application of their abilities.

Achieving and sustaining high performance requires you to evaluate yourself, make changes and adjustments, stick to a plan of action, follow through on what you set out to do, and work with others. You won't do this without high character and integrity. High performance requires responsibility and accountability to yourself, and it requires responsibility and accountability to others in working together. Being a person of high character and integrity is the foundational quality that ensures the honesty and the consistency needed to achieve high performance. This cannot be assumed or taken for granted.

Principle 2—Be Able to Access a Resourceful State

To be in a resourceful state means that you feel capable of responding positively and successfully to whatever challenges you're facing. A resourceful state is a "find a way, make a way" mindset, given your circumstances. It's when you feel confident, competent, capable, centered, grounded, and clear in your thinking. It is not simply what is commonly referred to as a "positive attitude." A positive attitude is a colloquial term that reflects a general disposition. It may reflect "who a person is," or it may be an attitude that someone adopts for a reason, but it is not the same thing as a resourceful state. A resourceful state is a mindset intentionally accessed with an outcome in mind. The outcome is high performance.

The principle is that you have an ability to access this state when desired. This is a deliberate, intentional process. It's preparation by design. This is important in two respects. First, it's important to be in a resourceful state as you think about and prepare for your performance. It would be important to approach principles 3 through 9 in a resourceful state, so you bring "your best thinking" to bear for each. As you consider what you want (principle 4), as you examine your abilities and how best to manage them (principles 5 and 6), you want to be in a mindset that allows for your best thinking.

Imagine evaluating your strengths and weaknesses while in a negative frame of mind. Imagine the impact on your aspiration and ambition if you think about your goals in a distracted state.

Second, it is critical to perform in a resourceful state in order to execute your performance with the feelings, thoughts, and intention needed to perform effectively. Who wouldn't agree that they give themselves a much better chance to achieve high performance when they do so with feelings of confidence, competence, and capability? To achieve and accomplish at a high level, you must think, feel, and believe, "I can do it." Achieving and sustaining high performance requires a mindset commensurate with that level of achievement. It cannot be assumed that this will happen automatically when it's time to perform, or that you know how to access this state. It's a learned, practiced, and rehearsed mindset.

Principle 3—Be Driven by a Sense of Purpose

Purpose is what grabs you at a deeper, visceral level, and it compels you to act. It's not simply the surface reason why you do something. It's a feeling of deeper meaning, cause, and mission that is strongly motivating and inspiring. Everyone understands what purpose feels like. Almost everyone feels purpose in some area of their life. You can feel a purpose that is more specific, like the desire to coach youth soccer. Or, you can feel a purpose that is more general, for example, the desire to help and serve others.

We're talking about purpose as it relates to your performance and what a difference it makes to feel that deeper meaning. Purpose cannot be given to someone or imposed on someone. Some people feel purpose about their performance, and many people do not. There are people who come to us who already feel it and have it, and many who do not. The point here is twofold. First, purpose can be found, drawn out, uncovered, cultivated, and developed. Purpose is not something you have or don't have. You can work to discover and develop purpose for what you do.

The second takeaway—purpose matters because with it comes greater energy, drive, focus, concentration, stick-to-it-ness, all of which enhance the ability to perform at a higher level. People who feel purpose in what they do "bring more to what they do." Purpose heightens and amplifies the qualities needed for high performance. As we say, be a "purposeful performer" in whatever it is you do, and you will find that you bring a higher-quality commitment, attention, and desire to it.

Principle 4—Translate Purpose into a Plan of Action and Tangible Outcomes

Purpose provides a very powerful underlying energy and drive for people who have it. It's the wellspring of performance. But it doesn't necessarily address specifically what you want to achieve, when you want to achieve it, and how you want to go about it. Purpose doesn't automatically mean that you have defined goals, objectives, outcomes, and a plan of action with timeframes and benchmarks. Achieving and sustaining high performance requires this kind of more defined planning. It requires you to bring a degree of analytic thinking to bear on what you're doing in order to get more defined and specific on what, where, when, how.

Having a purpose without this type of accompanying definition is like having a business without a business plan. Purpose does not always provide the specificity needed for evaluating and developing performance. Achieving and sustaining high performance requires heart and mind. It requires a degree of analytic thinking so that your methodology for success is laid out in a clear pathway of expectations, measurements, steps, and checkpoints. This, of course, enables you to know if you're on course, progressing, and sustaining what it is you aim to achieve.

Principle 5—Understand Your Ability, Talent, and Limitations at a High Level

To achieve high performance, you must have a very sophisticated understanding of your ability. This includes your strengths, weaknesses, and blind spots. It's an understanding of what you do well, what you don't do well, and the areas where you need to improve, grow, and develop. It is every bit as important to understand your limitations as it is your strengths. This is not a static understanding. It's not something you understand at a single point in time. It's dynamic and ongoing. It requires ongoing self-evaluation and learning.

This is a kind of meta perspective. It's a mindful awareness. It's not done with casual reflection. It's a process that is deliberate and intentional. It requires time, reflection, introspection, and a measured approach. It requires a degree of detachment so you can "see clearly" in a process of self-evaluation. It means going to some tough places and thinking about experiences that weren't always positive.

It also requires getting perspectives, input, and feedback from multiple sources outside of yourself. These multiple perspectives have to be calibrated and aligned to get a fair and accurate picture of your ability. Your own perspective of your ability is simply one data point. What you think about yourself can't be the only data point.

This principle is about having a cognitive, rational, and logical understanding of your ability and talent. You cannot be a generalist about yourself and expect to achieve high levels of sustained performance. You have to be analytical about yourself and accurate. Ultimately, achieving top performance in any field requires you to manage your abilities and talents in the context of what you do. You cannot do this unless you first understand yourself in a very accurate and sophisticated way.

Principle 6—Be Able to Effectively Manage Your Capabilities and Talents in Context

Performance is inseparably linked to context. This principle is about having the ability to work with "what you know about yourself" (principle 5) and performing effectively when it counts. This principle is about applying your knowledge and understanding to make it work "live" and in context. Principle 5 is about "knowing," and Principle 6 is about "doing."

Having a good understanding of your own ability and talent is not the same thing as being able to utilize and apply that talent in a context. You can have a very good understanding of yourself but not do a good job of managing your talents and abilities when it's time to perform. If you don't start with a good understanding of your ability (principle 5), you may be managing the wrong things (principle 6). To achieve high performance, you must be able to make the transition from the process of researching, analyzing, self-assessing, and gathering input (principle 5), to actual performance (principle 6). You must be able to make the transition from "assessing and understanding" your performance to "doing it." Easy to say, not easy to do.

There's a great deal of complexity in going from principle 5 to 6. Principle 6 requires self-management and self-regulatory skills. It requires an ability to access a resourceful state (principle 2) from which you can operate and function. But it also requires an ability to manage emotion, focus, and tension as you go. Principle 5 is thinking about performance. Principle 6 is about performance in real time when a lot of variables come into play. It means having the ability to make adjustments in your performance as it unfolds. To achieve and sustain high performance, you have to be able to "know your game" and then be able to consistently "play your game." To "play your game well," whatever it is you do, requires that you be able to transition from your self-understanding (principle 5) to an application and execution in a dynamic context (principle 6).

Principle 7—Be Able to Sustain Yourself Amidst Difficulties Over Time

This principle is about resilience, endurance, and determination. To achieve and sustain high performance you must have an ability to sustain yourself despite negative experience. Setbacks, pitfalls, disappointments, and failure are a regular part of performance. The road to high performance is filled with these experiences. Top performers are not exempt from setbacks and failure, but rather, they have an ability to persist and sustain themselves in spite of these. They have an ability to recover from these adverse experiences and keep going. In the process, they learn and adapt from these experiences.

For top-performing people, negative experiences are not simply discarded, but they serve as a source of insight that leads to improvement and growth. Negative experiences are a source of feedback, not failure. Having the ability to sustain yourself is essential if you are to establish long-term success.

Principle 8—Be Able to Develop Greater Capability in Yourself

To achieve and sustain high performance requires ongoing improvement in the short term, but it also requires development over time. Development is about increasing and enhancing your capability to perform in a way that fits with a plan for performance. It's not simply refining an already existing ability. It's about developing an ability that doesn't already exist. And it's about developing an ability that fits into a larger purpose for successful performance. This won't automatically happen organically. It needs to occur systematically. You must have an ability to develop your performance in a deliberate, intentional way over time. Otherwise, improvement and development may, or may not, happen. And even if improvement occurs naturally, it may not fit with the systematic growth you need to achieve and sustain high performance.

This principle means having a way of processing your experience that compiles and extracts what's useful for growth and getting better. In any field, it means having a plan for long-term performance. It requires the ability to gather multiple sources of feedback, being able to triangulate feedback to distill what's most important, acquiring the resources needed, and then being able to apply and integrate feedback into what you're already doing to make it better. It means engaging in reflection and introspection in an ongoing way, so you can benefit from comparison and contrast over time. But the development of more capability is not an end in itself. It's a means to an end, with the end being the ability to achieve and sustain high performance over time. Developing more capability only makes sense in relation to a larger plan for success.

Principle 9—Maintain Overall Health and Wellbeing

You cannot achieve and sustain high performance without maintaining your overall health. The fundamentals of diet, eating, sleeping, rest, recovery, and staying free of illness underlie top performance. These are easily taken for granted. You must attend to and proactively manage your overall health in order to achieve and sustain high levels of performance in any field.

Taking care of your health doesn't guarantee performance, but failing to manage your health will certainly undermine performance. Missing considerable time due to illness, poor diet and nutritional habits, failing to get proper rest, and not respecting the need for recovery time away from performance will ensure that your performance is less than what it could have been. There are a lot of components that make up overall health. It is common for people to do well in one or another of these aspects, but to struggle at managing their full array of health needs. It takes a lot of everyday focus and concentration to do this at the level needed to achieve and sustain top performance. It doesn't just happen on its own. You must be thoughtful and proactive. Your overall health and wellbeing is foundational to your ability to achieve and sustain high-level success in any field.

Final Thoughts

For purposes of this chapter, we've laid out a set of principles that highlight the preparation needed to achieve high performance in a wide variety of fields, industries, and settings. We don't claim to have truth with respect to preparation and performance. These principles simply reflect our experience in working with people who have demonstrated success over time.

These principles are simply "a way to think about performance." They are not entirely sequential in the way we've presented them, there are some principles that precede others. If you don't start with high character and integrity, nothing else matters. You won't have the internal compass needed to assess and develop your performance, or to work effectively with others in the process. You have to know yourself really well "before" you can manage your abilities effectively at a high level. If you can't bring a resourceful state to what you do, whether it's thinking about your performance or your actual performance itself, you will undermine yourself and get something less than your best.

It's not difficult to lay out these principles in an abbreviated form. It's very complex and challenging to make all of these principles work together effectively and sustain them over time. As we expressed at the beginning, our hope here is to "point the way" for anyone who would like to go farther into the exploration needed to achieve and sustain more success in whatever their field or endeavor.

About the Authors

Tom Perrin, PhD, is President and CEO of Perrin & Associates, Inc. Tom provides management consulting services to organizations in a wide variety of fields and industries including manufacturing, healthcare, banking, higher education, and construction, among others. Tom works with employees at all organizational levels but focuses primarily on CEOs, presidents, business owners, and leadership teams. Tom also provides sport psychology services to highly competitive coaches, athletes, and teams in intercollegiate, professional, and international sport. Tom has worked with both the men's and women's US soccer teams, and with head coaches and teams in the NBA. Tom has worked with many national championship head coaches in intercollegiate sport over the past 35 years.

Website: https://www.tomperrinconsulting.com/

Emily Perrin is the founder and CEO of Perrin Wellness & Performance. She is a mindfulness and performance coach who works with people through mindfulness, meditation, breath work, and yoga. She is a certified mindfulness meditation teacher, certified breathwork coach, and a registered 200-hour yoga teacher. She also completed Duke University's Integrative Health Coaching Program and is currently getting her master's degree in clinical social work from the University of Denver. She played college soccer at the University of Virginia and went on to coach collegiately at the University of Pennsylvania. The majority of Emily's work includes helping elite athletes and coaches address their health in a holistic way, in order to enhance their performance. She has worked with teams at Duke University, NC State, Towson University, the University of Virginia and Johns Hopkins, as well as various individual professional athletes in the NWSL, PLL, and MLS.

Website: https://www.perrinwellnessperformance.com

CHAPTER 22
YOU CAN'T WIN ALONE

By Theo Pickles
Olympic Strength and Conditioning Coach
Amsterdam, Netherlands

*Teamwork is really a form of trust. It's what happens when you surrender
the mistaken idea that you can go it alone and realize that you won't
achieve your individual goals without the support of your colleagues.*
—Pat Summit

It's Thursday afternoon at the Bosbaan Olympic Training Centre in Amsterdam,
the training centre for the Dutch national rowing team. The women's eight are
filtering into the gym to start their second training session of the day and their
tenth session of the week, with six more sessions to go this week. For the most
part, they are in good spirits even though when I ask them how they are, they
all respond almost in unison, "Tired!" That's okay, they should be tired, but
I'm looking for something more, the way they walk, how they hold themselves,
and I make sure to engage with each of them.

As they start their warmup, we have some banter about the upcoming race
this weekend and their latest test results. At this moment, I see that one of the
women, usually animated, is not herself. I take this as a queue to go have a chat
and check if something may be bothering her. It turns out her back has been
sore since this morning's session. Together we have a look at the plan for the
session, and we agree to make some modifications and take a couple of things
out. I explain to her that if she feels anything during training that she's not

happy with, she should stop immediately. I advise her to book an appointment with the team physiotherapist.

Overall, it has been a strange season with the postponing of the 2020 Tokyo Olympics. We should have been riding on the back of a successful Olympic campaign in Tokyo, with some of the team retiring and making space for new talent, and others consolidating their training base to become seasoned elite athletes going into the next games. But this is an unprecedented time in elite sport. After the intense training environment in the six months before the Olympics, here we are still training for an Olympic Games.

For younger athletes, this is a positive story as it is another year to develop, gain experience, and train load tolerance, and some may be going to the Olympics sooner than they thought. Seasoned athletes have one of two choices. Some will choose to remain fit and stay motivated to train hard and avoid injury for another year. Others who have been nursing injuries for the last two or three years of their career will decide it's time to focus on other aspects of their life such as study, a career, or family.

While the world watches amazing Olympic efforts and moments on our screens once every four years, the reality is, many more years go into creating that performance, that moment. In rowing, preparation for an athlete's first Olympic Games will have started when they were around 16 years old, and they will probably be about 24 when they go to their first Olympics. They may go to three games, perhaps four (for those resilient enough), meaning approximately 20 years in the pursuit of excellence in one very specific skill. It entails early mornings, early evenings, and a complete lack of social life while being constantly sore, tired, occasionally injured, and sometimes disheartened.

I have often wondered what keeps the athletes at Olympic level going under such circumstances. What defines these athletes that allows them to endure huge workloads, discomfort, injuries, and setbacks? At the same time, how can we, as coaches, manage the emotion, tiredness, injuries, and general bad days, and keep top athletes motivated to achieve an Olympic medal?

In my view, and most importantly, an Olympic athlete has an underlying drive, a determined spirit to win, with some being passionate about rowing and others about competing. However, passion ebbs and flows, and there are a few other ingredients that go into sustained effort of this magnitude in addition to drive. These ingredients are the right genetics and a strong support network, both professional, in terms of coaching, and personal, when it comes to family and friends.

Where we as high-performance coaches can help is to support that passion should it dwindle, by celebrating successes, giving comfort in the losses, and providing constructive feedback. The environment must be demanding yet nurturing. An athlete is successful in part due to their drive and in part due to the team of experts around them. This team would normally consist of the sports coach, strength and conditioning coach, sports scientist, nutritionist, physiotherapist, sports masseur, team manager, and psychologist. What all of these team members have in common is a strong desire to help the athlete succeed by creating an environment of discipline, self-analysis, and self-improvement, and bring a new perspective to the problems athletes face.

So how do I, as a strength and conditioning coach, contribute to this network? On the one hand, it is the application of the latest scientific knowledge to get the best possible physiological reaction; on the other hand, it is getting the athlete to buy into these ideas and perform as effectively as possible. There is a set of both hard and soft skills at play.

I'll give you an example of how I might coach a squat. For those of you not regularly lifting weights, a squat is the movement that we use to sit on a chair and stand up again. Typically, an athlete will lift more than their own body weight while executing a squat, so a barbell with extra weight is positioned on the shoulders during the movement. So how would I correct this movement should I see a problem? Below is a bullet list of statements that the athlete is likely to hear from me:

- "Great squat!" I tell them it is good; an endorphin spike makes them more receptive to what I am going to say next.
- "Strong hip drive!" Now I tell them why it is good; another endorphin spike increases the strength of that neural connection in the brain.
- "Keep your chest up." Now I give them a corrective point but word it as a solution rather than a problem. I've also directed their mind to a solution rather than dwelling on a problem, much akin to "Don't think about the pink elephant."
- Before the next set, I reinforce these points: "Here we go, another great set, keep that hip drive going and lift the chest."
- I've now attached a lot of meaning to the word "chest." During the set, at the key moment just before I expect the chest to drop, I say (forcefully), "Chest!"

Providing feedback in this way has a positive learning effect, resulting in a constructive interaction. Another technique I commonly employ is using questions to encourage learning. You will notice in our gyms the cameras and televisions near lifting areas. These systems are providing live delayed feedback, just long enough so that when the athlete completes their exercise it will be automatically replaying for them. This provides me with the opportunity to coach with questions that might sound like this:

Me to the athlete: *Good set, what do you see that went well?*

Athlete: I kept my back straight.

Me: Your back looked really good, what can you do better in the next set?

Athlete: I need to make sure I keep my shoulders in front of the bar.

Me: Great, let's do that!

What I hope is clear from these examples is that being a high-performance strength and conditioning coach is not about shouting "motivational" words at athletes, but it is about creating a positive environment where an athlete has a positive experience and can learn new things, and as a coach, I can build on their innate motivation.

Coaching is about feedback, delivered in a structured and systematic way designed to elicit changes in behaviour and performance. Each member of the coaching team delivers that information to the athlete in a manner that is kind and encouraging but holds the athlete accountable. The relationship between the athlete and the coach is built on trust, which is central to the process and hinges upon constructive feedback so as to facilitate learning and the fostering of that rare spirit of the competitor.

Feedback is key but needs to be delivered in a way that provides solutions while also encouraging positive behaviours leading to better performance. As such constructive feedback creates an environment in which an athlete can excel, with the coaching team being an important piece in its delivery.

What also sets an Olympic athlete apart is a genuine enjoyment of what they are doing. It is a combination of talent, enjoyment and interest, and finding a passion. Wanting to invest time and effort in that passion is more likely to deliver success. However, no amount of passion will make your legs or arms longer. Olympic rowers are genetically gifted. They have long arms and long legs, an extraordinarily low resting heart rate (some as low as 25 beats per minute, where the average fit adult has a resting heart rate of around 50 to 60 beats per minute) and a naturally enhanced ability to absorb and use oxygen. They have an ability to tolerate, recover from, and adapt to the enormous workloads that are placed upon them.

A great athlete not only had the right parents from a genetic point of view but also from a support point of view. Their parents were willing to drive them around the country, early in the morning and late in the evening. They never pushed too hard and let their child find the sport they wanted to do and nurtured that passion. From there, the athlete found a coach who created a love for the sport long before anyone knew how good they would be. A space was created where they were allowed to try and fail, yet they were held accountable for aspects of their performance that they could control. They also learnt discipline, turning up on time, and not taking shortcuts. It was in this environment that the raw talent was nurtured.

In any work environment we need to look at the people around us and our relationships with them. Your network is the key to developing greatness in the pursuit in which you are passionate. This means family, friends, and colleagues. If you have found your passion, and this passion is something that you want to have incredible success in, do the people around you want that as well? This means, will they encourage you when times are difficult? Help you to come up with solutions? Expect a strong work ethic from you and hold you accountable when you slack off? In regard to colleagues, are they experts in their field, and do you all as a team complement one another to be a group of high performers?

Just like peak-performing athletes, success in anything requires multiple layers of support. If your spirit is driven to perform in some elite area of athletics, school, business, or life, seek out the people who can help you get to and remain at your level of peak performance.

About the Author

Theo Pickles is an Australian strength and conditioning coach who currently works with the Netherlands National Rowing and Swimming teams. His professional experience spans 15 years, five countries, ten sports, and three Olympic Games. Over that time, he has worked with a number of European, World, and Olympic champions. Theo completed his bachelor's degree at Southern Cross University in New South Wales and his master's at the University of Queensland in Brisbane. In addition to his work with the Netherlands Olympic Team, Theo is also an educator for the Australian Strength and Conditioning Association, the organization through which he holds his professional qualifications. Outside of coaching elite athletes, Theo volunteers as a rugby referee on weekends and lives with his wife, baby, and two dogs in Amsterdam.

Email: theo.pickles@me.com

CHAPTER 23

THE QUANTUM SHIFT SYSTEM OF TRANSFORMATIONAL LEADERSHIP

By April Qureshi
Leadership Coach, Keynote Speaker
Vancouver, Canada

Even though it seems as though the world is trying to steal our focus and our energy, ultimately, in each moment, it's our choice to make.
—Seth Godin

I'm on a mission to uplift human consciousness, one intentional conversation at a time, transforming our challenges in business and life into a path for growth—and you're going to join me.

I've carefully curated the Quantum Shift System of Transformational Leadership from more than two decades of experience as a leader, entrepreneur, a third-degree black belt in aikido, and more recently as a meditation and mindfulness teacher and coach.

I'm going to challenge your current habits and beliefs about your leadership.

I'll outline a proven system to help you to reach your full human potential as a leader who has the power to ripple out a positive impact on people at your work, home, and in your community.

I'll share actionable exercises you can apply right now and coaching questions that will stretch your awareness for reflection and insight. We'll try to ignite the fire in your spirit as you understand that you are limitless in your potential. You'll open yourself to a "possibilities orientation" and a solution-focused mindset. We can't always avoid growing pains, but we're going to have fun and celebrate while doing it!

Who am I?

I'm a peak performance coach and visionary. I've spent the last 25 years mastering the inner game and a winning mindset for success as an entrepreneur, martial artist, yogi, speaker, and writer. I've worked with leaders, entrepreneurs, and executives in the sports and fitness, non-profit, health, construction, and finance industries as a coach, trainer, mentor, and leader.

My clients appreciate my ability to gracefully motivate and support them to overcome unconscious blocks and inspire incremental change without judgment or drama.

I'm a gen-Xer who values freedom and trust, and an expert-level Pong player. And, I'm not surprised that Inspector Gadget's spy tech tools now exist in reality.

Ultimately, I'm passionate about fulfilling my life mission as a visionary leader and coach by helping leaders reach their full potential and realize more enjoyment in life.

Clarity, Performance, Wellbeing

My clients consistently achieve higher levels of clarity and focus that fuel awareness and insight for better decision-making and clear communication with their teams. With clarity comes a vision and values worth rallying around as a team and organization. Time and energy are redirected to increase employee engagement, motivation, and satisfaction, resulting in more productive teams. On a cultural level, leaders learn to unlock the human potential that lies within each individual creating positive, realistic behavioural change that supports workplace wellness and a sense of community and connection.

A well-balanced lifestyle between work and home life is possible. That doesn't mean there aren't times of stress and tension that come with deadlines, conflict, and lack of capacity. But at least you'll have the skills and confidence to deal with these challenges in a positive way.

I'll share with you the Quantum Shift System of Peak Performance Leadership where leaders master their inner game for outer success and shift from change to transformation. We'll journey along the path of peak performance visiting the four foundational pillars of vision, mindset, resilience, and mastery.

Plus, you'll learn the secret weapon of disrupting your default mode of consciousness and how to train your brain for increased capacity to focus attention, problem solve creative solutions, and find balance between stress and relaxation.

The Quantum Shift System of Peak Performance Leadership

The path to mastering success is not without its challenges. But it's a journey worth the discomfort that comes with change. Once you take ownership of the journey, you can apply the same system to achieve outstanding results with your teams and organization.

The Four Leadership Shifts for Self-Mastery

Imagine for a moment that you have a brand-new car. It's the most amazing car you've ever owned. You've dreamed about this car, and now it is a reality. It has all the accessories and upgrades just the way you like it. It is the perfect colour, size, and model. It's a perfect match for your personality. It's sitting in the driveway ready for you to hit the road! Now, all you need is a map to your favourite destination, fuel in the tank, and the coolest, sexiest sunglasses to match your outfit.

The leadership shifts are just like you and your brand-new car. (1) Story shift is your ability to envision and map out the future and where you want to go. Next, you are the leader in the driver's seat, and you possess the growth mindset and leadership skills for an (2) identity shift. Then, you fuel your leadership style with the (3) energy shift of resilience necessary for navigating the way ahead with compassion and understanding. Eventually, you make your way to your final destination marked by a (4) quantum shift of mastery for maximum output and productivity.

I should add that you're welcome to take a friend along with you. Studies have shown that having an accountability partner increases your chances for success.

Now, we're going to park the car at the top of the mountain.

If you're reading this, you're most likely not content with the easy path. Strolling around the base of the mountain just isn't your thing. You want to climb to the top and find all the possible different ways to get there. And once you're there, you want to share your experience with others. You love the exhilaration of polishing your spirit and engaging all facets of your multidimensional life working together to accomplish a long-term goal.

Let's dive deeper into the journey of self-mastery for high-performance leadership. We'll stop along the way and touch on the foundational pillars of peak performance, including vision, mindset, resilience, and self-mastery.

FOUR PILLARS OF PEAK PERFORMANCE

Your vision must be fueled by imagination, nurtured by inspiration,
and driven by a desire to make a positive difference to the world.
—Oleg Konovalov

Create a Compelling Vision

Leaders who have the ability to create a compelling vision are able to attract the right team members, opportunities, and situations critical to moving a vision forward. A vision designed with intention and anchored to a set of common values is worth rallying around. A compelling vision brings the opportunity to shift the story from where you are now to where you want to be.

Vision

A vision consciously created with intention has a cascading effect on your identity as a leader, on your values, beliefs and assumptions about yourself and your team, on your motivation for action, and on the type of environment and culture you design. Vision provides the jumping-off point for setting goals, milestones, and actions. It sets up expectations for roles and responsibilities, drives performance measures, and is the summit to aim for providing clarity, focus, and purpose.

Let's do a visioning exercise.

- Breathe in and breathe out.
- Repeat two more times.
- Feel yourself relax with each exhaling breath.
- Close your eyes and imagine yourself three years from now (repeat for five, ten, and 30 years).

What do you see? Who is with you? Where are you? Who have you become? What have you achieved? How did you achieve it? What action steps did you take to get here? What values are you living? Who benefits from your vision? What legacy are you leaving behind?

Now open your eyes and write out, in as much detail as possible, the vision you have created for yourself. If you manage a team, repeat the exercise with them.

Values

Values are fundamental beliefs about yourself that guide your motivation and behaviour. Just like your pet cat is fundamentally self-motivated and directs its own day, dogs on the other hand are people pleasers motivated by a sense of achievement and reward. While cats and dogs are both loveable family members guided by a desire to belong, cats value a self-motivated existence while dogs value pleasing others. Just as you might treat your cat and do differently, knowing your values and the values of your team members can give you a deeper understanding of their character and beliefs which will help you align your leadership style to meet the specific needs of your team.

One of the biggest benefits of having a set of values to hold firm to is the ability to quickly make decisions and direct tasks based on priority. When you say yes or no to a request, you know exactly how you came up with your decision and why it's important or not. When a decision is anchored in your values, it feels right and requires no waffling and rehashing.

Linking values between individuals, teams, and the organization creates familiarity, sameness, and the trust and safety of being a part of a community. Emotional barriers and unconscious biases are reduced. People feel part of a family, and you have each other's backs. Your capacity to help others is enhanced when linked by shared values.

Here's another exercise.

To find your values, ask yourself: what are the guiding principles in your life? When you're operating at peak performance, what values are you living? What characteristics do you value most in your team and organization?

Next, make a list of values that are important to you. Then narrow your list down to your top eight values. From there, narrow even further and draw out your three core values—those values that if they were missing from your work or life, you'd be living only half of yourself. For example, my three core values that I cannot live without are freedom, trust, and passion.

Values can be individual or created as a team. Ideally, your personal values align with your team and organizational values in some way. That way you feel good about waking up each morning. You're engaged and making a significant contribution to your team and organization knowing that you hold true to yourself.

The foundation of vision and values set the stage with clarity and focus that will attract qualified experts needed to build a team to help you carry out your amazing vision as a leader.

You have power over your mind. Realize this, and you will find strength.
—Marcus Aurelius

Develop a Growth Mindset

Your mindset shift is the secret weapon for disrupting your default mode of thinking. When you master the mind, the body follows. It's an integrated approach that uses brain plasticity to create new pathways of thought and possibility.

The challenge is that the mind produces a constant stream of thoughts—and it can be overwhelming! The good news is you have a choice of what thoughts you put your attention on. With practice, you can grow your capacity to be with a multitude of thoughts, sensations, people, and situations. Your mind wants to take the easiest route to any destination. But the betrayal is, the mind only sees the world through the lens of the past.

It's as if you're using a personal computer that runs on Mac OS 8. You'd never run your business on an operating system from 20 years ago. And yet, your mindset is running on old files created from childhood, which are then reinforced as an adult. It's time to start clearing out old files, apps, and systems.

The freed-up space can then be converted into more time and energy for your best work as a leader.

In essence, you change the relationship with your thoughts. You are in control. As the pilot, you consciously direct your thoughts rather than the other way around.

Between stimulus and response, there is a space. In that space is the power to choose our response. In our response lies our growth and our freedom.
—Viktor Frankl

Strengthen Emotional Resilience

Emotional resilience is a core competency for today's world of leadership. If you aren't aware of your own emotions and feelings, how can you lead others through the complex and diverse world of workplace relationships?

A year ago, almost to the day that I wrote this chapter, the global pandemic of COVID-19 hit. It was March 2020, and the world was at a standstill for two weeks. For the first time in decades, perhaps centuries, the canal waters of Venice cleared and dolphins frolicked, smog clouds parted to reveal the peaks of the Himalaya mountains, and city centres around the world experienced a resurgence of wildlife on the city streets. Nature's ability to bounce back from adversity was clear.

During this time, while the global business community searched for answers, I decided to put together a leadership summit. I interviewed 17 global business experts for their best tools and advice on how business leaders can pivot to stay ahead of the change curve during challenging times.

What emerged was a consistent message that for businesses to thrive, the shift to an environment of compassion, transparency, courage, and agility are critical to innovation and growth.

From Reaction to Resilience—A Framework

Use this simplified three-step mindful response framework to help you master the skills needed to build internal resources and self-awareness to be resilient in any situation. You'll shift from your habitual unconscious reactions to conscious choice responses. You'll establish compassionate communication with yourself and others.

- **Get Aware.** When you notice yourself reacting, become aware of your thoughts and feelings.
- **Breathe.** Initiate a relaxation response. Inhale and exhale, breathing deeply into the abdomen. Repeat three times. Notice yourself relaxing with each exhaling breath.
- **Choose.** From this place of relaxed awareness, choose to respond versus react.

Building emotional resilience as a leader is key in creating a culture of trust, compassion, and authenticity. This three-step framework will help you build that resilience.

> *"Misogi" is a removal of all obstacles, separation, and negative thought. One returns to the very beginning, where there is no differentiation between oneself and the universe.*
> —Morihei Ueshiba

Clear the Path to Self-Mastery

The path to mastery is fraught with challenges from all angles, but there is a sense of satisfaction in growing your skills, understanding, and capacity as a leader. Ultimately, the path to growth necessitates letting go of what's not working and allowing the quantum shifts to integrate and become a part of the person you are becoming as a transformational leader. Boiling water becomes steam. Then, when cooled and condensed, it turns back into water. But, add coffee beans to boiling water and you fundamentally change the essence. Forever.

With the quantum shifts, it's impossible to be the same leader you started out as. You change your story and the relationship with your thoughts. You shift identity from habitual and unconscious to intentional and conscious. You adopt new behaviours in new environments. You free up energy to serve your highest purpose. As you become the leader the world wants you to be, you see the world through a different lens. You are fundamentally transformed as a leader. And your whole world is better for it. The ecology of your actions have a powerful ripple effect on the people around you.

The world needs skilled leaders who are courageous enough to set a new standard for themselves and their organizations. It's possible to have a clear direction with performance-oriented outcomes and a culture that supports workplace wellness.

Now is a pivotal time in our history. It's time to step into the future as a leader of leaders. I'd love for you to continue on this amazing odyssey with me.

About the Author

April Qureshi is an award-winning entrepreneur, certified professional coach, speaker, writer, meditation and yoga teacher, and martial artist. Known as the Peak Performance Optimizer, April Qureshi is the creator of the Quantum Shift System that inspires courageous leaders to master the inner game for results-driven growth. She helps leaders transform their people into high-performance teams that positively affect the bottom line.

April brings innovation and vision with fearless energy to everything she touches. She is a dynamic leader and creative force who has a strong ability to connect and intuit a client's needs, and deliver results.

April is passionate about giving back and serves as VP on the board of ICF Vancouver and coordinator of giving at 100 Women Who Care Sunshine Coast.

April has been featured in numerous magazines, TV shows, and podcasts, and is a contributing author of the bestselling book *Simple Success Strategies for Women Entrepreneurs.*

If you enjoyed this chapter, April would love to hear how these transformational shifts have been of value to you. Send her a message via email or connect on social channels. April is passionate about your success. Her clients continue to work with her because she helps them make progress and get results. She helps leaders build the confidence, skills, and resilience to stand out as in-demand global leaders.

Get access to free resources exclusive to this book, including videos, worksheets, guided audio, and more at the Peak Performance Leadership Academy https://bit.ly/30NnUEI.

Contact information:
Email: april@coachaprilria.com
https://coachaprilria.com/
http://aprilspeaks.ca/
https://leadfromwithinsummit.com/

http://inspiredleadershipcanada.ca/
https://www.linkedin.com/in/april-qureshi/
https://www.facebook.com/aprilriaqureshi/
https://www.amazon.com/April-Ria-Qureshi/e/B00HER9L8Y

CHAPTER 24
A CONSCIOUS EVOLUTION

By Ahad Raza, MA, CPT
Professional Athlete, Performance Coach
Toronto, Canada

God grant me the serenity to accept the things I cannot change, courage to change the things I can, and wisdom to know the difference.
—Reinhold Niebuhr's Serenity Prayer

It's really happening.

Not in a million years did I think life would unfold this way. Lacking grand aspirations or inspiration, my life seemed destined for mediocrity.

Others: What do you want to do when you grow up?

Me: I don't know.

Others: What do you enjoy doing?

Me: I'm not sure.

Others: What do you want to study in university?

Me: I really don't know.

That sums up my level of awareness and insight as a teenager, throughout my twenties, and truthfully, into my thirties.

How do you want to be remembered when it's all said and done?

The first time I reflected on that question, I was floored. I thought. Truthfully, I wasn't sure how to respond. What I do know is that my 20-year-old self would have tucked his tail between his legs and run. Now, as a "mature" individual (so I tell myself sometimes), regular reflection has become second nature, leading to conscious choices for my life's direction. But let's take a look at life without regular reflection—starting when I was a teenager.

As a teenager, I started playing the racquet sport of squash with my father and a group of other wonderful people at a community centre near my childhood home. The first time I stepped on a squash court, held that tacky grip, and heard the thunderous sound of the ball hitting the concrete walls, I fell in love with its individualistic, gladiatorial nature. It was all up to me—win or lose, persevere or give up. My mental fortitude was tested repeatedly. Frankly, I often came up short.

Early in life, I developed a strong work ethic. I think I did this because my life was filled with joy, so by working persistently, I could extend happiness and curiosity in all directions. My wonderful parents created a positive, love-filled environment in which my sister and I could be honest, supported, and have fun. Physical activities made blood course through my veins—figuratively and literally. My passion was stirred. In studying the notion of grit in recent years—a fundamental requirement for success—it became clear that I had unknowingly cultivated its elements of interest, purpose, deliberate practice, and hope. Squash embodied all of those attributes for me.

In my late teens, when I truly fell in love with squash, I distinctly remember thinking, "My goal is to catch up to so and so." Over a decade later, after lots of perseverance and practice, I achieved my goal. However, recent reflections made me wonder if I had set the bar too low. I had. Our mind is a powerful resource, and whatever we believe, we will achieve, as long as we truly want it. We begin to see everything through that lens, searching for solutions. How would things have unfolded if instead my affirmation had been "I will be the best player in the world"? Would my actions, decisions to seek out world-class support, and outcomes have differed?

Truthfully, I was naive and scared, thus setting the bar too low. I learned that lesson the hard way. Nonetheless, I worked my tail off. During my university years, I struck a deal with my parents that would allow me to train full-time throughout the four-month summer holidays, conditional upon receiving certain scholarships. With the achievement of my goal, four years of summer training included four to six hours of daily training, five to six days each week. I cycled, lifted weights, completed core-specific exercises, and practiced technique and accuracy, daily! What was the result? Definite improvement. However, without fail each summer ended with an injury and the feeling of being burnt out.

At that time, I was heedless. "No pain no gain," right? Wrong! The priceless wisdom of balancing effort and rest was not a conscious thought. It was buried somewhere deep down inside, but the subconscious fears of scarcity and never doing enough governed my behavior. By the way, I was totally unaware of all this at that time. Only in recent years, as I have chosen to consciously evolve, grow, and reflect, has this become obvious. "Reflection and deconstruction—what do those words mean?" That summarizes my mindset back then.

Fast forward to 2016. "Is time running out? I'm 30 years old ... It's now or never. If I don't do this, I'm going to regret it for the rest of my life!" By this time, I was competing provincially and nationally while working in a corporate environment for eight years. By all conventional measures, I was successful with a promising career, a reasonably high level of squash, a wonderful wife, and a decent amount of money saved up. I must have had it all figured out, right? Wrong again.

Fear and doubt continually manifested themselves, making me feel like an imposter in spite of tangible success. Why? Because, years earlier, I began playing squash as a teenager while my peers had begun seven to ten years earlier. Others were professionally coached given their affluence. I was not. Many were national junior champions. I had never played a junior tournament. Imposter syndrome kicked in hard. "Do I really deserve to be here? Am I fooling myself and wasting my time? Maybe I should just stick to my 'real' job? It pays well and it's stable. I have responsibilities after all." The mental chatter was draining. Truthfully, I was scared.

In fact, the mental chatter kept me up at night and made me aloof during the day. Then, at the height of the doubts, a calming voice emerged and interjected. It was my intuition, divine guidance, if you will. "I will regret this if I don't do it. I need to live out my dream. I need to prove to myself that I can do it. I will find a way. I don't want to be 40, or 50, or 60, wondering what could have been." With that revelation and the support of my loving wife, I had a difficult conversation with my corporate manager and took the plunge.

The rest is history-in-progress.

Everything changed instantly. My income immediately decreased four-fold, the days lacked structure, but I was happier than ever. I was made for this. I regained control over my destiny. My effort would determine my success. And so, I embarked on the newfound journey of my life.

My professional squash career was always going to be short lived. It began at age thirty after all. Over three years, I traveled to several beautiful destinations to compete on the PSA World Tour. I had the honor of representing my province in the Canadian team championships, my country in a squash specific Pan Am event, and most importantly, I lived my dream, regret free.

Grasping, Repetition, and Letting Go

As a professional squash player, the lessons were plenty. For starters, I discovered that I often crumbled under pressure. Closing out matches was challenging. Competing against athletes who were slightly below my level was unnerving. In time, I became aware of the folly of shifting my focus from the process to the outcome, then grasping at the outcome and judging myself for the performance, often at precisely the wrong time. "You're almost there, Ahad. Win this game, and you've won the match. I wonder who I'll play tomorrow." Yikes. Not the sort of internal dialogue you want at pivotal times, in anything. The subconscious self-sabotage meant inconsistent success, without my ever even knowing it at the time.

Another lesson: "Rome wasn't built in a day, but they laid bricks every hour." Three years and a dozen or so professional tournaments doesn't even come close to the amount of time or experience required to truly excel at a world-class level. That takes decades of perseverance, the right support structure, and a dash of luck. *Setting appropriate expectations and taking daily action is crucial.*

Despite having coached for a decade by this point, my patience, compassion, and desire to fix situations were often tested. Students would appear, and I'd find myself thinking, *Not another person who says they want to improve but then doesn't do the required solo training, inner work, and fitness.* What we see in others is often a reflection of our own inner beliefs. There had been countless situations in my life when I'd thought I wanted something, I would get excited, dabble, and then fade. Upon reflection, I realized *the importance of passion and purpose in cultivating perseverance.*

In April 2019, my wife and I were blessed with the arrival of our radiant daughter. I played my last professional event (without knowing it at the time) in July of 2019. Ironically, my body and heart produced some of my best squash ever. I played for the love of the game, from a place of joy, without expectations. All this with many sleepless nights and limited training. The structure I strived to create went out the window with the arrival of our daughter—something any parent can attest to. Ironically, my performance rose. So, another example of happiness and joy making everything better, and that letting go of control can be hugely beneficial at times.

Every Challenge Contains the Seed of Opportunity

In early 2020, COVID-19 officially hit the world, hard. What continues to be a devastating and monumental time in history has truly been a blessing for me personally. Did I have moments of fear? Absolutely! But I looked at it as a once-in-a-lifetime opportunity to use the time I had been given more effectively. We all have a choice.

I strive to live each day with purpose, clearly identifying my top priorities. I rise around 4:45 am, getting into a state of flow during the morning silence and stillness. From 6:00 am onwards, my wife and I put on a majestic demonstration of tag team parental duties—tagging the other in just before submitting to our daughter. In the absence of COVID-19 lockdowns, frankly, it would have been impossible to cultivate such a deep bond with my daughter—dancing with her in my arms, staring into her eyes, and telling her how much I love her. Additionally, many fears that have now surfaced through journaling and reflection would still be wreaking havoc under the surface of my visage, continuing to sabotage my definition of a successful life.

Most weeks I exercise twice a day, five days a week, read one book, and diligently work away on several projects. I created the Life-Strong program which is "your treasure map to a fulfilled, successful life." I contributed to this wonderful effort you're currently reading, took on new coaching clients, and I am happier than I have ever been. All the result of a choice to shine a light on my fears and consciously choose bravery in the face of my insecurities.

I share this not to gloat or to rub my success in anyone's face. My sincerest hope is to show you that anything is possible. It all stems from the mind and spirit. Presumably that is why you are reading this book. Right?

For me, a successful spirit is one that will naturally evolve over time as I do. My definition is: the awareness and courage to listen to our intuition faithfully, assess our emotional blueprint honestly, define our true north genuinely, and reach our destination joyfully, in a nonjudgmental, non-grasping, action-filled manner, with loving relationships.

I genuinely believe that each of us must be vulnerable, honest, and willing to peel back the layers of our life experiences in order to grow. Approaching every situation with a beginner's mind and spirit; a sense of openness, curiosity, and wonder, regardless of how capable our knowledge is. This is one key to success.

Discoveries for Fulfilment: Journaling, Growth, and Environment

Each morning, as I crack open the pages of my trusty companion—a journal—I envision our forefathers. People like Marcus Aurelius writing his meditations, or Paulo Coelho transcribing his enlightenment in *The Alchemist*, I reflect upon my successes and failures, to learn and grow from each one.

However, to do so takes energy, and lots of it! I wish sometimes I could be the Energizer Bunny, running around with endless energy while beating my drum. All joking aside, we truly are human batteries. Just like all plants and animals—the sun, fresh air, food, and water give us energy. Activities and stress drain our energy. Given our higher faculties of intellect, the people, books, movies, social media, and podcasts we consume have a significant impact on our mindset, our thoughts, our actions, and in turn our momentum. Research has shown that the friends of our friends, friends, friends have an impact on us. Every day, I listen to (or read about) Buddhism, poetry by Rumi, and/or some inspiring, growth-oriented book. I'm currently reading *The Presentation Secrets of Steve Jobs*. I encourage you to be very deliberate about what enters the permeable membrane of your being. You choose what you are filling yourself with.

I encourage you to imagine a puzzle with thousands of pieces. How long will it take to complete it and see the beauty of the picture? It certainly won't be a day, or even two. It will take patience, commitment, a vision of the destination, and daily effort—strategies, moving you in the "right" direction.

Consider that the sum of our days creates our lives. If we merely take three to five small steps each day (mini goals) toward our destination, we will lead a fulfilled life, much like gradually completing the puzzle. At the end of each day, I encourage you to reflect in your journal by asking yourself, "Am I better today than I was yesterday?"

Discoveries for Fulfilment: Purpose, Reflection, Awareness, and Intuition

"Hold the coffee!" Once we identify our purpose or calling, we will never need another espresso. Previously unimaginable perseverance and flow become our constant companions. Work becomes play.

I encourage you to ask yourself the questions this chapter opened with:

- "How do I want my eulogy to sound?"
- "What legacy do I wish to leave behind once I'm gone?"
- "How do I wish to be remembered?"

Regular reflection, and a genuinely open, curious approach to life promotes exploration. I encourage you to discover the things that truly bring you joy, peace, and presence. For me, being out in nature, journaling, exercising, mentoring, meditating, reading, and spending time with family are my saviours—especially dancing with my wife and daughter! These activities revitalize me. I ensure that each and every day I engage in two or more of these activities.

How often have you heard about entrepreneurs and other successful individuals claiming that they work less and earn more? I used to think it was nonsense. I mean, come on. Here's what my experience has made clear: through greater awareness and deliberate choices to engage in our revitalizing activities, our productivity increases exponentially, and we end up working less. There's also the metaphorical element of working less, in that working on our passion doesn't feel like work.

That being said, balancing rest and recovery is absolutely critical. If we're caught up with an unquenchable desire to "do more," "get more," or "be more," a deep-seated belief of unworthiness, scarcity, or some other fear is governing our behavior. I'd encourage you to examine this with love and without judgment by reflecting through meditation or journaling—simply write your thoughts without stopping your hand.

And, thus, we arrive at the related ideas of non-grasping, mindfulness, and simply being present. At first these ideas were counterintuitive to me. How does it make sense to set goals and then not grasp or reach for them? The truth is that we must set goals, and then let go. Our highest-level goal, our purpose, is our destination. The thing we enter into the GPS of our life. Without it, we're floating aimlessly. Once the goal is set, however, the key is to spend each day (remember the daily three to five tasks we discussed earlier?) incrementally working towards our destination by focusing on the process, finding a state of flow by being present.

Mindfulness and meditation practices help tremendously in this regard. I consciously remind myself to get grounded and practice mindfulness through-out the day, as often as I can remember. As I write, I am again reminded of mindfulness, and now I consciously feel my fingers striking the keyboard, my bum sinking into my chair, my left foot resting on my right foot, the edge of the chair pressing against my hamstring, and the bottom of my palms resting against the laptop. This is an example of being present, here, as I write. I am involved with my surroundings.

And then there's intuition. The idea of faith. It's hard to put this into words, until you've watched *Star Wars*: "Close your eyes. Feel it. The light … It's always been there. It will guide you."

I hope you read this chapter with an open heart and an open mind. I hope that you are ready to reflect upon your own life, your choices, and their outcomes. I hope that you experiment with the suggestions I've shared. I hope you cultivate joy in your life by discovering the activities that invigorate you. I hope you discover your true north and then seek the necessary support to achieve it. I hope you find the love that connects us all.

About the Author

Ahad Raza is the Excellence Alchemist. Ahad aspires to be the mentor that he never had by cultivating the possibilities we can't currently fathom. Ahad builds his practice on inspiring possibilities, empowering change, and guiding transformation, to fulfill our potential and live a life without regret. Ahad's philosophy is one of conscious evolution. He earnestly strives to cultivate a successful mindset every day and guides his clients with love and respect to do the same.

Ahad has positively impacted countless youth and adults through the Life-Strong program—*your treasure map to a successful, fulfilled life*. Several of Ahad's students are currently attending and competing at Ivy League

Universities. Ahad is also committed to guiding and mentoring underprivileged youth regularly. Ahad lives in Canada with his wife and daughter.

E-mail: ahad@arproformance.com
Website: https://www.arproformance.com
LinkedIn: Ahad Raza (AR Proformance)
Instagram and Facebook: @arproformance
YouTube: ARProformance
Life-Strong Program: https://www.arproformance.com/life-strong

CHAPTER 25
SUCCESS VISIONING

By Flemming Rontved
Behavioral Scientist, John Maxwell Certified Coach
Dubai, United Arab Emirates

If you change the way you look at things! The things you look at change.
—Wayne Dyer

The Day Life Began

Sixteen of January 2010. That day is very clear in my mind.

Eleven in the morning, I woke up in the streets of Copenhagen. It was a very cold day at minus 19 degrees Celsius. Wow, it was cold. My body was stiff. The ground was hard, and winter had snuck into my body, along with depression and anxiety.

I could barely move. I couldn't raise my hands. I was hungry and thirsty. It would be nice to find a place with some warmth. Where to go, what to find, how? I had not eaten for a couple of days. I looked up. Was there a sunny spot somewhere, just to get a little warmth into the body?

A spot. It was shielded from the ever-blowing wind, 100 meters away. I moved over there, put up my sign, "Homeless," and situated my cup for money.

Not many people were out in the day's cold weather. Suddenly, I saw a family walking toward me. Hope raised in me. Perhaps they had a few coins or some notes? I waved, begged for money. They stopped.

The man asked, "How are you? Looks like you could use a hot meal, a warm bed, a bath, and a winter jacket."

Wow, just my thought!

I said, "That would be wonderful."

The woman said, "Wonderful, we would be happy to help. Let's go to our car. We will bring you to our home."

I was so grateful. It had been months since I had met such nice and caring people.

We went to the car and drove for half an hour, arriving in a small city outside Copenhagen. We went into their house, which was nice and cozy. I took a bath and put on some clean clothes. It was wonderful. I could not remember the last time I had clean clothes and was in a warm house.

The family had four children, ages four, eight, 11, and 14. They set the table and the mother was making dinner, chicken and potatoes, salad, and more, while I was sitting in the living room, talking to the father, thanking him for their hospitality.

After we finished talking, he showed me the room where I was going to sleep. When we dined together, it was like becoming human again. It was wonderful. The small children were put to bed, and it was only the oldest son and the parents left talking.

It was nine in the evening. The father went to the bathroom, but he came back in a hurry and asked, "Has anybody lit up the fireplace?"

"No," we answered.

"But it smells of fire in the bathroom?"

A small fire had started in the corner of the bedroom where the smallest children were sleeping. We closed the door. The father ran to the kitchen for a bucket of water. I asked the oldest child to call 911 and to wait for us outside the house.

We ran back to the bedroom and when we opened the door again, the fire had exploded. This is because when we opened the door the first time, we gave it oxygen. The mother looked for the children inside the room. She found the girl but could not find the youngest boy. Finally, she found him. I told them to get out of the house. I told the father to find his remaining son and get out of the house.

During the time I'd been aiding the family to escape from the house, the fire spread quickly, growing bigger and bigger, eating more and more of the house. I was now in the kitchen; the light was gone—total darkness—I could not get out because the exit way was blocked by fire.

I shouted to them, "Are you all out? Are you safe?"

They answered yes.

Wow, wonderful. Now it was time to think about me getting out.

The family was scared and wanted to make sure I was still alive, so we kept yelling to each other. I called 911 from a mobile phone left on the table.

"We are busy, please leave a message" was the response I got.

I did not know the layout of the house, but I found a door. It had no handle and could not be opened. I tried to use my shoulder. Hopefully, I could break it. One shoulder against the door, I ran into it again, and again. Nothing happened.

I started kicking the door, and then I suddenly heard a voice in my head, "You—you have no friends. Even your family left you. You have nothing to live for. Nobody likes you. You have no place to live, no money, and a debt of one million dollars. There is nothing for you. Just lie down on the couch and relax. You will find peace!"

Shortly after, I heard a second, friendlier voice: "Come to me. There is more. Just come to me. Just come to me!"

I did not respond to the first command. But the second caring, welcoming voice sounded nice. We had a long conversation about life, of the things I had been through, of love, boundaries, generosity and forgiveness, humility, prosperity, and most of all, responsibility. The one thing I especially remember is—forgiveness.

The voice said, "You do not even forgive yourself, which means you put yourself above God. He forgives you, but you cannot forgive yourself for failure and mistakes, which only leaves you in a place of shame and guilt, and makes you confused and without direction. You cannot control everything; you need to pause, think of what you are thinking of, reflect, listen, and learn, and most of all—have patience. Follow me, and you will see—life has so much to give you."

I said, "If you can reverse every thought—every feeling in me ... I will follow you."

The voice said, "Take my hand and walk with me."

Suddenly, I was standing in front of a large, heavy wood and glass door. I barely touched the handle. The door slid open, but I still couldn't find my way out of the entryway. The fire was reaching over ten meters up into the sky. The father heard me yell again, and he found me. We grabbed each other's hands, and he pulled me outside.

An ambulance arrived, the paramedics came with a stretcher and oxygen. Then I was put into the ambulance, and we were speeding to the hospital.

In the ambulance, the paramedics told me, "You are a living miracle. By first breathing in the smoke, your lungs were filled with carbon monoxide, and by breathing in fire, your lungs should be burnt. You should be dead." We made it to the emergency room.

In the ER, I had a lot to think about, quite a message to consider and quite an experience to go through—to be reborn by the universe, God, the quantum, the field. I am not going to project faith upon you—but I found God gave me his hand on this night, and I have so much to live for, so much to do, so much to investigate, and so many areas to grow. I found my purpose and passion this night—to unlock potential, to ask open, curious questions, and to know the answers are within us—to succeed and to experience personal growth.

After 24 hours of oxygen, the hospital sent me out into the world, and I was a totally different Flemming Rontved. Different behaviour, attitude, a person with gratitude, grace. In 24 hours everything was turned around, reversed—moving from guilt and shame into love and hope. The circumstances outside of me were not changed, but my thinking, my thoughts, my values, everything inside of me was reversed.

When I came out of the hospital, I went directly to visit the house. It was blocked and locked, wooden boards were in front of the windows, but I managed to get inside. Inside the house, I felt thankful to be alive, an extreme gratitude for life and victory.

Here are a few things I came away with after the fire:

- *Gratitude* changed my perception of life—my navigator. When you are thankful for what you have, for every day you are given, for the roof above your head, and for the clothes you are wearing, everything will change.
- *Forgiveness* is even better. Forgiveness, especially of yourself and others with no strings attached, ensures that no one is in control of you and your life, but you.
- *Never let a day end with anger.* Always do a mental cleanup. Every day.
- *Changing thoughts changes perception*, allowing you to get out of your comfort zone, the prison of habits.

Belief Systems

Where did I come from? How did I end up homeless? The answer starts with growing up in a home of negativity. I remember my father telling me, "No matter what you do, it will never be good enough." He would rather do everything himself. I remember my uncle telling me, "I can easily understand why nobody likes you." Those two things became my reality, my truth, my context, and they colored every aspect of life.

When we are gripped with this kind of conditioning—let's call it B-type (unconscious) conditioning, the programming from birth to seven years that's obtained through our five senses—it becomes hardwired into our subconscious. This can be positive or negative. The external circumstances and ideas in the conscious mind, which I'll call an A idea (conscious thoughts), must be in harmony with the unconscious conditioning; otherwise it will be rejected, neglected, and dismissed. Getting our unconscious wiring in alignment with our conscious thoughts and driving them in a positive direction is essential to live a life of success and abundance.

In my case, a change in my navigator, perception, and comfort zone happened overnight. Within 24 hours after the house fire, everything in my life changed—moving from guilt and shame into love and hope—such that I came into harmony with A ideas, a new perception navigator of life, and harmony happened. Self-leadership came into my life. You see, my perception of life had previously been wrong based on negative comments from my family during childhood. I was living in a healthy environment, but my perception and interpretation of what I was experiencing was unhealthy.

That changed when my self-worth was reinforced by the voice I heard during the fire, but really—whether God was driving it or not—the voice was in my head. I was faced with choosing, either (1) to believe in myself and my abilities to change my perception of the healthy environment I could choose to see or (2) to continue to believe in the unhealthy conditions I let myself live in that drove me to homelessness. Once I made the mental shift, I could take steps to make my life better.

One thing that often holds people back is that they may wait for the circumstances to change on the outside before being willing to even start to make a change on the inside. So they are literally thinking in reverse, external to internal rather than internal to external. This is a fundamental error in goal setting and goal achievement because ... the world does not give you what you want; the world gives you who you are. The world simply reflects back at you—and your beliefs. If you wait for changes to happen on the outside, nothing will change.

When I accepted myself, just as I was, I positioned myself for growth.

Our brains can be used most effectively in constant change, and there are some core techniques to do this. These include:

1. Understanding the basics of your brain
2. Unlearning
3. Growing your self-awareness
4. Developing resilience

Let's look at each of these four core techniques.

Core Technique One—Understanding the Basics of Your Brain

Develop an awareness and understanding of the ladder of Inference, a way of understanding the brain as developed by Chris Argyris. The ladder of Inference describes the brain's processing according to the following seven rungs:

1. It takes action.
2. It adopts beliefs.
3. It draws conclusions.
4. It makes assumptions.
5. It adds meaning.
6. It selects data.
7. It observes data.

While all this is happening, we should pause at each of the brain process rungs and ask ourselves, "What if … I am wrong? What if there is something I'm missing?"

We need to do this because we don't always believe what we see. Our beliefs are the truth; the truth is obvious; our truths and beliefs are based on real data, but *we* select the data we see. By periodically and intentionally slowing down to think about what we are thinking about and why, we can sometimes gain a better perspective.

Core Technique Two—Unlearning

Your brain loves well-worn pathways, and the more successful or unsuccessful you have been, the more your brain wants to stick to the same trail. As humans, we are pattern-seeking, structure-loving animals. The good news is that we can create whole new pathways, structures, and frameworks constantly. This neuroplasticity requires the crucial ingredients of time and intention.

Typically, in unexpected change, we go through various phases, including:

- *Shock*: a sudden upsetting or surprising event or experience occurs. "What is this?"
- *Denial*: we look for evidence that it is not true or won't affect us. "This can't be true!"
- *Frustration or anger*: things are different and unfamiliar. "I don't like it! Here is why it won't work."
- *Depression or a lack of energy*: we withdraw or disconnect. "I'm just going to check out and wait. I don't have to do this."
- *Accept and begin to experiment*: we consider new ways and ideas. "I'm going to think about this in a positive way and consider how it can work."
- *Integrate*: we work with the new parameters or situations, and become more positive. "I'm going to do this now (to move forward)."

The tricky part is that we experience wave after wave of change, tossing us back to the beginning, which means we are experiencing shock constantly. This gets us stuck. We can easily get caught up in the loop of shock > denial > frustration > depression. When this happens, recognize where you are in these cycles and help others to recognize where they are in the phases as well.

It is important for us to keep in mind that *change is external*, an anticipated or unanticipated event, and that *transition is internal,* a personal reaction—and this is something within our control.

Core Technique Three—Growing Your Self-Awareness

Here is a list of things that can help with our self-awareness, especially through change:

- *Be positive.* Beliefs, setbacks, and failures are temporary, limited to given situations.
- *Be flexible.* Demonstrate the ability to surface, test, and if necessary, change deeply-held beliefs and assumptions about past issues and new issues.
- *Be focused.* Get interested through engaging your imagination and generating intrigue in all subjects. Ask yourself questions that stimulate new thoughts.
- *Be proactive.* Ensure commitment and understanding of resulting decisions.
- *Be organized.* Formulate clear decision criteria; evaluate options by considering implications and consequences, and choose an effective option for whatever situation you're faced with.

Core Tactic Four—Developing Your Resilience

Resilient people are positive, focused, flexible, organized, and proactive. To cultivate resilience, do the following:

- Display a sense of security and self-assurance that is based on your view of life as complex but filled with opportunity (positive).
- Have a clear vision of what you want to achieve (focused).
- Demonstrate pliability when responding to uncertainty (flexible).
- Develop structured approaches to managing ambiguity (organized).
- Engage change rather than defend against it (proactive).

These are the characteristics of "winners" in the world of change. Resilient people experience the same fear and apprehension as everyone else when they engage in change. However, they are usually able to maintain their productivity and quality standards as well as their physical and emotional stability while achieving most of their objectives.

It is fundamentally important to continually maintain a clear vision of what you want to achieve. Focus on the target. For example, ask yourself, "What does winning look like?" Bring goals to life by establishing what it looks like when the desired results are achieved, and define winning/excellence with as much detail as possible.

When I was homeless in Copenhagen, I had no direction. I allowed external factors to dictate my actions, and I held a mindset of failure. However, as soon as I made the internal transition, I started moving out of my situation. I began to see positivity and hope in not only myself, but in my perception of my environment.

Since that day in the fire, I've gone on to live in multiple countries, I've trained to work with others, so that I could share my message. Now, as I look out of the large windows in my warm and comfortable house in Dubai, I exist as I was designed to exist—filled with comfort, authority, ambition—and I'm glad that I get to help others break out from their negative (or stagnant) thinking that is holding them back in their lives and their businesses.

You don't have to die in a fire, like I did, to wake up. All you have to do is decide that you want to change and understand that change is within your control. Take charge of your thinking, your language, your actions, and see the positivity and possibility within your environment as you take on your winning mindset to create your own success.

About the Author

Flemming Rontved guides leaders and their organizations to achieve greater success by leveraging their brains and the brains of others to

- Create clarity on what winning looks like and execute with excellence
- Master how to think differently and to be truly innovative
- Engage their entire organization to accomplish more
- Increase skills required to thrive in today's hyper-paced world

As an experienced business leader and behavioural scientist, Flemming has a combination of academic training and in-the-trenches experience working with leaders across the globe unlocking potential for high performance and establishing their legacy.

As consultant, Flemming is frequently hired by companies to help them compete effectively in uncertain markets. He provides support in strategic planning, operational excellence, and organizational alignment to help them achieve higher profits and more success.

In entertaining, interactive keynotes, Flemming blends the 30,000-foot view with hands-on experience along with practical tools creating immediate, lasting change, drawing from his deep knowledge of the neurosciences to help people succeed in business and improve their lives.

Email: Flemming@esqlworld.com
Websites:
www.flemmingrontved.com
www.esqlworld.com

CHAPTER 26
SUSTAINED MOTIVATION AND LONG-TERM GOALS

By Stefan Due Schmidt
Olympic Athlete, Long-Track Speed Skating
Copenhagen, Denmark

Most people overestimate what they can do in one year
and underestimate what they can do in ten years.
—Bill Gates

To be able to sustain motivation over long periods of time is an essential and rewarding skill that must somehow bond mind and body through a spirit of dedication. It enables you to get value from your daily work and have success in big, ambitious goals. Long-term motivation is necessary for long-term effort, which makes it possible to achieve long-term goals. This is true in any area of life, but it is extremely evident with elite athletes and Olympic ambitions. Achieving athletic success on this level can take decades of commitment. To have a lot of motivation, but for a short period of time, is not helpful towards achieving a goal of this type. Ensuring a sustainable motivation, not only makes it more likely to succeed with long-term goals, but also makes it more enjoyable and rewarding throughout. The fire of motivation has to burn not just strong, but long!

From the outside, when people watch athletes fulfil their life-long dreams at the Olympics, that might spark a strong inspiration and motivation in that given moment, to try to achieve that same thing. However, what people see at the Olympics are athletes reaping the fruits of their life-long dedication to their sport. They don't see the daily training regimen, the setbacks, and all the sacrifices over the years that are necessary leading up to that. It takes motivation, commitment, and consistency over long periods of time to get there.

So, how do elite athletes put themselves in extreme physical discomfort daily, every day of the week, for many years, just to get a shot at their Olympic goal? This very singular difficult goal, which is only possible every fourth year and without any guarantee of making it, needs strong reasons to begin with. Equally important, it also needs strong reasons to persist. The challenges of committing to a goal like this put a high demand on your ability to sustain motivation. If you don't succeed the first time, are you ready to continue to work hard for another four years, or eight years, to maybe get there? To start the fire of motivation in your spirit is easy, to make it burn long and strong until you succeed, is the art.

A Happy, Naive Kid on Skates

Without my knowing, my Olympic journey started all the way back in 2000 when I was a happy, naive five-year-old kid playing around on my first pair of inline skates. Everything I've done since then has led to my first Winter Olympic Games in the sport of long-track speed skating, 18 years later, when I was 23 years old. When I was 13 and stepped on the ice for the first time, the idea of making it to the Olympics got stuck in my imagination, even without ice facilities for long-track speed skating in Denmark.

When I made it to the Olympics, I had already trained as an elite athlete for 15 years, the Olympics had been a dream of mine for the last ten years, and I had been on a structured plan towards that specific goal for over five years of my life.

When my 18 years of skating gets summed up like that, I might sound like I am a very result-oriented athlete, who is mostly motivated by setting big goals. However, my parents raised me to compare myself, not to others, but to myself. I am, for the most part, a very process-oriented athlete, and I simply love my sport. People who know me, even to this day, describe me as a "happy, naive kid on skates."

I started skating because I love to skate. In the beginning, that was the only thing. I still love to skate; however, there are now many more things that have value to me. Whenever I give more time, energy, and commitment to skating, I have gotten so much more in return over the years. Not necessarily results, but experiences, challenges, and opportunities. These have helped me to grow as a person and as an athlete. Because skating is not "only" about my love of skating or "only" about the pursuit of an ambitious goal, I have been able to create a daily life as an elite athlete that is both rewarding and sustainable. The single main thing that has contributed the very most to my athletic success has been my consistency in effort over the years, which I have been able to carry out because of my sustained motivation.

That journey from being a five-year-old kid on skates to becoming a 23-year-old first-time Olympian has been that cliché of blood, sweat, and tears, but it has also been so much more. At most times, it has been so enjoyable that it has felt almost effortless to do ridiculously hard training sessions and committing fully, day after day after day. On the contrary, at other times it has been so incredibly difficult and hard. The hardest things throughout the years have not been those brutal five-hour bike trainings or the all-out skating intervals that made me puke. The hardest things have been to keep my commitment, to make the necessary priorities, and to keep trying to focus on what to improve, even in periods of setback. I will for the rest of my life continue on this dynamic journey of learning how to fuel and sustain this fire of motivation and use that in every other aspect of my life going forward as well.

The Antidote to the "Effort in, Results Out" and the "If It's Hard, It's Good" Mindsets

"If you work hard enough, you can achieve anything."

I hate this over-simplified statement. Don't get me wrong, I love all the classic sports movies: *Miracle*, *Remember the Titans*, and even the original *Rocky*. But what I really don't like is hearing people adopt or promote that so-called "effort in, results out" mindset of thinking that if you simply put the effort in, that will make you reach any big long-term goal. I have heard that statement from athletes I know, who have succeeded and have attributed that 100 percent to their own effort and nothing else. It might be tempting when you have success to simply reward yourself by over-simplifying it like this. However, it is not that simple. Hard work might be *one* of the most important factors within our control, but it is not the only factor. I know fellow athletes who have put so much effort in but haven't gotten a lot of results in return. Earlier, I was that athlete as well.

Succeeding at something is more complex than just "effort in, results out." I've tried to follow the philosophical teaching from stoicism of understanding what is and isn't within our control, and acting accordingly. I can control my choices, actions, and effort. What I cannot control are chance, circumstances, and my past. My athletic results, I can only partially control by trying to make the best choices, actions, and efforts towards that. Through trial and error, I can build experience and continuously make better choices, actions, and efforts that give me a better possibility of getting better results. That trial-and-error feedback loop also develops your resilience, adaptability, and integration of learned lessons.

The "effort in, results out" mindset is oversimplified. The antidote is realizing and accepting that it is more complex and not everything is within our control. Because of that, however, there is also so much more learning, development, and reward to be found in the pursuit, luckily.

The other mindset that I hope I can persuade you to give up on is the one built on the notion, "If something is hard, it must be good." Getting the training done on days where the motivation is not one hundred percent present is something that should be encouraged, celebrated, and rewarded. Motivation is dynamic, and day-to-day variation is very natural. Motivation is, however, also a limited resource that you have to use wisely, but which you can also nurture to grow yourself. Being unmotivated for months on end is a completely different story and not a sustainable model. With this kind of struggle, it is necessary to try to understand the underlying causes of this more persistent state, instead of just continuing training and forcing it through. Here it might be tempting to try and trick yourself into believing that because it is hard right now, great things will come later from this struggle. I am not saying that great results can't come after periods of pushing through without motivation. However, it should not be expected as a certainty, so that your motivation is relying on that result in the end. It is a very fragile foundation to try and build long-term success upon. That short-term success from pushing through right now, might even come at the price of your long-term success.

For me, pushing through for longer periods of time without motivation has mostly resulted in suboptimal physical performance and an exhaustion of mental resources. After having experienced these negative results from pushing through without addressing root issues, I've instead tried to adapt the "happy head, fast legs" approach, where I try to make a positive mindset the dominant one. Not only is this approach more productive athletically, it is also a lot more enjoyable and sustainable.

Goals, Prioritizations, and Values

So, why should I even pursue an ambitious long-term goal? So far, most of what I have highlighted addresses all the years of commitment it takes and all the complexity involved with how to succeed with a major long-term goal. First of all, I am not saying definitely that you should find a long-term ambitious goal, or even that you need to find a goal at all. Neither am I saying that if you are an athlete, that the Olympics should be your goal. I just know that for me, goal-setting and committing to that long-term goal, has been the most rewarding thing I have chosen to do with my sport. However, the action should not be reduced to an instrument to that goal. There is still value to be found in the activity itself. Thus, the goal should be an extension to that.

If you commit to a difficult goal, any goal, it is important to make sure that the process towards the goal and the goal itself are actually worth more than the priorities and sacrifices that necessarily have to be made. It is easy to make choices on what you want to prioritize, but is a lot harder to make the necessary choice on what you then cannot do. It is also important to make sure that your goals are aligned with the journey you want and the values that you want to live by. Your educational, working, or athletic life will still have to be in balance while you try to commit to the parts that you have your big goals in.

The process towards the goal can also help you develop skills you can use in the other arenas of your life. By getting value from the process itself, you have made the path a part of the goal as well. The definition of "success" at the end of your goal is then not only defined by the result of a win, podium, or ranking, but in knowing that there has been value created in giving your best effort. When it is all said and done, I wish that you can evaluate your own success based on not just results, but also your development as a person and your realization of your potential. If you can evaluate success like that, it will also be easier, when it's time for something else, to then move on with peace of mind, feeling proud of what you did and knowing you got as much value from it as you possibly could.

My Olympic Journey and Handling Setbacks

In the summer of 2013, I had just won my third European title on inline skates, and I was entering into my fourth winter season on ice. I had developed a lot on the ice, surprisingly putting me in the position where qualifications for the Winter Olympic Games in Sochi 2014 had become a real possibility and a goal. I bought all the best new custom-made skating equipment, participated in many more training camps, and trained a lot harder that ice season. And, as it turned out, it was my first ice skating season since I had started with no major improvement. I failed at my goal. I was far from Olympic qualification and was disappointed, but more motivated than ever to make sure I would qualify in four years from then.

After the 2014 Olympics, I moved to the Netherlands to skate full-time on ice for the next season. I invested all my energy, money, and priorities in getting closer to that goal of the Olympics in 2018. That ice season was my worst ice season to date. I was putting so much effort in, and I was getting so little results out. It was not just that my level was flat-lining; I was even skating more slowly than I had three years earlier! I was mentally exhausted from forcing myself through every training that winter, I had used up all my money, and I was very close to quitting ice skating and my Olympic dream altogether. I moved back home to Denmark and decided to make sure to get my love for skating back by taking a step down from ice skating. I did one single race on the ice that winter and then went to Colombia to inline skate for the rest of the winter.

The following ice season, I returned physically stronger, mentally energized, and was ready to try to prioritize ice skating fully again. I enjoyed ice skating again, I improved, and I qualified for the Olympics in 2018.

At the Olympics, I made the final on the mass start and performed well, finishing thirteenth. I was relieved. A dream had come true. As soon as I passed the finish line, I just broke down in tears of joy. I had tried and failed in 2014, almost given up on ice skating, then I took a break and tried again, only this time for it to succeed. The feeling was indescribable. I was so proud, so grateful, and so happy. After that, I had zero doubts as to what my plan was going to be for the next four years. I wanted more.

Just as I thought I had fully picked the lock of motivation and understood all the dynamics at play and how to bounce back from setbacks, another challenge arose that I did not know how to handle—"Olympic blues." I had heard a disclaimer for this phenomenon from other Olympic athletes earlier and rejected the idea that it could ever happen to me. I had plenty of things I had sacrificed or put on hold that I wanted to do and catch up on after the Olympics.

However, after the 2018 Winter Olympics, I had a spring and summer where I struggled with some depressive tendencies and had a hard time getting back on track. None of my process goals or part-goals were exciting to me anymore, and racing regionally, nationally, or even internationally had become a very "flat" feeling after having raced at the Olympics. So, I remembered what I did three years earlier, and I decided to skip that ice season and go to Ecuador to return to my roots of inline speed skating. I needed to find my love for the sport again that could also bring me back to the joy of ice skating and help me towards my goal of the 2022 Winter Olympics. I once again returned stronger and hungry for more.

So now, I know, for myself, finding my full potential as a speed skater and trying to put all that potential into success at the Olympics is what I have chosen as my individual long-term goal at this point in my life. I am now 26 years old, currently number eight in the world ranking and preparing for my second Olympics in 2022, one year from now. The goal is to give my 100 percent at my chance of skating for the Olympic title. That is achievable, exciting, and meaningful to me. That is what excites my spirit and makes my fire burn. What makes your fire burn?

About the Author

Stefan Due Schmidt is a Danish professional inline and ice long-track speed skater who competed at the Winter Olympic Games in 2018 in Pyeongchang, Korea. He is currently number eight on the world ranking in his favorite discipline, the "mass start," and is preparing towards the Winter Olympics in 2022 in Beijing, China.

Stefan started his sporting career with inline speed skating back when he was just seven-years old, but later started ice skating in winter as well to chase his Olympic dream on the ice since inline speed skating is not on the Olympic summer programme.

While competing professionally, Stefan has finished his bachelor's in nutrition and health, and is currently taking a dual-career approach studying a master's in global health. Stefan is also the host of the podcast *The Due Power*

Podcast, where he talks with fellow athletes about mindset, experiences, and skills learned from elite sports.

Email: stefands1994@gmail.com
Hashtag: #DuePower

CHAPTER 27

THE POWER OF AUTHENTICITY—BE YOU AND BRING YOU

By Scott Span, MSOD, CSM
Transformational Consultant, Leadership Coach
Silver Spring, Maryland

Be yourself, everyone else is taken.
—Oscar Wilde

Have you ever had someone say to you, "Who do you think you are?" Perhaps you had a parent yelling the question at you when you were a teenager? And let's keep it real—how many of us had the self-awareness at that age to really know who we were?

I recall my mother asking me that question frequently when I was growing up. And in retrospect, I thank her. Though I'm sure it wasn't her intention at the time, she got me thinking about authenticity. She caused me to reflect on what is important to me and why. She also encouraged me to ask myself, "Who do I think I am and who do I want to be, and why?"

Authenticity—the meaning of this word has become a bit convoluted. It's become a term that businesses associate with branding and marketing. It's become a social media buzzword. Merriam Webster defines "authenticity" in several ways, including "true to one's own personality, spirit, or character." In

The Gifts of Imperfection, author and researcher Brené Brown refers to authenticity as a daily practice:

> *Authenticity is the daily practice of letting go of who we think we're supposed to be and embracing who we are. It is a collection of choices that we have to make every day. It's about the choice to show up and be real. The choice to be honest. The choice to let our true selves be seen. Choosing authenticity means cultivating the courage to be imperfect, to set boundaries, and to allow ourselves to be vulnerable ... mindfully practicing authenticity during our most soul-searching struggles is how we invite grace, joy and gratitude into our lives.*

And really, who couldn't use a bit more joy in their life?

Much has been researched and written on authenticity. I'm not going to rehash and espouse various theories. Instead, I'll share my point of view from my personal journey and professional experience accessing my authenticity and becoming my authentic self.

Back to the question my mother used to ask me, "Who do you think you are?" Our values, beliefs, and mindset all make up our authentic self. Giving thought to that question will help you define what authenticity means to you. And that is a step toward accessing your authenticity. This will help you be and bring your authentic self.

I choose to be authentic in everything I do.
—India Arie

As an adult, I've worked hard to define what authenticity means to me and how to access my authenticity to be and bring my authentic self. A combination of coaching, education, therapy, peer dialogue and support, reflection, and hard work has helped me in this process. It's a journey. And, in the words of Michelangelo, I'm still learning.

It takes courage to grow up and become who you really are.
—e.e. cummings

Do you know who you are?

And I don't mean your name or any basic characteristics listed on your driver's license. I mean, do you know YOU? Your values? Your beliefs? Your boundaries? Your preferred style? Your triggers? Your way of being? These are all characteristics that make up our authentic selves.

I value authenticity (obviously), transparency, honesty, accountability, creativity, diversity, determination, and empathy. My beliefs align with my values. My boundaries support my beliefs and protect me from any infringement of my values. My preferred style supports my values, beliefs, and boundaries. My triggers are usually set off when a misalignment occurs. And all of those make up my way of being and interacting in the world. I keep it real. I tell hard truths, and I get stuff done personally and professionally.

As you give thought to these things, it's also important to understand and acknowledge that not all experiences, relationships, job roles, client work, or situations may align with your values, beliefs, and mindset. And that's okay. These are good realizations. Being and bringing our authentic self is important to a healthy mind, body, and spirit. Not knowing who we are, what and who brings us joy, and what and who frustrates us (and why) can cause us to feel lost, isolated, unmotivated, unsuccessful, and unfulfilled. And those feelings have an impact on our mindset, our goals, our relationships, our health, and our spirit.

A successful spirit—and life—is all about alignment, and we can't achieve alignment without authenticity. In my personal life, my family, friends, and peers know who and what they're getting when they interact with me. They've come to appreciate me for my authentic self. They know when they need the ear of someone who can cut through the noise, the voice of a straight shooter, someone who provides empathetic, no-BS feedback, brings a sense of humor when needed, listens without judgment, and can be a thought partner who will support them to take action and get stuff done—that's what they will get from me. I'm consistent with being and bringing my authentic self, and they know it. In my professional life as a people strategist, consultant, and coach, my clients know what they're getting as well. And they're on board. If people are not on board with my authenticity, they won't achieve the best results, and they rarely become long-time clients.

Life can be amazing, but it isn't always exactly what we expect. Perhaps you have experienced some of these situations:

- You dread going to work every day. You get tense. Stomach knots. You find yourself being terse. Disengaged. You're just over it!
- You have a relationship, personal or professional, that causes you to get anxious or annoyed every time you have to interact with a certain individual.
- Each time you're in a particular situation or experience a certain interaction, you find your energy level is drained and your mind is exhausted.

These are just a few examples of situations that cause a misalignment between your values, beliefs, and your authentic self. And it doesn't feel good, does it?

I've had these moments. For example, I worked for one client organization supporting a technology implementation performing change management and user adoption work. The executive leadership was in flux when the work began. Culture, politics, and process issues were already apparent. However, several of my colleagues asked me to take on the work as they felt my expertise could help improve things. So, I agreed.

Several roles were being filled in an interim capacity by executives from other parts of the organization. Midway through the engagement, the organization selected a new CEO. He walked into the middle of a firestorm of changes and a culture that could use some change. His appointment also caused anxiety, uncertainty, and ambiguity throughout the organization. And the executive leadership team refused to add additional skilled resources to support his leadership transition and mitigate risks to operations and the employee experience.

I liked the new CEO. I thought him to be a good leader in multiple areas. I found my interactions with him to be in line with my authentic self. However, I also felt from day one that he wasn't going to last. I perceived the organization, their politics and culture, would not allow him to be his authentic self. I was right. He lasted less than a year. Similarly to how I observed the new CEO having an authenticity misalignment with the organization, I began to feel the same for myself. Instead of being appreciated for my expertise and my authentic self, I was being minimized and undervalued. I felt my work was not being given priority. I no longer felt supported or that I would be as effective as I could be in achieving results. And thus, I resigned from the project. It was the best decision for me professionally, and it was also the best decision for my health—mind, body, and spirit.

I've also experienced similar misalignments in my personal life between my values and beliefs. I've been in situations where misalignments occurred between my authentic self and that of family members. Every time I would have to deal with certain relatives, I became anxious, tense, and annoyed. I found myself feeling manipulated and treated with disrespect. I was not getting back the same level of effort, concern, and authenticity that I was providing. And sadly, these relatives lack the self-awareness to understand and the apparent desire to care. So, I made necessary adjustments in my interactions. This was another great decision for my mind, body, and spirit.

Whether it be work- or family-related, each time we encounter a misalignment with our authentic selves, we learn more about who we are, what we value and believe, and why. We can also learn more about who we want to be and who we want to spend our time with.

So, how do you identify what authenticity means to you? How do you begin to access your authenticity to be and bring your authentic self? Here are some strategies:

Reflect

Reflection is important in general. Giving ourselves the space and making the time to just be with our thoughts and reflect on our experiences provides us a great opportunity for learning and growth. Reflection also provides us an opportunity to not just think but to feel how our body reacts to certain thoughts and feelings.

Reflection can bring about memories from past experiences. Memories from childhood experiences can surface. As we think about these experiences and interactions, we may feel a sense of joy at some and feel negatively triggered by others. We may even discover patterns that contribute to how we feel and deal in the present.

Figuring out what makes us angry, what causes our veins to bulge or our shoulders to tense, and what causes us to feel a sense of calm and reduces the knots in our stomach is an important step in accessing our authenticity. And it's an important step in maintaining a healthy mind and a healthy spirit. Some clients I work with prefer to journal as a method of self-reflection. Some prefer to do yoga or practice mindfulness exercises. Me, I put on my "Reflect and

Reboot" playlist and go where the energy takes me. Sometimes that's a walk in nature with my dogs, sometimes it's a creative outlet like painting, and other times it is journaling. Find what works for you and roll with it.

Seek out that particular mental attribute which makes you feel most deeply and vitally alive, along with which comes the inner voice which says, 'This is the real me,' and when you have found that attitude, follow it.
—William James

Define

As you continue to reflect, give thought to the traits, characteristics, behaviors, and patterns that bring you the most joy, peace, and satisfaction. Also become aware of the traits that don't. This can lead you to uncover and begin to define what you believe is right and what you believe is wrong. Consider why certain things resonate and feel right, and why certain things trigger you or feel wrong. Identifying these things helps you define your values and beliefs, and access your authenticity. You can use various tools to help with this. When coaching clients, I often recommend mind mapping as a more visual tool to help in the process. However, some of the more linear clients I work with prefer an Excel spreadsheet. There is no right or wrong way. It's about continuing to build on what comes out of your reflection time and getting your thoughts organized in a way that works best for you.

You attract the right things when you have a sense of who you are.
—Amy Poehler

Test

After you have reflected and after you have further defined the traits, characteristics, and behaviors that bring you the most joy, the most peace, and the most satisfaction, and those that don't, you need to validate and test your assumptions, thoughts, and feelings. Practice being the new you. Most prefer to test this new way of being amongst those they are comfortable with and those they trust. This could be family, close friends, or selected peers. This is not a tool or framework type of exercise. It's a way of feeling, being, and interacting. Pay attention to your feelings, and be conscious of new behaviors that support your mindset of authenticity. Be intentional in your interactions. Observe. Ask for feedback if desired.

Understand, not everyone may be happy with the more authentic you as you begin experimenting with the way you interact with others. Your boss may not be happy you're more vocal about certain things. Some friends and family may feel the same. Not everyone is a fan when we use our voice or set boundaries. Not all people will cheer on the authentic you. Some may even get upset when you start accessing your authenticity. Some will be frustrated. Some will be confused. Some may even change or end their relationship with you, and you may change or end certain relationships with others. Accept this. Wave a swift goodbye to the haters.

Accessing your authenticity and being and bringing this new you can be a place of muck, change, and transformation. As long as you're not harming other people in this process, it's your life to live. Being your authentic self is not about the happiness of other people. It's about your own happiness. And your happiness can radiate to others. As the expression goes, we attract what we put out into the world. And you want to attract those who align, support, appreciate, and encourage your authentic self. Those are your people.

I've always loved the idea of not being what people expect me to be.
—Dita Von Teese

Live

Accessing your authenticity and being and bringing your authentic self does not mean living your life as a jerk. Though some may perceive it that way, especially if they haven't experienced you in this way before. The only way to find out who will be comfortable, encouraging, and supportive of your authentic self is to be you and bring you. Live your authentic life. Pay attention to your feelings. Your interactions. If something doesn't feel right or your authentic interactions are not resonating with people the way you intended, supporting your achievement of desired goals or increasing your happiness, then it may be time for further reflection, testing, and feedback.

We are constantly invited to be who we are.
—Henry David Thoreau

Learn

Accessing your authenticity and being and bringing your authentic self is a marathon not a sprint. Figuring out what authenticity means to you, accessing your own authenticity, and being and bringing your authentic self is a journey. It's an iterative process. It's not a one and done. You'll encounter bumps. You'll encounter roadblocks. You may feel frustrated. You may feel challenged. You'll also encounter aha moments. Attract what you put out. Forge or enhance genuine and supportive relationships. Cut the dead wood. Expand your perception, and learn and grow as a human being. The choice is yours.

> *Authenticity is about being true to who you are.*
> —Michael Jordan

As you pursue opening up your authentic self to the world, you are unlocking your successful spirit. Here are some things that happen when you access your authenticity and bring your authentic self:

- You have deeper and more meaningful relationships and experiences.
- You have greater health and wellbeing of mind, body, and spirit.
- You begin to feel and share more compassion and empathy.
- You attract the right things and the right people for you.
- You define and communicate your boundaries.
- You have an increase in confidence.
- You learn to be kinder to yourself.
- You strive less for perfection.
- You live a more joyous life.
- You recognize your worth.

Being your authentic self is not a popularity contest. If you are being your authentic self, you have no competition. It's your life. Be you and bring you. In the drama called life, don't be an extra or an ensemble cast member. Don't even settle for being an actor. Be the director.

About the Author

Scott Span, MSOD, CSM is a people strategist, coach, and change and transformation consultant. Scott believes that people are the greatest asset to any organization and that happy employees make for happy customers. His work is focused on people, supporting clients to create people-focused cultures and a great employee experience. Scott brings his empathetic, direct, authentic style and sense of humor to his work. He assists organizations, leaders, teams, and individuals to prepare for, adapt to, and overcome changes, both personal and organizational changes. His coaching work focuses on increasing self-awareness, identifying patterns and ways to shift perception and change behaviors to overcome obstacles and accelerate performance. Scott is an author on various topics of organization development and leadership. He holds a masters in organization development (MSOD) from American University and the NTL Institute. He is a certified Scrum Master (CSM) and member of the International Coaching Federation (ICF.)

Email: Scott.span@tolerosolutions.com
Website: http://tolerosolutions.com

CHAPTER 28

READY, STEADY, GO: FINDING YOUR SWEET SPOT FOR A SUCCESSFUL SPIRIT

By Jenny R. Susser, PhD
Sport and Performance Psychologist, Executive Coach
Ocala, Florida

*A man with outward courage dares to die; a man
with inner courage dares to live.*
—Lao Tzu

It is other-worldly, the feeling. Indescribable, like an out-of-body experience. You are suspended in time, as if gravity has no pull; you can do no wrong, and the thrill takes over your entire being, infusing you with pure energy. We love this feeling, this space, this moment because it is not the ordinary daily grind of trying to get through it all, and it is when we connect to our spirit.

The first time I "lost myself" and tapped into my successful spirit, I was facilitating a room filled with executives (people I was usually afraid of). I experienced a feeling I will never forget. I had found this place repeatedly as an athlete but never thought it possible without the physical element. After a few years of hard work, trying to set myself and my ego aside to really *be there* for the group, suddenly, it felt like slow motion, as if the walls and chairs and everything separating our bodies seemed to disappear. The group cohered as the conversation moved from purely intellectual to a deep connection between beings, spirit to spirit. None of us were the same after that day, and I left in wonder from the experience … and then wondering how to recreate that magic.

While there are a thousand roads to Rome, there are perhaps more to a successful spirit. As you work to discover your connection to spirit, know this is a life-long endeavor, with twists and turns of the expected and unexpected kinds. It is worth it, as I'm sure you are already sensing, so welcome to the journey.

You bought this book because something is eluding you, some secret to success you think you are missing, and you are convinced it is the reason you aren't further along or moving faster on your path. Others have it, but they don't show you where to find it or how to wield it, so maybe, just maybe this book will. How do I know this? My shelves are filled with books I just knew had the answer, and I have devoured or discarded them accordingly. Decades of reading, learning, fretting, and working have revealed to me, while there is no simple answer, the quest remains the important part.

Spirit is a funny word and for every person defining it, there is a different meaning. It's the same thing with success. I wonder if we have given away our control for our relationship to spirit to greater "authorities," be it religion or family or a person we have followed or trusted, while the irony is, we all have a natural connection to spirit. We long for a direct line to our inner magic yet have turned to looking for it outside the self, but that is not where it is to be found. It is right there inside of us. Inside of you. This chapter is about connecting to your successful spirit.

Early in my career as a sport psychologist, I was all about the toolkit, the "stuff" you needed to *do* to be successful. And while developing and expanding your tools and skills remain important, the mystery of "being" versus "doing" has taken on a more powerful role for me both personally and professionally. It has had a profound impact on my work and my "success." It is in this space of "being" that your connection to the power of spirit lives. The irony is that there are things to do and steps to take to get you to spirit. At first, it will be clunky and slow as you learn, and your confidence in yourself and your process will ebb and flow with your failures and successes, so be ready for it.

Everyone would be successful if it were easy; however, it is complex, challenging, and requires something beyond normal effort. Now add to it the word "spiritual" and you are not only trying to succeed, but now you are trying to succeed at something that lives out there in the ether. It is as dynamic as an ocean tide chart, ever-changing, always adjusting, and under the influence of countless external factors that you may or may not be able to account for. But here's the thing, you are not trying to be "spiritually successful." You are trying to *use your spiritual connection to foster your success: the successful spirit*. When you bought this book, you declared a desire to seek success through spirit and your connection to it. And you are right, when you are connected to spirit, it is hard not to be successful.

You will need a couple things to be able to use this chapter. One is an attitude combining curiosity and determination. The curiosity isn't only during the beginning stages, being curious while struggling (because you will) is an incredible mental ally. When you pair determination with it, you quit less. Einstein was famous for saying, "It's not that I'm so smart. But I stay with the questions much longer." So, hang in there longer than usual, and you will produce an "unusual" result. Two, you need a powerful way to dream, design, track, and celebrate your path. Many of us try to do this all in our head, but that is another mistake. You need a system, so you can see your work, as well as having something to help hold you accountable. For this, I recommend writing. I am a huge fan of writing *with pen and paper* not only because of the powerful way it impacts your brain as shown by Pennebaker and associates in a 2003 article in *Annual Review of Psychology*, but also because it supports an action plan better than anything else I have found. So, grab a pen or pencil you love to write with and a special notebook or journal for this work. This is not ordinary stuff you are working on, it's your life and your passion, so honor that with a special place to discover and document this process.

There are countless elements contributing to high performance and to get there, we need a method, a consistent pattern of focus, work, skill development, and personal growth to move our body, mind, and spirit into this place. Because of the elusive nature of spirit, most people chock it up to happenstance, yet there is a way to harness this power, and here is a process I have used with top performers in sport and business for over twenty years. Getting all the way through the three steps is a *process* and the most critical element is time, so as you settle into this material, notice your desire to rush. Each part is important and supports the others, so be patient with yourself, the process, and your growth. There are three things you need to do:

- Plan
- Prepare
- Deliver

Step I: Plan

There are two important elements in the plan: your goals and defining what success looks like. The more clarity, the greater your power, so be thorough in this step. A critical element people don't spend enough time on is goal setting, and when this is the case, they not only fail to have a powerful end game but can lose vision and confidence because something as simple as a hiccup can derail them. Stated powerfully, goals turn dreams and desires into a roadmap, setting you up for action instead of a wishy-washy, "maybe" or "I wish I could."

I am a big fan of SMART goals as outlined by Edwin Locke in 1968. A quick internet search will provide all you need to know to design your goals. This task is not to be skipped or overlooked on the way to fulfillment because without a clear picture and powerful connection to that which you seek, success is impossible. Your potential needs a target, and each target has a bullseye, so what is your target? And then, with all the courage you can muster, what is your bullseye? Use your notebook or journal to work this out on paper.

There is a lot of information and opinions out there on success and defining success, enough to leave you wondering where to start with this mountain of a concept. The question I want you to think about is, what does success for your goal look like? Spoiler alert: it isn't always reaching your goal. Honestly, if you aren't failing at a significant percentage of your goals, you aren't setting them high enough. We learn through failure, so we need it to succeed ultimately. *NOT* reaching a goal can produce some of the most successful feelings ever. Many times, I've failed at something, only to find something positive, even a learning experience, from the failure.

There is also the flip side, reaching your goal and still feeling rather unsuccessful. Naomi Osaka's first Grand Slam win in 2018 against Serena Williams fits this description. During this match, there was an unfortunate disruption, ultimately taking Williams out of the game, both mentally and physically. Osaka was declared the winner, but because it wasn't from play alone, there was a weirdly unsuccessful feeling as she accepted the trophy. I doubt this matched her fantasy of winning her first Grand Slam, and she admitted, "It wasn't necessarily the happiest memory."

Begin creating a vivid picture of what success for this goal looks like to *you*. Write it down and as you go, watch it evolve from pure thought to feeling and vision. This may take a few passes, so work on it, set it aside, and then work on it some more. Curating ideas involves letting them "cook," so resist the urge to simply check this off your to-do list and really dig into your mind.

Step II: Prepare

In real estate, the saying is location, location, location. In sport psychology, it is preparation, preparation, preparation. This step is all about identifying skills and then training them. How do you consistently perform from a place of spirit? Athletes train to prepare for competition, musicians prepare for performance, executives prepare for execution of strategy. A good question to ask is, how do you know you are in this performance state of spirit-inspired flow? Look to the past to create the future because I promise that you have performed from there before. Start by writing out a description of a time when you felt connected to your spirit or spiritual energy. What did you feel in your body? What did you think in your mind? What were you focusing on? What was driving (motivating) your energy? Why was this moment important? You get to say what this is, how it looks, and what it feels like, and it should be in the realm of amazing, by the way, so don't hold back.

Keeping body, mind, and spirit in balance is what creates the ultimate performance state for most of us. It starts with either body or mind. Look at the description you just wrote and ask yourself, what space do you need to be in to be at your best and connected to your spiritual energy? Do you need to have your *body* ready first or is it more important for your *mind* to be ready first? Here is what this means. I worked with an executive of a major company, and her spiritual jam came from her physical or *body* energy. Thinking no one knew, she often snuck out of the office for a midday run. The funny part is that everyone knew, and whether or not she had her daily run had a big impact on the success of their team meetings. Once the cat was out of the bag, her runs became part of the team's jam, with the physical or body part helping to set the stage for the mind and then the spirit, creating one of the most successful teams in the company (a Fortune 500 company).

Conversely, I worked with an Olympian who needed to be fully connected to his *mind* to train and perform well—not what you would expect from an athlete. He practiced meditation to center himself and then wrote profusely in a journal daily to clear his mind of the clutter and then set his vision, connecting his training to competitions.

This book is the third in a series, perfectly setting you up for success. Look to *The Successful Body* to help you discover the tools you need to help you ground there. Look to *The Successful Mind* to develop a masterful skill set with your mental game. This book, *The Successful Spirit*, helps you close the circle, creating a powerful connection to spirit. Do this work to figure out how body, mind, and spirit combine to have you firing on all cylinders and be your best. Then, *train* this routine until it becomes reliable.

It would be great if we could all click our heels together three times and be amazingly connected to a successful spirit, but the truth is, you have to practice. The body and mind can be used to set the stage for the spirit and are much easier to maneuver, at least in the early days. This is how you create a language of the spirit, and then you need to speak it every day until it speaks to you. Be Einstein and stay with it longer than you think you can.

Step III: Deliver

The deliver step is about always (well, as much as possible) being in a mindset where your connection to spirit drives your performance … and ultimately, your success. As you get ready for a test drive, being aware of when you are connected, when you lose connection, and how to get it back are the keys to performance. This cha-cha-cha never ends, by the way, and the great performers know this. You worked in the first step to identify what you are after with your goals and created your definition of success. That vision sets your focus and helps you line up the actions to take on the way to achieving "success." Then, in the second step, you worked to figure out your jam or flow to get you into a connection to spirit, using the body and mind to prepare you to perform from a place of spirit. When you are in this space, creativity flows and actions come from within, seemingly without effort. It is here where the great insights and ideas are "stumbled" upon, but the truth is, they are really intentional once you own this space because you can now make them happen. As you become more and more agile with getting yourself here, success becomes more and more frequent. If you have ever looked at someone and thought they were ridiculously lucky, perhaps it is just that they had mastered this process.

Delivery is not a one and done; it is a fluid process that will evolve and change with you. One of the myths of great performance is that it should be seamless and while it may *look* that way sometimes, I assure you, it is not. The endless practice of losing it and getting it back, over and over again, is what allows for the blending of actions into one movement during performance.

After outlining the steps, I often feel like a broken record when I say, "Now, there is work to do." So many people with so much to offer the world get stuck in the no-man's-land between knowing what to do and actually doing it. Where you are now is as good a starting point as ever, so I implore you, grab a pen and paper and start writing, create a vivid picture of what you truly seek, tune into your body and mind to connect to your spirit, and use the power of your spirit for your focus and drive to be the success you want to be. I will be rooting for you and watching out for the one with the successful spirit.

About the Author

Dr. Jenny Susser may not use "successful" in a bio, but she would definitely admit to having a successful spirit. In the world of high performance, this mindset led her to become a four-year All-American at UCLA and a US National Swimming Team member. Once firmly back on land, a PhD in clinical psychology with a specialization in sport psychology put her on the other side of the mental sport game, helping athletes to find their best performances, with athletes ranging from high school to NCAA Division I teams to international and Olympic individual athletes to the 2012 US Olympic Equestrian Team. When Jenny discovered high performance is not only owned by athletes, she took her "game" to the corporate world. She now straddles both worlds, using a dynamic mixture of psychology, neuroscience, and intuition to help people find what makes them train, perform, and live better.

Email: DrJenny@DrJenny.com
Website: www.DrJenny.com

CHAPTER 29

TURNING FRUSTRATION INTO YOUR GREATEST FRIEND

By Kamille Rose Taylor, BCC
Peak Performance Coach, Forbes Coaches Council
Pasadena, California

Where you stumble, there lies your treasure.
—Joseph Campbell

"Why are you crying?"

"Because he hit me!" I replied through heaving breaths, tear-drenched eyes, and water-soaked clothes.

Soon after my younger cousin ran through the swinging screen door yelling a similar cry of injustice, "No! It's her fault. She wouldn't share the water gun with me!"

My grandmother looked at both of us with a calm and a strength that only comes from someone who has lived through some intense moments in life and found the gift of faith. She then asked, "Okay, now what is the truth?"

My younger cousin and I, all but four and eight years old, looked at each other in confusion.

"What do you mean, 'What is the truth,' Grandma? I just told you what he did," I sheepishly replied.

"But she was mean to me first!" my cousin snapped back.

"Yes," my grandma said to both of us, "but there are three sides to every story. Yours, his, and the truth."

When I think about that moment, it astonishes me because a personal life principle that I now live by—*to learn how to find truth by listening to all sides, including the ones not spoken*—was instilled in me during a moment of great frustration and anger.

Today, as a peak performance coach to driven entrepreneurs and business leaders all over the world, I personally can attest to my grandmother's wisdom as I have had hundreds of conversations with business leaders about how they found some of their greatest opportunities of growth after taking time to learn the whole truth and wisdom from a frustrating situation.

Frustration is a funny friend, but when you learn to work alongside her instead of against her, she can be your greatest ally on the journey towards a massively successful life.

It is my belief that the most successful individuals on this planet have reached top levels in their field because they learned to turn painful moments into purposeful opportunities. They were able to transform negativity into a driving force that allows their true spirit to shine.

Read the stories of Oprah, Michael Jordan, Dr. Martin Luther King Jr., and Ray Dalio, to name a few. Each massive success story also had a major painful moment, if not several. Yet, each of them found a way to use those painful lessons to propel them forward into purpose.

You now have the opportunity to do the same, but there is a way to make that process more productive, so you don't spend years of your life having to relearn the lessons that lady frustration is trying to teach you.

In this chapter, I would like to give you the three tools to use when you're feeling frustrated. These are the same tools I use with my private clients, and it will change your business, your life, and your relationships for the better.

Tool #1: Focus in Front of You

Developing a winning mindset begins with learning to focus on what's right in front of you.

I recently picked up golfing as a hobby with my husband, which, by the way, was something I thought I'd never do! My sport growing up was basketball, but I loved all performance sports where I could "muscle" my way through. I enjoyed the physicality of them because if a certain technique wouldn't work, I could run faster, swing harder, or use my stamina to compensate. However, with golf, I noticed 70+-year-old women at the range driving the ball further and straighter than me without ever breaking a sweat in their swing.

While I was hacking away at this tiny little ball getting absolutely nowhere, I would watch these women and men at the driving range cracking 150, 200, and even 300 yards with a swing that looked effortless. I was certainly younger and probably stronger than most of them, and yet I was getting nowhere fast. It was frustrating, to say the least.

Then one day my husband watched me swing and said, "You're lifting up your head too fast, and you're not watching the ball."

"What do you mean? I *am* watching the ball. I'm watching to see where the ball is supposed to go!" I replied in frustration from feeling so defeated by this sport that I couldn't seem to get.

My husband smiled lovingly at me and explained that what's most important for me right now is to not take my eye off the golf ball. "Focus on what's right in front of you," he advised. "Don't worry about where it's going yet. Just stay focused on the ball."

I stared intensely at the golf ball, swung, and kept my head down still looking at the same spot long after the ball had disappeared.

"Kamille, awesome hit! You got about 150 yards on that!" my husband cheered.

In shock, I looked up and didn't even realize how far it had gone. Honestly, I was just happy that I hit the darn thing! Swing after swing, I kept focusing only on the ball, and every time I did, I had a solid hit. With every swing, I got better and started to build my confidence at this new sport. However, every time I lifted my head too quickly to see where the ball was supposed to go, I would miss it completely or have a terrible hit.

At that moment, it struck me that another life lesson was being taught to me by my dear friend frustration. Well, and my husband.

Focus on what is right in front of you.

Admittedly, like most of the entrepreneurs I coach, I tend to be futuristic with my thinking. I compare my chapter one to someone else's chapter 21 and feel "far behind." I see what can be and try to do too many things at once. I want to get there faster, but I haven't even excelled at the fundamentals yet.

I've learned that top entrepreneurs, leaders, and game changers in their industry have learned the discipline of focusing and excelling at what is right in front of them. These successful individuals do not waste time comparing themselves with others. While they may draw inspiration, motivation, or even a competitive fire by seeing what others are doing, successful leaders are hyper-focused on their game. Simply put, they know to focus on what is right in front of them and master that through consistent practice.

Is there something that is right in front of you that you are looking past too quickly? Are you jumping to too many things all at once out of fear that you might miss out? Are you comparing your early chapters of growth to someone else's experienced years of hard-earned development?

It's normal to feel that you're not succeeding fast enough, but let me encourage you to see that the solution you are looking for might be right in front of you. There may be an opportunity, a skillset, a client, or an unresolved matter that needs your focus and attention. However, because you keep over-looking it trying to jump ahead, the same issues keep arising.

Why hack away at the golf ball when all that is needed is a slight adjustment in your focus? If you are willing to focus on what is right in front of you and practice becoming masterful at it, success will start to look effortless in your hands.

Tool #2: Forgiveness Is Freedom

When you hold on to the past in anger, you cannot move forward into a life of freedom.

When my grandmother finally got my cousin and me to calm down from our bickering, she repeated the question, "What is the truth?" She continued to explain that my cousin got mad at me because I wouldn't allow him to play with me and our other cousins, and that hurt his feelings. Then she explained to my cousin that when he continues to hurt people, no one wants to play with him.

She didn't take either of our sides. Instead she helped us to see the truth that each of us contributed to the situation. Then she asked us to apologize to one another knowing that we couldn't have a healthy relationship if we both held on to the weight of anger and hate.

Forgiveness cannot be overlooked in your journey towards a winning mindset and a successful life.

I have seen so many cases of intelligent entrepreneurs being held back in their peak performance because of a lack of forgiveness with someone in their past or even with a lack of forgiveness towards themselves. There is no other tool that will transform a person's life more significantly than forgiveness.

Now recall that my grandmother never asked us to say that what the other person did was right, justifiable, or even okay. Forgiveness does not mean you're giving someone a free pass for what they have done.

Forgiveness is about letting go of the poison, anger, and hatred that you are holding inside you.

You may think a grudge punishes the other person, but sadly there is a cost, and the cost is your peace.

I've worked with so many high achievers who got to places of success because they wanted to prove something to someone, or they were motivated by their anger/pain, or they felt that success was the best revenge, but in every one of those cases, their fuel of hatred ran out. Sure, it works for a while, but there comes a time when you can only be angry for so long until it starts to eat at you. At that point, your progress, momentum, and success become capped.

Do you feel like there is a glass ceiling on your success right now, and you can't figure out what it is that's holding you back? Are you outwardly successful to everyone else but not finding much fulfillment, joy, or peace within yourself?

If you said yes to any of those questions, then think about who you are still angry with. Who do you need to forgive? The answer may jump out at you right away, or you may have no clue as to who it might be. A note of consideration: sometimes the forgiveness work you need to do is with yourself, especially if you often feel guilty or ashamed.

Whatever the case may be, know that your freedom to get to your full potential only happens when you are willing to let go of the chains of anger that are holding you back. I highly recommend working with a forgiveness specialist, coach, counselor, or therapist if there is deep work that needs to be done.

The bottom line is to remember that forgiveness and fully letting go of the anger within you is the next step to turning that painful moment into purposeful opportunity. When you finally let the anger go, your spirit will become light and you can enjoy, play, and be free once again.

Tool #3: The Follow-Up Question

Change your questions, change your life.

It sounds simple enough—ask better questions, get better answers. But when you think about it, how often are you really assessing the types of questions you ask yourself? Do you really think about the quality of the questions you ask yourself? Do you even realize how many questions you ask yourself on a given day?

The other day, I was making my bed and I smacked my shin into the side of our bed frame, to which I yelled in my mind, "What the heck? Why do I keep doing that? What's wrong with me?"

That seems like a harmless response to a painful, frustrating moment, right? Maybe not.

Try this exercise. Pretend your brain is a search engine like Google. You are the user and every time you ask yourself a question, you are typing that question into the search engine that is your brain. Let's see what I just did.

"What the heck?"

In this scenario, I asked my brain to look for answers to the question, "What the heck?" My brain then provides the search answer results as: "The 'heck' you are currently referring to is the pain from the bedframe you just hit."

Okay, thanks brain. Fair and accurate answer but doesn't do much to move me forward or alleviate my pain.

Next inquiry … "Why do I keep doing that?"

I type that new inquiry into the search engine that is my brain, and it looks for an answer. The brain responds: "Okay, here is a list for why you keep doing this …"

Now I have a list for why I keep doing this, which is not a very direct or efficient way of finding a solution as I still have to find the patterns in the issue, but it's a starting point.

Last one … "What's wrong with me?"

I type that final inquiry into my search engine brain, and here is what it tells me: "Here are all the things that are wrong with you …"

Granted I didn't actually want to know everything that I believe is "wrong with me." It was just an expression, but the brain is doing its job and simply taking orders from the user, aka me.

What is a better way to do this?

While I can't always control the reactionary question that pops out imme-diately, I do have control on my follow-up questions. You see, peak performance is all about the preservation of energy. We cannot achieve high levels of performance if we are constantly running low on energy. So as a peak performance coach, I help high achievers find leaks in their energy. I find patterns where an achiever might be expending more energy than is necessary or getting drained of energy by a poor habit. One bad habit many people have is asking poor questions.

This is why your final tool when dealing with a frustrating moment is to ask a great follow-up question. I say "follow-up" question because often the initial question that gets blurted out is reactionary. However, what you choose to ask after the reactionary question is what matters.

I recently coached a top real estate agent who couldn't figure out what was causing him to fall short of his goals that quarter. He was working harder than he ever had before, he was reading self-development books, meditating every morning, working out, eating healthy, and had a great team, but he was still losing focus and falling behind financially. I asked him what he asks himself in situations like this. He replied, "I ask, what is the biggest chokehold in my business?"

When I asked him why he chose that question, he replied, "So that I can fix it."

Fair enough.

So, I challenged him with this thought, "What is an even better question you could be asking that would take your business to a new level?"

He thought for a moment. His face was plagued with struggle and then he said, "Hmmm … how can we make our services even better for our clients so that they would stay with us longer and become raving fans for life?" When I asked him how he felt about that question compared to the first one about the chokehold, he said he felt energized again.

Immediately, he started brainstorming new ideas and collecting feedback from his clients. Within a few weeks, he partnered with a new agent, added to their company's services, and started growing their business almost three times that month. All this from a simple follow-up question that was even better than the first.

How can you start asking even better questions in your life today? Instead of asking your brain to search for "Why do I keep failing?" ask yourself, "What would energize me to work towards succeeding in my goals?" Find the questions that provide the most energy to you and expend the least.

You may not be able to control the initial question you ask from a frustrating situation, but do not underestimate the power of your next question, the follow-up. A winner's mindset starts with winning questions. Practice those powerful follow-up questions today.

Frustrating moments are going to happen in life, and I have seen that those who succeed in life are the ones who have mastered these tools in those moments. As I mentioned in the title of this chapter, frustration is a great friend, but it only becomes a friend if you use the tools I've set before you.

Remember, if you keep your focus in front of you, acknowledge the need to forgive, and practice powerful follow-up questions, your spirit will be strengthened and success will be inevitable.

There is a third side to that frustration story you've been telling yourself, and I'm positive that once you realize the wisdom in the truth that is there, you will get to new heights you never even thought possible.

About the Author

Kamille Rose Taylor, also known as the "CEO Whisperer," is a leadership strategist, highly sought-after speaker, and top peak performance mindset coach to entrepreneurs, leaders, and high achievers.

Today, Kamille is the CEO and founder of The Ultimate LYFE, a leadership coaching company that has helped thousands of entrepreneurs and driven individuals achieve ultimate success in their personal and professional life. In addition to personal coaching and consulting, she is also a keynote speaker for Fortune 500 companies and national conferences, and continues to expand her research on human peak performance as a member of the Forbes Coaches Council, Harvard's Institute of Coaching, and her travels around the world speaking to diverse communities on how to master their mindset.

Currently Kamille resides in Pasadena, California with her husband and enjoys board game nights with family and friends, really good guacamole, and going on road trip adventures in "TARS the Tesla."

For coaching, podcast interviews, speaking engagements, and consulting:

Email: Coaching@TheUltimateLYFE.com
Website: www.TheUltimateLYFE.com

CHAPTER 30

SYSTEMS THINKING: CONDITIONING THE MIND AND BODY FOR SUCCESS

By Gabrielle Thomas
Professional Athlete in Running
Austin, Texas

A goal without a plan is just a wish.
—Antoine de Saint-Exupéry

We all want success and recognition. It's like a breathtaking view on the top of a mountain. People only post the pictures of the view—but how did they get there? The only way to see the view is to climb. No shortcuts; there's only one way up. You can learn to love the hike, struggle through it, or not take it at all. Reaching the top takes an accumulation of small steps—one step at a time until you make it. Similarly, success is not one grand achievement; rather it is an accumulation of smaller achievements.

On March 10, 2018, my life changed forever. Or at least I thought that was the day that it did. That was the day that I won a Division I Track and Field NCAA Championship and broke a ten-year collegiate record in the 200-meter on national television. I became the first Ivy League sprinter to win an NCAA Championship. Followed by that performance was interest from shoe companies, agents, coaches, and plenty of media attention.

What I've come to realize is that March 10, 2018 was not *actually* the day that my life changed. My life changed long before I sprinted for 22.38 seconds at Texas A&M University. It changed before I even warmed up for that run; before I threw on my uniform and laced up my spikes. In fact, it actually started changing each day that I showed up to the Gordon Track at Harvard University where I practiced for three years. It was changing. Each day I prioritized my physical and mental health. Each day that I kept up my good habits and fought off my bad ones. As a matter of fact, I didn't go to bed anxious or nervous about that championship race the night beforehand. That's because before I ever stepped to the line to win that history-making race in College Station, Texas, I already knew that I had won. My competitors just didn't know. I was already successful.

The interesting thing about track and field, or any other sport, or anything in life, really, is that eventually you will get to a point where everybody around you is talented. Have you ever heard the saying that goes, "Hard work beats talent when talent doesn't work hard"? The only thing is, a lot of us don't know *how* to work hard. I mean, if improvement were easy, everybody would be fluent in multiple languages, have Olympic medals, maintain a perfect body weight, and generally float through life with ease. This is not the case. Improvement is hard. And messy.

Many of us struggle with achieving goals because we try to change everything at one time. We focus on the monumental moments instead of the smaller ones. We choose to ignore the environments we are in. Being success-oriented is great, but it sets you up for constant failure due to the arbitrary nature of its metrics. When we decide on a goal, we have decided in our minds that we will not be successful until we achieve that goal. Consequently, when we are not "successful" in conquering that goal, we become disappointed. This becomes a cycle where we constantly live in a state of disappointment and pushing off our own success. Therefore, instead of tying our success to arbitrary goals, we should tie it with a plan, or a system.

Systems Thinking

Everything we experience works within a system. The lights in your house, the plants growing outside, etc. Nothing happens without some type of system preceding it. The same applies for our outcomes. In the words of W. Edwards

Deming, "every system is perfectly designed to get the results that it gets." That means if you don't like your results, change your system.

Building systems means developing consistency in your actions that are conducive to a desired outcome. Basically, a system will be a set of habits, physically or mentally, that you build into your life. For example, if your goal is to lose weight, then your system is to run two miles every day. You can't decide how your body is going to look, but you *can* decide your lifestyle choices, and those choices will decide how your body looks.

Systems are surrounded by and influenced by their environment. So, think about your current one. Take a moment to identify parts of your environment that are working well for you and some that are unnecessary or actively unhelpful. Creating a sound physical environment is the key to building a foundation from which your success will stem.

First ask yourself, what will this achievement look like? What are you hoping to accomplish? Be realistic with yourself and develop a metric. Maybe you want to run for 20 minutes, five days a week.

Now, how do you set yourself up physically to achieve success? Have you allocated time in your schedule? Are there people around you who are hindering you or motivating you?

A team, an individual, a group, will not improve or find success without clear intentions to do so and a clear plan to execute. It does not have to be written down, but the answers to these questions will help to build your foundation physically to achieve your goal.

That being said, our mental environment also needs to be conducive to our goals. We spend the most time with ourselves, so training our minds to work in a healthy environment is just as important, if not more.

As a professional runner, I've fallen in love with building systems. If my goal is to run sub 11 seconds in the 100 meters, then I am developing habits that are aligned with that goal. That means I am getting an adequate amount of sleep, buying and consuming healthy food at home, practicing meditation, etc. It doesn't mean that I'm going to be perfect, but I am going to be committed to this system that I built. Because if I only focused on my goals 100 percent of the time, I would've lost my mind a long time ago.

Here is a general five-point framework to consider as you develop a system that works for you as you train your mind and body to achieve success.

Point One: Redefine Success in Your Mind

We love to celebrate big achievements in our lives—graduations, promotions, marriages, etc.—but what got us to those achievements? I can't just show up to a track meet and expect to win a race. I have to train for weeks and months and earn it. Why? Because every athlete has that same goal of winning. What separates the winners from the losers is how we prepared for the race. We should normalize focusing on the small accomplishments that lead up to those big moments. Let's put more emphasis on the process. Because that's the part that *really* matters.

Instead of waiting for these big moments where we can finally say that we've found "success," we can redefine what success actually looks like to us. Instead of defining it as a grand, monumental achievement, maybe we define it as a string of smaller achievements. For me, success looks like having a great acceleration rep last Tuesday at training. Or maybe it was me making time for treatment last Wednesday instead of going home to take a nap. If we continue to wait for our arbitrary measures of success, we will constantly live in a state of unhappiness and unsettlement. Let's find success in committing to a system.

Point Two: Focus on Things You Can Control

As I write this, I'm a professional runner for New Balance. How do I improve my times on the track to win races? By not focusing on improving my times.

Yep. That's right. Instead of focusing strictly on the goal ahead, I focus on everything that is within my control to achieve it. I will never be able to control whether I win a race or what time is going to flash at the finish line. I can control how I position myself to better my chances of achieving the goal. I can train my mind to train my body. If every runner spent their energy every day focused solely on winning a gold medal, they would never get better, and perhaps even worse, they'd never be happy. In reality, runners must focus on the actual journey to getting the gold medal—which will be training, nutrition, recovery, etc. These are variables that are within our control. When we fall in love with the system, or the process, we can work towards our goal and be happy while doing it.

Point Three: Positive Self-Talk

I recall an experience I had at the gym in 2020. It was test day. That means we had to lift as much weight as we possibly could in each exercise—max out. I stepped up to test my power cleans. I was working my way up to a max. I looked at the bar and counted the weight—155. I figured I could probably knock out at least two or three at this weight, so I went for it. I hit one rep before dropping the bar thinking I needed to get my strength back up! It wasn't until afterwards that I realized the bar actually had 175 pounds on it. Why is this significant? Because I had tried to lift 175 pounds earlier with no success. As soon as I thought that I was lifting 20 pounds less, my body was able to do it. Interesting. All this to say, if you think like a champion, you will train like a champion, and then you can become a champion.

Like I mentioned before, we are products of our environment. Where do we spend 100 of our time? In our own mind. So, if you aren't kind to yourself, then you've already defeated your own self in your mind. If you've lost the battle in your mind, then you've lost the reality of achieving your goal.

Develop the habit of acknowledging negative thoughts in your mind instead of feeling bad about having them. Once you've acknowledged those thoughts, you can then choose how you are going to respond. Practice telling yourself that you are enough, that you are prepared, that you are fantastic. The cool thing about our mind is that if you say it enough, you start to believe it. Positive thoughts can trigger chemical reactions in our brain that eventually lead to noticeable changes. I'm a firm believer that your body gets you in the race, but your mind gets you the medal. Train your mind to talk to itself with growth and encouragement.

Let's talk about how powerful the mind is for a second. I studied neuro-biology at Harvard. The human body is actually capable of so many things, but it will not achieve any of those things with a weak mind. In the words of Henry Ford, "Whether you think you can or think you can't, you are right." This quote applies to track and field perfectly; if you go into a race without confidence that you can win, you will most likely lose. Like most things in life, you've got to have confidence to be successful. Confidence begins in your own mind, and it's a choice.

Point Four: Be Comfortable with Being Uncomfortable

Most of us have learned to run from discomfort. We need to unlearn that. The easiest way to do this is to decide what you want. Write down what it will take to get there. Start with small, incremental changes. And repeat until they have become lifestyle changes, and you have become comfortable with the changes. For example, let's go back to the goal of wanting to lose weight. You'll need to find some time to exercise. That might look like waking up at 7:00 am instead of 7:30 am each day just to make time for it. This might seem uncomfortable in the beginning, but once you've done it over and over, it becomes a part of your routine—just as getting up 7:30 am was previously. Habits don't just happen; we develop them. Champions don't just win; they train themselves. Success doesn't just appear; we work for it.

Now being comfortable does not mean it will get easy. It just means that you have developed discipline. That discipline is what you're left with when motivation leaves. We can't be motivated every day—not even the most successful people feel motivated every single day. There are days when I do not feel like training. But there is never a day that I feel like sucking. So when my coach tells me to repeat 300s at a pace that I've never run before, I lace up my spikes and do it despite my discomfort, because I am used to pushing myself past my comfort zone. It's still uncomfortable (and actually can be very painful), but that is what it takes for me to be successful.

Point Five: Repetition

This process is where most people get stuck. The first thing that I want to note about this part of the framework is that mentality is 90 percent of the battle. You must form key habits—with your mind first, then the body will follow—then you will find excellence. Our habits become our actions. Our actions become our behavior. Our behavior becomes us.

One thing is certain. We need to be just as committed to building the system as we are to the goals. Nobody likes repetition. We get bored of wearing the same clothes, watching the same TV reruns, or eating the same food. I get it. We like to switch it up every day. And that's what makes it difficult to condition the mind and body to be great. Anybody can do all of this for a few days, weeks, months, or even a year, but repetition and consistency must become a part of a greater lifestyle.

Building systems is the most important thing that we can do to achieve success in any aspect of life. Now that you've read this chapter, stop what you're doing. Think about what success looks like for you—at work, in school, a relationship, etc. Now reflect on the process that it will take to get there. What has to change? What will remain the same? What is within your control? What are you realistically willing to do each day? You are building your system. Commit to that and see where it takes you. You just might be pleasantly surprised.

About the Author

Gabrielle Thomas is a professional runner for New Balance training for the 2021 Tokyo Olympics. During the 2017–2018 season, she became the first Ivy League athlete to make an indoor NCAA sprint final and win an indoor national championship title while breaking the indoor 200-meter collegiate record with a time of 22.38. Gabrielle became the first female sprinter to be sponsored by New Balance in 2018. She graduated from Harvard University in 2019 with an undergraduate degree in neurobiology and is now pursuing a master's in public health from the University of Texas Health Science Center at Houston. When she is not training or studying, she is exploring Austin with her pug, Rico, or experimenting with new recipes at home.

Email: Gabbythomas18@gmail.com

CHAPTER 31
THE BEST IS YET TO COME

By Joey Wagman
Professional Baseball Player, Olympian
Los Angeles, California

When I have truly been searching for my treasure, I've discovered things along the way that I never would have seen had I not had the courage to try things that seemed impossible for a shepherd to achieve.
—Paulo Coelho, *The Alchemist*

What I am about to share are lessons and skills I have learned throughout my life and my baseball career. I am constantly learning and refining these practices, but I would like to share foundational aspects and stalwarts of my mindset. Everything in this chapter includes things I have put to use to achieve success. Each aspect is learned and can be applied to numerous life situations. The discovery and implementation of these practices have been fundamental to my growth from an un-athletic, non-prospect to a professional baseball player and Olympian. There is a reason I have performed at some of the highest levels while still considered "underwhelming" as a pure athlete in my sport. I lack the physical abilities many of my counterparts are blessed with, but what I lack physically, I make up in spirit, mental strength, and discipline. As the quote from *The Alchemist* alludes, it is vital to have goals in life, but most important is what we find in pursuit of those goals. I am happy to share what I have found on my journey.

In this chapter, you will read much about goal setting, so let's start by setting goals of our own. Upon conclusion of this reading, you will be able to train your mind and clear the path for success. My journey to success has been found through three main practices—goal setting, building confidence, and mindfulness. We will examine how these ideas relate to each other, and the effect they have on achieving success. Throughout this chapter we will be focusing on how my experiences have shaped how I train the mind, and how I have learned to use the mind as a tool to propel me toward who and where I want to be.

Setting Goals

In order to set a goal, we first must understand what a goal is. A goal is defined as an end toward which effort is directed. Constructing this "end" can be tricky. This expected result should be something simple and easy to understand. Having a way to measure the goal is important, there should be no doubt as to whether it has been accomplished or not. The goal needs to be loosely realistic, but who am I to say what is possible? Dream big! Most importantly, the goal must be meaningful. This will help us stay committed and keep us in sight of the reason we are putting in all this work.

Now, we know a goal is a noun, and to set a goal is a verb. I want to show how true, effective goal setting is not an action or a thing. It is a feeling. It is an emotion. First and foremost, we must believe we can accomplish this goal. We must commit fully and trust it can and will happen. If we believe we can accomplish this goal, we are correct. If we do not believe we can accomplish this goal, we are also correct. Our attitude and approach are drastically improved if we believe we can achieve it. Conversely, our effort is lacking when our attitude is one of non-belief. When we set our goals, we should be able to visualize ourselves accomplishing the task. Visualize it so strongly that it feels real. Adding sensory details help paint the picture; no detail is too small as long as it aids in making our vision come to life. We want this picture to be so clear in our mind's eye, we can produce the feeling of what it is like to achieve our goal. Visualizing a feeling may seem contradictory, but the distinction is important. Allow me to clarify.

Imagine I am in a classroom with a group of people. Imagine it has been weeks, maybe months since I have clipped my fingernails. I walk over to the chalk board and quickly extend my fingers to form a claw as I reach out toward the chalkboard and swiftly move my hand downward without actually touching the board. The reaction of this group of people, and perhaps yourself if you have taken the time to make this visualization real, is the same as if I had actually scraped the chalkboard. You cringe, you pucker, you produce the feeling as if this action has genuinely happened, although it has not.

Our brains have difficulty distinguishing the difference between reality and imagination. Through visualization we can use this to our advantage by essentially "tricking" our brains into thinking we have achieved our goal and what it would feel like to do so. Having this goal clearly recognizable in our minds along with the overwhelming joy of accomplishing it, gives us direction and inadvertently provides a starting point in our journey toward success when we otherwise would feel aimless.

Instead of looking for somewhere to begin the process of achieving our goal, I found that starting from the end and working backwards is a much more effective method. We do not need to overcomplicate the process. Simply draw up a goal, commit to it, and constantly keep that goal front of mind, and this will dictate our day-to-day actions. Ultimately, we use our long-term goals to drive our short-term actions. Allow me to share how I have turned my goals into reality. It started with building confidence.

Building Confidence

The connotation with confidence is generally viewed in the present tense. If I am seen as confident, I am confident right now in this current moment. To an extent, this is true, but it is only half correct. We must ask ourselves, "How do I become confident?" The reason I am confident in the current moment is because of all the work I have done in the moments leading up to this point.

Confidence is built steadily over time. It does not show up randomly or just because we need it. Confidence comes from consistency. Being persistent in sticking to our routines and trusting we have done the work necessary to accomplish the goal.

During my junior and senior years of college, I was our team's Friday night starting pitcher. This meant I pitched once a week, every Friday night. Each week I would set goals for what I wanted to accomplish on Friday night and work backwards. With those goals in mind, I would start to map out what I needed to do each day to achieve them, essentially creating a routine. I would leave no stone unturned, jotting down everything from throwing programs, weight lifting exercises, and conditioning workouts, to blocking off time for visualization and planning what I was going to eat before the game.

As the week went along and game day approached, I was continuously checking off items that I had completed, each check mark acting as another weapon in my bag of confidence to bring to the mound on Friday. By game day, all the work was done and there was nothing left to do but have fun and trust everything I had done leading up to that point was more than enough to bring me success.

This is how we build confidence over time. We set a goal, we carefully map out what it will take to accomplish that goal, and we consistently complete items on the checklist to get us closer to achieving that goal. At this point, we should feel a sense of confidence, a sense of freedom from worries or negative self-talk that creeps in when we haven't done the work we know is necessary.

We have created a cycle. We set a goal. > We determine what needs to be done in order to achieve it. > We carry out those actions. > Those actions give us confidence to now achieve the goal in front of us. It works backwards as well. We are confident to achieve this goal because we have carried out actions we know will help us, after carefully thinking about the steps necessary to achieve what we really want.

Confidence truly is a byproduct of preparation. It is something that can be attained. Some people are more naturally confident than others, sure. But confidence is a skill that can be learned, and it comes from being well prepared, having a clear goal in mind, and consistent repetitions from a healthy routine in pursuit of our goal.

Confidence: Certain and Irrational

As we continue our practice of building confidence, a benchmark we try to reach is what I like to call an "attitude of certainty." What I mean by this is when we are so confident about something, we are absolutely certain it is going to happen. No ifs, ands, or buts. With an attitude of certainty, there is no other option. Failing does not even cross our minds. For instance, before I pitched on Friday nights as a junior and senior in college, I was a freshman at the bottom of the depth chart. To an outsider, it might have looked like I had no chance of becoming the number one starter or being a professional in the future. But that is exactly what I had in mind, and there was no question it was going to happen. I did not have the exact details of how it was going to happen, but I was completely convinced both of these things were going to come true. Anything else was just not an option. I had the goals in mind, and every decision from that point on was based on achieving them. Some call this irrational confidence, and I would wholly agree.

Irrational confidence is one of my favorite terms. It is usually uttered in a slightly negative way, as in "Why is this guy so confident? He has no reason to be." I embrace the hell out of this. In most cases that skeptical third party is correct; I have no reason to be confident. But that's the beauty of irrational confidence, it doesn't make sense to anyone else, and it's not supposed to. I fully believe in myself, regardless of the situation or what anyone else thinks. If I can't convince myself I am the best, that lack of belief will find a way to show itself on the field.

Your beliefs become your thoughts; your thoughts become your words; your words become your actions; your actions become your habits; your habits become your values; and your values become your destiny.
—Gandhi

Mindfulness

Maintaining discipline and conviction toward our goal is an important part of the practice, but it is challenging. There are a few main staples I use to stay on track. The practice of mindfulness has helped immensely. It is defined as the quality or state of being conscious or aware of something. Simple, right? Try taking one minute to solely be aware of your breath and notice how quickly your mind wants to attach to something else. To simply be, and not get consumed by the countless distractions available today, is difficult and empowering. It teaches the art of slowing down when things in a game or in life seem to speed up. One of my favorite teachers, George Mumford, relates it to being in the eye of the storm. Everything in the storm is chaos, but right in the middle is a tiny space of complete calm. That's where I like to live, and mindfulness is the tool to keep me there.

I find this most helpful when life is not so easy. I have battled my share of depression and anxiety. This has come from injuries, being out of a job, not knowing if my career was over, among other things. It is almost impossible to be confident and have goals from this place. Sometimes it's impossible to take a shower or go for a walk from this place. This is where mindfulness shows its malleability. Staying in the present moment and aware of the root of negative thoughts and self-talk is paramount in climbing out of the dark, endless pits of depression and anxiety. Mindfulness can be a fantastic aid when we lose our confidence or have trouble building some in the first place. It has allowed me to keep perspective, and when that anxiety spiral feels out of control, mindfulness taps the brakes and puts me back in control.

One of the most important lessons I have learned from mindfulness is how the mind works and how powerful it is. I have learned that I am the architect of my thoughts and beliefs. Although I might not always be able to control my thoughts, I am in control of how I react to them. I've gotten to a place mentally where I can recognize a thought or emotion is present but not attach to it.

Similar to the calm space in the eye of the storm, there lies a moment between when an action takes place and when we choose to react to this action. If I give up a home run, I don't get angry or feel sorry for myself. I focus my mind on making the next pitch better than that one. Two different reactions to the same action, it is my decision which one I choose. I can recognize that I am starting to feel angry, and instead of succumbing to that anger and attaching to it, I can acknowledge its presence and choose a more productive reaction. When I give power to an idea, I take away its power over me.

This experience is powerful with stress as well. I have found that when I am in a stressful situation, the basic idea of recognizing that this situation is indeed stressful and it is okay to be stressed, I immediately feel the stress dissipate. It is like I am cutting myself some slack for being stressed in a stressful situation, rather than stressing over the fact that I'm stressed. We all need a break sometimes, and there is no better place to take that break than in the state of mindfulness.

Putting It All Together

I would like to share the culmination of goal setting, confidence, and mindfulness as it pertains to my baseball career. Everything I have laid out in this chapter, and everything I had learned and practiced showed itself in the days and moments leading up to the biggest game of my career. In 2019, I helped lead the Israeli Baseball Team to its first Olympic berth in history. Along the way, I pitched in four separate international tournaments, with each tournament providing a win-or-go-home scenario. Before the opening game of the final tournament, the Olympic qualifiers, I was set to pitch against Spain.

Days earlier, I watched as they scored 16 runs to beat us in the prerequisite tournament. As I prepared for this career-defining game, I felt an overwhelming calm. I was less nervous for this game than any we had played prior. How was that possible? This was the biggest stage and the best competition I had played to date.

The answer is quite simple. I set my goals and used my practices of visualization, mindfulness, and breathing techniques with strong focus for a matter of months to this point. With these repetitions, I had become quite good at it. In the days leading up to this game, I was able to achieve intense sensations during my visualization sessions. It felt as if my whole body was tingling and as if I was floating above my bed where I lay to visualize. I had put myself in a trance where the only thing I knew was success. Nothing phased me, and I had a laser focus to the present moment. This has been referred to as "the zone," and I was completely entrenched in it. I pitched all nine innings and gave up zero runs—in baseball terms, a complete game shutout. A feat I had not accomplished in over six years, I had just performed on the biggest stage. I can attribute nearly all of this success to my mental preparation and visualization. When it came time to actually perform, I had felt as if I had already done it, which lifted any perceived pressure. There was no room to be nervous, I had visualized this success over and over again with such detail, I could feel it. I was able to clear the way for my body to follow what my mind had already seen.

Ultimately, everyone's goals are different; thus, the journeys along the way are unique as well. What is important is not that we reach the end, but that we strive to get there and absorb the lessons and skills taught down the path. I have learned that achieving success is a process, and I have full control over every aspect. Maintaining control over mood, thoughts, actions, and reactions is an ongoing practice. By no means am I done learning or feel as if I have mastered these teachings.

The successful spirit is found and defined in many different ways. Setting our goals properly, staying committed to those goals, and developing healthy habits to build confidence over time, all while staying mindful throughout the process guarantees us nothing, but is a hell of a good place to start. I have shared what I have soaked up so far, but the journey and teachings are far from over. If you are someone, who after reading this, feels as if some changes need to be made, Edgar Cayce put it best, "Don't feel sorry for yourself if you have chosen the wrong road, turn around."

The best is yet to come.

About the Author

Joey Wagman is a professional baseball player and Olympic athlete. Joey is a right-handed pitcher and has pitched for numerous professional teams, including the Chicago White Sox and Oakland A's organizations. He will be competing in the 2021 Summer Olympics in Tokyo for Team Israel.

Joey is a native of Danville, California, and attended Monte Vista High School. He was not drafted out of high school and received only one Division-I scholarship offer. He went on to attend Cal Poly SLO where he became a two-time team captain, two time First Team All-Conference pitcher, and an NCAA D1-All American. He holds numerous school records including Most Wins in a Single Season and Career Wins (D1). In 2013 he was selected by the Chicago White Sox in the Major League Baseball Draft.

Since 2013, Joey has competed at some of the highest levels of professional and international baseball, including the 2017 WBC for Team Israel. In 2019 Joey led the Israel National Baseball Team to qualify for the Olympics for the first time in history.

Email: Joeywagman@gmail.com

CHAPTER 32
PAIN TO PURPOSE

By: Kendrick Williams
Life Coach, Speaker, Servant Leader
Fairborn, Ohio

You can't beat someone who doesn't quit.
—Babe Ruth

"Kendrick, we don't think it's best for you to come back for the next semester. You should really think about finding another school."

Wait, what just happened? I shouldn't come back next semester? I need to find a new school? Wait, this was supposed to be my year! This was supposed to be the year all those years of hard work paid off! This was my time, but instead my basketball scholarship was revoked.

"Pick yourself up. Walk out the office. Don't say anything stupid," I said to myself as I got up and left my coach's office.

With every step I took, heading back to my apartment, my heart broke over and over again. There I was. My girlfriend had just cheated on me. My relationship with my father was at the worst it had ever been. I was struggling in school. And now, my coach was asking me to not come back after Christmas break.

I was a former high school basketball star who flew under the radar. Now, in my second year of junior college, basically, all I had to do was show up and not suck. Now here I was, getting my scholarship taken away. My whole life had been wrapped in my identity as an athlete. Now, that was gone. Here was yet another school, program, team, and family saying, "I don't want you." So I asked myself, "What do I do now? What's next for my life?"

So many of us athletes, after we're done playing, really have no idea what's next. We spend our lives pushing our bodies and our hours honing out athletic skills without imagining there could be an end. My mother is a teacher, and she always made it clear that I needed to think about life after ball. But what happens when the ball stops without any warning at all? How do you transition when life transitions you?

As I reflect on the journey God has brought me through over the past seven years, I see that being an athlete was pivotal into being successful in life. That day in my coach's office, December of 2013, was the worst day of my life. Now, as I look at it with 20/20 hindsight vision, I see how this tragedy has become one of the biggest blessings of my life.

As the year 2013 ended, I was forced to move back home to a little suburb of Dayton, Ohio called Fairborn, a city many in the area jokingly call "Fail-born." My mind was all over the place. Situational depression set in, and I had no idea who I was and why I was here on this earth. I feared I would simply become another statistic and that life would basically be over. For a month, as I entered into the new year of 2014, I soaked in self-pity and was ready to throw in the towel. That's when a man stepped into my life and challenged my way of thinking, which in turn, challenged and changed my life forever.

I woke up early January 16, 2014. I went to the gym for the first time since getting kicked out of school. I worked out and played basketball for the first time in over a month. As I was leaving, I was approached by a man named Mark Drake. Drake questioned me, asking if my career (and life) was over. He then asked me to come back and meet him the following day at 10:30 am. Apprehensively, I said yes.

Drake and I worked out on the basketball court for three years, and I began to realize he was training my mind just as much as he was training my physical body. He would have me speak positive affirmations about myself as we were training. Still to this day I speak things like "Instantaneous, spontaneous, simultaneous, elevation to any pressure of precarious situations." Another mantra was "Anybody, anywhere, any time, and any place." These mantras Drake would have me speak to get my mind to tell my body, "You can do anything and there's no reason to fear the unknown." Drake was helping develop the winning spirit within me.

So much of my thinking had been conformed to the patterns of this world. The facts of this world had been my driving factor in my thinking. I believed that because of the situation of losing my scholarship on top of family struggles, I could not do certain things. Drake challenged this way of thinking. He began to teach me that the way I thought about the situations in my life were going to determine the results I got in my life. I did not understand at the time, but he was preparing my mind to be ready for the unknown pressures of not only basketball, but of life.

The positive affirmations transformed my mind into believing that ALL things are possible to those who believe. Belief led to confidence, which led to success. This was especially important, because the success I knew I wanted in life would not start to manifest itself for more than four years. I had to change my thinking, so that I could actually steward success correctly, but it was a long process.

My thought process through lengthy suffering was truly cultivated during those four years, from 2013 to 2017, and I latched on to something from the Bible that helped keep me going, "The present suffering is nothing compared to the glory coming" (Romans 8:18). For four long years, daily, I would work out and train. I would read books about great leaders and athletes that Drake suggested. I would work two or three jobs at a time, just so I could have the resources to be able to take care of myself and still have time to train.

It was inevitable, however; weekly, almost daily somebody would suggest, "Man, you should just quit and go back to school and get a job." I would hear, "Your sports career is over," and "You'll never play again." The doubts would creep in, but by the new mindset that was being cultivated, I knew I could not settle for a life less than what I knew God had for me. I would have to speak that verse over to myself constantly, "The present suffering is nothing compared to the glory coming." Now as I reflect, patience and tenacity were being cultivated as core values that I would need for life. I had already learned these traits while being a high school star and collegiate athlete; but now I was having to go deeper into these beliefs and let them guide my life.

One day as the fear and depression were again setting in, I thought that I may never get the opportunity to play competitive basketball again. I saw a quote from Babe Ruth that changed my life. It read, "You cannot beat someone who does not quit." Drop the mic.

Little did I know that quote would help keep me inspired for one of the greatest opportunities of my life to present itself. It was the summer of 2017, and I got the chance to go play in a summer league in Jamaica. My mindset had been getting ready for this moment for four years. I stayed in the gym training even though I was not sure if I would ever get an opportunity to play competitively again.

That summer, I ramped up my training regimen. I began doing two-a-days, sometimes three-a-days. I would train, rest, repeat. For three long months, that's all I did. When my body became tired, weak, and exhausted, I would just say, "The present suffering is nothing compared to the glory coming." I pushed my body further than I thought possible. I kept pushing. Then because fear would try to creep in and say I wasn't good enough, I would have to say, "Anybody, anywhere, any time, and any place." Saying this helped me stay confident that my skills and training would prepare me for the competition I was about to face. My winning spirit was developing.

The hard work forging my mind and my body worked. On August 14, 2017, my teammates and I held a championship trophy over our heads. During the games, I played just like I had practiced, and I averaged over 25 points per game while dishing out many assists as well. After my Jamaica experience, I knew that all those years of hard work honing my body and refining my skills surely would pay off.

When I got back to the States, I started sending my film from the Jamaica games to every professional agent and team I could find. And every response was the same, "You look good, but we need more film," or "We're not sure you're good enough." Crushed. There I was again. Thoughts of quitting began to set into my mind. Luckily, there was a small, still voice reminding me in my spirit, "The present suffering is nothing compared to the glory coming," and "You can't beat someone who doesn't quit."

Finally, early in September, I got a call from the coach from a school in Broken Arrow, Oklahoma. "Broken what?" I thought, but he began to tell me about the school he coached at called Rhema Bible College. I had never heard of the school or the city, but it was the opportunity I had been waiting for. I decided to go.

The next two years at Rhema would be two of the best years of my life. I got to play ball again. I averaged 39 points a game, and I was named an All American two years in a row. I was also able to finish school. I was never sure this day would come. As I walked across the graduation stage, so many thoughts and emotions came back to me. The main thing I kept hearing on the inside was "See, the present suffering was nothing compared to the glory coming."

I never would have imagined that when I was a confused young man in my early twenties that one day, this season of my life that left me depressed would now be the driving force behind everything I did. Now, I am a life coach serving an organization called Athletes in Action, where I am fortunate enough to be able to use my testimony to help inspire others to keep chasing their dreams. The mindset and work ethic I was able to cultivate during those long four years of lots of work and uncertainty are now the tools and principles I use to guide myself and others daily.

As I leave you, I want to encourage you to complete whatever it is that you want to do. Your body and your spirit can do more than you could ever imagine, and that goes for the mind too. I want to remind you that *you cannot beat someone who doesn't quit*, and whatever suffering you are going through along your journey, it is nothing compared to the glory coming.

About the Author

Kendrick Williams is a life coach and pastor servant leader. After God radically changed his life in 2014, he has been dedicated to sharing the truth in love with everyone whom God brings in his path. Growing up a successful two-sport athlete, Kendrick uses the experiences of being a leader to help others reach their full potential.

After graduating from Rhema Bible College in the summer of 2019, Kendrick has been serving at Risen Hope Church as an administrative pastor, and he also works with Athletes in Action, a worldwide sports ministry. In college, Kendrick was an All-American basketball player majoring in Ministry Fundamentals with a focus in youth psychology. Kendrick believes his testimony and leadership skills can help to inspire the next generation.

Email: kendrick.williams@athletesinaction.org
LinkedIn: http://linkedin.com/in/kendrick-williams-834b83188

CHAPTER 33
THE SUCCESSFUL SPIRIT

By Erik Seversen
Author, Speaker, Coach
Los Angeles, California

*In the depth of winter, I finally learned that within
me there lay an invincible summer.*
—Albert Camus

As a writer, I'm commonly asked to produce material on a topic or a theme. This is easy for me. You want me to write about selling; I'm going to focus on value and what problem your product solves. You want me to write about serenity, I'm going to focus on emotional triggers that produce positive-feeling hormones like oxytocin, dopamine, and serotonin. You want me to provide a history or description of something; I can do this quickly and easily. However, writing about spirit is different because spirit is so foundationally present and yet so elusive as well. Add "successful" to this, and I'm at a double loss since success is, in many ways, just as indefinite as spirit. This is because success can be totally different from one person to the next.

As I begin to write about spirit, I'm haunted by specters of what spirit could mean. A person could spend years following rabbit holes in search for a concise idea of spirit. Many have tried. Starting with a quick internet search, I see that Merriam Webster's Dictionary lists "spirit" as an "animating or vital principle held to give life to physical organisms," and a "supernatural being or essence as in Holy Spirit." Dictionary.com defines "spirit" as the "principle of conscious life; the vital principle in humans, animating the body or mediating between body and soul and the incorporeal part of humans." The Cambridge English Dictionary puts "spirit" as "enthusiasm, energy, or courage." Thefreedictionary. com says "spirit" is the "vital principle or animating force within living beings, divine spark ..."

Whatever the definition of spirit, it always seems to be connected with something fundamental, essential, and vital. Even the etymology of the word "spirit" alludes to the idea that spirit is central to being alive as the word "spirit" comes from the Latin word *spiritus* or "breath." This is about as close to the core of maintaining human life as we can get. But life is more than a beating heart, lungs absorbing oxygen, and food being digested. There is something more. There are emotions which affect mood and determination, and I think this is where spirit begins to affect who we are, what choices we make, and how we go about accomplishing things. This is the type of spirit I want to focus on here.

An evil jailer or torture master has the ability to break any prisoner's arm they choose, but the torture master cannot break any prisoner's spirit. Because of the intangible nature of spirit, there is nothing there to break. Or is there? I argue that there *is* something there, and the evidence is found in the varying individual responses to people being tested. Along with the broken arm, some imprisoned people's spirits will be broken. They can not only get physically defeated, but they can become mentally and emotionally defeated. They can give up, and with it, they may either confess whatever the torturer is interested in finding out, or they may exist as an empty shell of a body caring not about self, others, life, or death.

While looking at torture and imprisonment as described by Holocaust survivor Viktor Frankl in *Man's Search for Meaning,* we can see that some people's spirits are breakable and others' are not. What is the difference? That is the main point of this book—to provide examples of people who followed the calling of their spirit to accomplish amazing things. While hopefully none of us will be tortured as prisoners, all of us will face external and internal challenges, and it is up to us to decide how to respond to these challenges. Whether our challenge is as somber as overcoming a terminal disease or as jubilant as trying to win a gold medal in the Olympics, it is up to us, individually, to choose how to overcome the externally-inflicted or self-imposed challenge at hand.

External challenges might be personal health issues, a family crisis, financial ruin, unreturned love, and more. Each of these challenges is a result of some action originating outside of our control. Internal challenges, on the other hand, might include a decision on whether to pursue a university graduate program, whether to pursue love with another person, whether to try again after loss of a business or home. The financial crisis from a failed business is an external challenge, but the decision to try again or to fight to pay off a debt is an internal challenge. The attraction to another individual with whom you're acquainted is an external challenge, but the decision to woo is an internal challenge. Being diagnosed with cancer, multiple sclerosis, or another chronic disease is an external challenge, but the manner in which you respond and the action you take is an internal challenge.

The decision on how to respond to external challenges is entirely personal, and only you are able to make that decision. This, I think, is where spirit comes in. What determines whether a person gives up after diagnosis of an illness or after failed love or business bankruptcy? Is there somewhere we can learn how to be more equipped to make strong, healthy decisions when faced with adversity? My answer to this is *yes!*

I believe each of us is born with spirit and through a combination of nature (the genes we're born with) and nurture (our upbringing), we are each equipped with an array of possibilities in regards to the level of our spirit's determination. However, I equally believe that spirit is something that can be taught, learned, and developed. This book, *The Successful Spirit,* was created for just this reason. As the third in *The Mind, Body, and Spirit* series, this book is meant to show how others have responded to adversity. You see, when things are going great, the spirit is often forgotten, but when there are things that need to be overcome, the focus, drive, and determination of the spirit is very strongly needed.

When I think of people whom I consider to have a successful spirit, a few names jump out at me: Dr. Martin Luther King Jr., Louis Zamperini, Mother Teresa, Gandhi, Winston Churchill, and Bruce Lee. Each of these individuals did extraordinary things. Maybe some were blessed with certain intellectual bents that allowed them to see possibilities where others didn't. Maybe some of them were blessed with a certain sense of compassion that allowed them to dedicate themselves to others. Maybe some were blessed with certain body-types that allowed them to excel in the physical spaces. But these individuals could easily have passed through history unnoticed and without affecting much beyond their immediate families if it weren't for their focused desire to see change in themselves and in the world, and to take massive action toward exacting that change. Each of these individuals put others above themselves in their passionate pursuit of a better world. King had a dream of racial equality, Zamperini's end found him wanting to share a message of true forgiveness, Mother Teresa dedicated her life to helping the unfortunate, Gandhi fought for inter-religious and inter-political harmony, Churchill sought to end the frightening expansion of fascism in WWII, and Bruce Lee dedicated himself to showing the world the beauty of Asian culture through his martial arts skill. These individuals stand out because they stayed true to their cause; they listened to their inner spirit and were uncompromising while pursuing their goals.

Similar to the historically renowned individuals like King, Churchill, Teresa, and Lee, the authors composing this book have faced challenges. From being mugged at gunpoint as a child in intercity Cleveland, to growing up not knowing where the next meal would come from in the streets of Accra, Ghana, to being diagnosed with multiple sclerosis as an adult or being born with cerebral palsy, to being homeless, to suffering in an upscale suburb with a quiet desperation that there should be something more, that life should be better. All of these situations and more are featured in this book and have contributed to the authors' strength of character and the desire to push for something better because better is a choice, whether it be striving to overcome illness or training to win an international sporting competition.

Every single one of the authors in this book knows how to push themselves in a way that is unique. They have overcome adversity, and they are proof that with a determined spirit, anything is possible. Some of the same people mentioned in the above paragraph have competed and won medals in the Olympics and Paralympics, have climbed the highest mountains in the world including Mount Everest, have found economic success, have started companies to help others find success, and have found joy in themselves and in spending time with their families. Each of them has a message about how to push through challenges to create the life you want to live by forging a successful path and continuing along that path with strength and confidence as well as joy, calm, and peace.

The successful spirit doesn't mean winning is an end-goal. Rather, the successful spirit is that connection to our inner force that allows us to know ourselves and to decide exactly how we want to live our lives in a manner that creates success within and around us. If there is anything in this book that you really connect with, I encourage you not to let your moment of enthusiasm die. Instead, immediately reach out to the author of the chapter. Directly contact them. Each author in this book would love nothing more than to help you develop your unique spirit. It is already within you.

Take a moment right now and ask yourself if you are pushing yourself hard enough? Or, maybe you're pushing yourself too hard, and you need a shift in direction? Ask yourself exactly where you want to be in life. If you are totally happy with where you are and where you are going right now, celebrate that. But if there is something else that you would like to see in your life, decide what you can do to get it. Anything is possible—anything—if you can see it in your mind, and you're willing to embrace your inner strength, your courage, your love, your drive, focus, and determination. You have a fiery spirit within you that is capable of more than you can ever imagine because your spirit is infinite, limitless. With something as simple as a thought and a decision to take action, you have the freedom to ignite a spark that will allow you to accomplish your most daring dreams. May you embrace your spirit right now and enjoy walking the path of success that is unique to you.

About the Author

Erik Seversen is on a mission to inspire people. He holds a master's degree in anthropology and is a certified practitioner of neuro linguistic programming. Erik draws from his years of teaching at the university level and years of real-life experience to motivate people to take action creating extreme success in business and in life.

Erik is an author of six books, keynote speaker, adventurer, entrepreneur, and educator who has traveled to 86 countries and all 50 states in the USA. His travels and intersections with people have been a deep study of love, struggle, and ways of thinking that Erik relies on to tackle challenges in school, business, and life. His most current ambitions are sharing the lessons he's learned with others and climbing mountains. Erik lives in Los Angeles with his wife and two teenage boys.

Email: Erik@ErikSeversen.com
Website: www.ErikSeversen.com

DID YOU ENJOY THIS BOOK?

If you enjoyed reading this book, you can help by suggesting it to someone else you think might like it, and **please leave a positive review** wherever you purchased it. This does a lot in helping others find the book. We thank you in advance for taking a few moments to do this.

THANK YOU

If you enjoyed reading this book, you might also like the first two books in The Mind, Body, and Spirit series:

Book 1:
The Successful Mind: Tools to Living a Purposeful,
Productive, and Happy Life

Book 2:
The Successful Body: Using Fitness, Nutrition,
and Mindset to Live Better

Made in the USA
Las Vegas, NV
01 September 2021